D1195122

Tropical Surge

Tropical Surge

*A History of Ambition and
Disaster on the Florida Shore*

Benjamin Reilly

Pineapple Press, Inc.
Sarasota, Florida

Iosco - Arenac District Library
East Tawas, Michigan

Copyright © 2005 by Benjamin Reilly

All rights reserved. No part of this book may be reproduced in any form or by any means, electronic or mechanical, including photocopying, recording, or by any information storage and retrieval system, without permission in writing from the publisher.

Inquiries should be addressed to:

Pineapple Press, Inc.
P.O. Box 3889
Sarasota, Florida 34230
www.pineapplepress.com

Library of Congress Cataloging-in-Publication Data

Reilly, Benjamin, 1971-
  Tropical surge : A history of ambition and disaster on the Florida Shore /
by Benjamin Reilly.
      p. cm.
  ISBN 1-56164-330-0
  1. Flagler, Henry Morrison, 1830-1913. 2.   Florida East Coast
Railway—History. 3.   Railroads—Florida—Florida Keys.
4.Hurricanes—Florida—Florida Keys. I. Title.

  TF25.F58R45 2005
  385'.09759'41—dc22

                                                                    2004025968

13 digit ISBN 978-1-56164-330-1

First Edition
10 9 8 7 6 5 4 3 2 1

Design by Shé Heaton

Printed in the United States of America

Contents

Acknowledgments

I am deeply indebted to the pioneering historians who have covered south Florida history before me, as well as the dedicated librarians and archivists who provided the necessary research materials. No historians were of greater assistance to me than John Viele, Stuart B. McIver, and Dan Gallagher, who not only provided vital data for my study, but also contributed by editing and fact-checking the work. Let me hasten to add that any errors that crept through are mine alone. As for research institutions, I would like to thank the staff at the USF library's Florida Study Center, the staff at the Miami Public Library, the staff at the European Reading Room of the Library of Congress, and Tom Hambright at the Monroe Country Public Library in Key West. I would also like to thank the photographic collections staff at the Florida State Archives for compiling and preparing the excellent photographic images that appear in this work, as well as the staff of the library's Special Collections department, including the Floridiana Collection, at the University of South Florida.

In addition, I would like to express my gratitude to several special people for their important personal contributions to the book's completion. My thanks to Rudy Hernandez, who not only opened his home to us in Miami but suffered through a six-hour lecture on south Florida history that was, though I didn't know it at the time, the prototype version of this book. Thanks as well to my son, Will Edward, whose very existence encouraged me to finish this book, if only so that I could include him in the acknowledgements. Most of all, my profuse thanks to Anita, who supported me financially, emotionally, and intellectually throughout the entire writing process. With her help, nothing is impossible.

Introduction

The Shipwrecked Train

Almost all books follow a crooked path to publication, but I daresay that this book's own genesis story is more roundabout than most. I first became interested in the topic, oddly enough, while reclining on a deck chair at a Balinese hotel. It was late July of 2001, and my lovely newlywed wife and I had just spent an exhausting day mountain biking down the slopes of an extinct volcano. The early evening found us enjoying a well-earned rest by the pool, she with a Tom Clancy novel, and I with *Tales of Old Florida,* a curious collection of turn-of-the-century magazine articles published by Castle Press. Anita had fished this book from a discount bin on a lark, knowing that we planned to move to Florida shortly after the end of our honeymoon.

Anita had hoped that the book would prove to be good vacation reading, but at first, the book barely scratched the surface of my interest; outside of a few well-written travelogues, it mostly contained articles penned by so-called "sportsmen," who gleefully recounted the indiscriminate, unthinking havoc they had wreaked upon Florida's dwindling populations of fish, mammals, birds, and crocodilian reptiles. My interest was piqued, however, by a 1908 piece by Ralph D. Paine concerning the status of a bizarre island-linking railroad that was then under construction between Miami and Key West. The project was already about four-fifths completed, Paine proclaimed, and the next step would be the erection of an unprecedented bridge to span the formidable seven-mile water gap between Knight and Bahia Honda Keys. Once finished, this rail line would offer passengers the unique opportunity of fishing directly from the window of the train or of witnessing the spectacle of flying fish skipping over the surface of the sea thirty feet below. It would be like nothing else in the world.

I remember putting the book down and staring vacantly past waving bamboo-mounted flags towards the lovely waters of the Badung Strait, pondering what I had just read. Why haven't I ever heard of this railway? I wondered. Was it ever completed? And if so, what happened to it? Why isn't it still running today?

These questions, obviously, were not likely to be answered in Bali, so I tucked them away for the duration of the honeymoon. Once we returned to the States, however, I conducted a brief web search and learned the fascinating truth. Yes, the island-linking overseas railway was completed—but it only remained in operation for a little more than two decades before being disabled permanently by the most powerful hurricane ever to strike the continental United States. Eyewitnesses to the awful scene described two-hundred-mile-per-hour winds so choked with sand they could strip flesh from bone. Worse yet, the hurricane heaved a tidal wave over the Florida Keys that swept away everything in its path, including the rescue train that had been dispatched to bring Keys residents to safety on the mainland. Hundreds died, and scores went missing. In the decades that followed, hardly a year went by without the discovery of ghastly skeletal remains tangled up in the dense mangrove thickets alongside Florida Bay.

My first reaction, upon learning the fate of the doomed railway, was one of surprise. Why had I never heard this story before? I had spent four years as an undergraduate in a Florida college only a decade before, yet somehow managed to stay entirely ignorant of even the existence of the so-called Key West Extension of the Florida East Coast Railway, often called the "Overseas Railway." I was determined to learn more—but in the meantime, I was distracted by other more pressing concerns, including our impending move back to Florida and the deadlines my doctoral committee had set for the completion of my European History dissertation. The story of the shipwrecked rescue train would have to wait.

Such was the state of my affairs when September Eleventh burned itself into the American national psyche. Like many Americans, I suffered badly from nightmares in the weeks that followed, but I am willing to bet that mine were different from most. In my dreams, I was at the helm of the doomed rescue train, buffeted by heavy, howling winds, surrounded by an impenetrable midnight murk. As I clattered along the railway, the train's headlight cast a feeble light on the swirling seawaters ahead (a historical inaccuracy, as it turns out—I did not yet know that the rescue train actually backed its way into the Keys). Then, with an awful suddenness, a tremendous wave roared out of the gloom, towered above me, and smashed down upon my helpless head. I grabbed onto the heavy locomotive engine for dear life, desperate to save myself from the suffocating flood. I have no idea what happened next; by that point in the dream, I had generally been scared awake.

After several such nightmares, I decided that I wanted to write a book about the life and death of the Overseas railroad, if only to purge my mind of the lingering shadows of September 11th. As soon as I completed and defended my dissertation, therefore, I took advantage of my status as an alumnus of the University of

South Florida and began to make almost daily trips to the USF main campus library in Tampa, Florida, in an attempt to ferret out as much information as possible about the ill-fated railway. At first, I focused my efforts primarily upon the construction and destruction of the railroad itself. As time passed, however, my interests became more far-reaching, and I became curious about the circumstances that had brought about the building of the railway in the first place. What on earth possessed Henry Morrison Flagler, the oil magnate who bankrolled the Key West Extension, to expend so much of his fortune on this curious railway? What was so special about Key West that justified the construction of railway bridges across the open sea? And how did the rail line influence the growth of the modern-day metropolis of Miami, the mainland terminus of the Extension railway? Answering these questions, in turn, raised still more questions, and I found my research interests coiling in an ever-expanding spiral around my original topic of the Key West Extension railway.

As a result of these inquiries, I came to the realization that the story of the Extension railway was just one vivid chapter of a much larger epic—the perennial clash between human ambition and geographic realities along the southern Florida shore. I have always been interested in the role played by geography in history, both in terms of the ability of the climate to shape human lives, and the tactics which people employ to change their environment to suit their own needs and desires. South Florida, I soon discovered, offered particularly striking examples of this process in action. The unique resources and industries of south Florida, including turtles, sponges, and wrecking, all left an indelible imprint on the history of the region. The area's most important resources of all, however, proved to be its wide-open, unsettled acreage and its splendid climate, which together tempted scores of developers to south Florida's shore. Flagler's Extension railway was just the most grandiose example of a hundred similar projects, each of which sought to carve out a plot of paradise in the American subtropics.

Unfortunately for these ambitious dreamers, however, the same factors that made Florida such attractive terrain for development also made it especially vulnerable to the terrifying reality of the West Indian hurricane. The Florida peninsula resembles nothing so much as an enormous ironing board, flat and nearly featureless, rising no more than a few hundred feet at the highest from the warm subtropical waters that surround it. Worse yet, this ironing board protrudes dangerously into the Gulf of Mexico and the Atlantic Ocean, which are prowled from June to October by some of the most powerful storms to occur anywhere on our planet. As a result, Florida bears the brunt of more hurricanes than any other American state, and when these hurricanes do strike, Florida's inherent low-lying flatness makes it particularly vulnerable to the systematic devastation that these horrifying storms inevitably bring in their wake.

The goal of this book, then, is to chronicle the dramatic clash between human ambition and subtropical hurricane realities that took place between 1831 and 1935 along the south Florida shore. Flagler's Extension railway will serve as a vital central thread to the story, since it weaves together the histories of Key West and Miami over a distance of both space and time. Nonetheless, as we shall see, there is far more to the story of southernmost Florida than the triumphs and tragedies of one doomed rail line. In the first five chapters, we will explore the founding, development, and growing ambition of Key West and Miami, the two towns that would eventually anchor the southern and northern ends of Flagler's Key West Extension railway. Chapters six through eight, in turn, will examine the greatest flowerings of human achievement along the Florida shore, with particular emphasis on the completion of the Extension railway, the founding of Miami Beach, and the halcyon days of the Miami real estate boom of 1925–1926. Finally, in the last three chapters, we will examine the hurricanes that shattered south Florida's fragile prosperity, especially the Key West Storm of 1919, the Great Miami Hurricane of September 1926, and the incredible

Labor Day Storm of September 1935, which brought both the Extension railway, and a whole era of Florida history, to a sudden and violent end.

One final note: although I did spend quite a bit of time in the archives collecting source materials, I never intended the present volume to be a major work of new scholarship. This book will contain no great new revelations for those already well acquainted with the history of southern Florida, nor was it my intention to provide such revelations. My goal, rather, was to weave the many strands of the history of south Florida into a single, coherent story. It is, I believe, a fascinating tale, full of human achievement and human tragedy, exotic people and exotic locales, milestones and body counts. What is more, I believe that it is a uniquely American story; the historical actors we will encounter in the following chapters, such as Henry Flagler and Carl Fisher, were motivated by the same characteristically American mixture of greed, ambition, and self-confidence that put American astronauts on the surface of the moon and American soldiers into the rice paddies of Vietnam. It is American in another sense as well—the story of south Florida serves as a grim reminder, if one is still needed in the aftermath of September 11th, that America's unmatched prosperity and power cannot protect it from unforeseen catastrophe. The mightiest always have the farthest to fall.

At least, I am happy to report, my nightmares have stopped.

Tropical Surge

1

A Land Apart

June too soon
July stand by
August look out you must
September remember
October all over
—traditional Florida mariner's poem

In the 1830s, the railroading age had just dawned in America. At that time, only a few hundred miles of track had been laid in all of the United States, and only a handful of trains were yet lurching their slow, experimental way across the American landscape. Yet even then, Key West was sure it wanted a railroad. Indeed, as early as 1831, a call appeared in the editorial column of the *Key West Gazette* for the construction of a railroad to connect the island of Key West with the Florida mainland.

A bold plan, certainly. But also a ludicrous one. Had anyone on that upstart island actually consulted a map? Key West was separated from Cape Sable, the closest point on the Florida mainland, by over seventy miles of open sea. Even if this gap were somehow bridged, the railroad would have to contend with endless tangles of dense coastal mangroves and the waterlogged muck of the Everglades, which was still virtually unexplored and had a sinister reputation. As it passed further north, and struck dry ground, this theoretical railroad would have had to somehow navigate the country of the Seminole Indians, who had been defeated in 1818 by Andrew Jackson and his rough militia, but who still held stubborn dominion over a large territory in central Florida. Clearly, the Cape Sable route offered no outlet for Key West's railroad dreams.

Another possible route existed, to the east, but it was little better. Key West lies near the western end of a ragged archipelago of islands, called the Florida Keys, which string themselves along for over a hundred miles before finally joining with the mainland. There was some dry ground here, such as on Big Pine Key, but there were also many miles of open water, including one seven-mile gap between Little Duck and Knight Keys. Furthermore, many of the "islands" that did exist were barely worthy of the name and consisted of soupy mudflats stitched together by mangrove thickets. Still other keys were mere outcroppings of inhospitable coral rock, which one contemporary observer, Dr. J. B. Holder, described as "black and jagged, looking like rotten ice," rising barely above the water line. Even when the ground was solid, it was inhospitable; mosquitoes abounded, yet paradoxically, fresh water was scarce, conditions that would make the life of a railroad laborer all but unbearable. Once the mainland was reached, the land became more solid, but a prospective railroad-builder would still have to contend with the formidable Seminoles, who were unlikely to suffer the construction of a possible route of invasion through their territory.

Given these geographic realities, one can only agree with the assessment of Jefferson B. Browne, customs collector at Key West, that "the traveler approaching Key West . . . cannot but wonder" why so many people had "congregated on a spot so manifestly and completely isolated from the rest of the world." The fact that Browne wrote these words in 1896, following six decades of rapid settlement in the Florida peninsula, only underscores Key West's profound isolation in the 1830s. At that time, the closest American cities of any size were the panhandle port of Pensacola and sleepy old fort-town of St. Augustine, and both were nearly four hundred miles to the north. Tampa and Miami, the two cities that would later exert a powerful influence on Key West's destiny, did not yet exist in 1831—indeed, another half century would pass before the Miami pioneers finally declared themselves to be a city.

An objective observer in the 1830s, in fact, might have guessed that Key West's future lay not with the Anglo-Saxon north, but to the Latin south. The Cuban city of Havana had become large and prosperous by the 1830s, and a mere ninety miles of water separated it from fledgling Key West. And indeed, Key West's history would be profoundly shaped by its nearness to Spanish Cuba. Nonetheless, it is the railroad, and not the Spanish Caribbean, that captivated Key West's ambition in 1831.

Even if these geographical problems could be overcome, any railroad would still have to contend with the reality of the hurricane. South Florida boasts some of the world's best weather, but it is also particularly vulnerable to the terrifying storms that periodically sweep in from the mid-Atlantic tropics, leaving horrific devastation in their wake. In 1835, in fact, just four years after Key West first announced its railroad dreams, the first recorded hurricane in Key West's history raged through the city, bringing with it waves of astonishing height. Low-lying areas on the island were flooded, and the heaving seas dashed at least a dozen large vessels onto the reefs of the Florida Straits.

The 1835 storm, however, was a mere teacup tempest compared with the Great Hurricane of 1846, which Jefferson B. Browne later called the "most destructive of any that has ever visited these latitudes within the memory of man." After leaving hundreds dead and thousands homeless in western Cuba, the Great Hurricane swept due north and unleashed its full fury on Key West on October 11. A naval officer aboard the revenue cutter *Morris,* which happened to be in Key West's port at the time of the storm, later reported that at the storm's height, "the air was full of water, and no man could look windward for a second. Houses, lumber, and vessels [drifted] by us—some large sticks of lumber turned end over end by the force of the current." Another observer, the customs agent and future Confederate Secretary of the Navy Stephen R. Mallory, claimed that "slates from roofs, boards, and even heavy pieces of timber were driven through the air like straws, and one piece of plank, nine feet by fourteen inches wide, came from a distance like an Indian arrow and penetrated the weatherboards and ceiling into one of the Customs House rooms."

As if to add insult to injury, the '46 hurricane played a particularly ghoulish joke on Key West. Not content to trouble the living, the hurricane outraged the dead as well: the storm surge tides accompanying the storm uncovered the cemetery on the southern shore of Key West and scattered skeletal remains through the town. According to one horrified observer, "after the storm subsided, one coffin was found standing upright against the bole of a tree, the lid open, and the ghastly tenant looking out upon the scene of desolation around, as if in mingled wonder and anger that its rest had been so rudely disturbed." These old bones were eventually laid back to rest alongside a new batch of corpses, as the storm killed an estimated twenty-five people out of Key West's two thousand–odd inhabitants.

Even if the problems of geography and weather could be overcome, sheer human arithmetic seemed to dictate against a Key West rail line. In 1830, the year before the *Key West Gazette* first championed the idea, Key West had only 517 inhabitants: 368 white, 83 "free Negro," and 66 enslaved. By the standards of the rest of the country, Key West was a mere village in 1830, and it would be anoth-

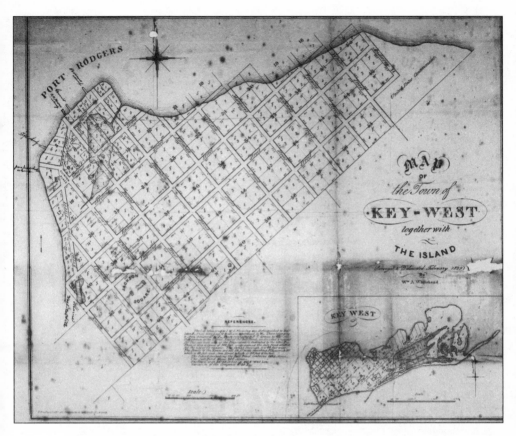

This 1829 map of Key West by John Whitehead, one of the early settlers, was more plan than realization, as most of the population of about 500 was clustered near the port. (P.K. Yonge Library of Florida History)

er two years before the town even declared itself to be an incorporated city. Perhaps if Key West was undergoing a population explosion during the 1830s, its desire for a railroad would be understandable, but this was just not the case. Between 1830 and 1840, in fact, the population of Key West increased by only 171 people, or 17.1 per year, which is hardly an impressive statistic. If located elsewhere in the country, a town of Key West's size would have counted itself lucky if a railroad deigned to notice its existence. Yet Key West expected a rail line to be delivered to its very door, even though hundreds of miles of howling wilderness, open water, and trackless marshlands separated it from the rest of America. What cheek! What presumption!

Key West's desire for a railway connection with the mainland in 1831, therefore, seems to verge on madness; the logic of geography, constraints of the climate, and the reality of demographics all dictated against it. Yet Key West's railroad dreams would not die. In 1835, a second Key West newspaper, the *Inquirer,* published an editorial calling for the construction of a Key West rail line. Fifteen years later, the idea gained a powerful champion in the person of Stephen R. Mallory, now graduated from customs agent to U.S. Senator, who urged the Federal government to run a rail line to Key West, or "America's Gibraltar" as he put it, due to its dominating position in the Gulf of Mexico. Mallory was banished from American politics after picking the wrong side in the Civil War, but later Florida politicians followed his lead, and in 1879 they went so far as to charter a rail company with the ambitious title of the "Jacksonville, Tampa, and Key West" railroad line. This act of the legislature, however, by no means precluded other attempts to run rails to Key West. In both 1880 and 1883 entrepreneurs from Georgia declared themselves willing to attempt the project, only to be thwarted by the sheer scale, and astronomical cost, of the undertaking. The time was not yet ripe for the realization of Key West's long-cherished railroad dreams.

Why was such a minor town afflicted with such a grandiose ambition? Key West's early history provides few clues. By all accounts, in fact, Key West's origins were quite humble and gave little indication of the island's illustrious future.

Key West was "discovered" by the Spanish in 1513, but they were far from its first inhabitants, as the Spanish themselves knew all too well from painful personal experience. Although stories of contact between Native Americans and Europeans generally revolve around the wrongs done by the white man upon the red, Native Americans actually enjoyed the upper hand in south Florida well into the modern era. Consider, for instance, the fate of D'Escalante Fontenada, a Spanish boy shipwrecked in southern Florida in 1547.

Fontenada and several shipmates survived the wreck only to find themselves forcibly captured and enslaved by the tribes of Florida's southeast coast. It would be seventeen years before Fontenada finally escaped the captivity of the south Florida natives.

By the seventeenth century, however, the Native American population of the keys had plummeted, primarily due to the ravages of Spanish-brought diseases, and the Spanish had begun to refer to Key West as "Cayo Hueso," Spanish for "island of bones," since the key was reportedly strewn with great piles of human remains. The modern-day name of Key West, in fact, is most likely a bastardization of the Spanish designation: *Hueso* became West over the passage of time.

With the natives slain by European diseases, Key West remained for years an obscure and neglected corner of the vast but ramshackle Spanish colonial empire. A small fishing colony, founded by Cubans to feed the hungry city of Havana, was long the only habitation in the area. In 1763, control over Key West and the rest of Spanish Florida passed to the British, but the British were as neglectful as the Spanish, and did little with the newly won territory. During the English interregnum, in fact, the town of Key West vanished entirely, since the few Spanish settlers of the Keys evacuated both themselves and the remaining Indians rather than submit to British rule. Following the American Revolutionary War, the territory reverted to Spain, but the already tottering Spanish empire, which had done so little to develop the island even during the height of its power, had no resources to spare on Cayo Hueso during its years of decline. Eventually, the Spanish governor of Key West granted ownership of the island to a certain Juan Pablo Salas in 1815, but he did nothing with it. Seven years later, one year after Florida was purchased from Spain by the U.S. government, an American businessman by the name of John W. Simonton acquired title to the territory in a Havana café for the sum of $2,000. At least in theory, then, Key West was now the property of an American.

Simonton's purchase of Key West was no whim, but rather an

informed gamble; he and his business associate, John Whitehead, envisioned that Key West would become an important American port and naval base. As Simonton wrote to the Secretary of the Navy, "if this place was made a Port of Entry it would in all probability become a place of deposit for the productions of other Countries . . . as it may be termed a key for the whole of the Bay [Gulf] of Mexico and the north side of the Isle of Cuba." The secretary of the Navy, impressed by Simonton's letter, dispatched Lt. Matthew C. Perry to examine the naval possibilities of the island, and to formally take possession of the island on behalf of the U.S. government. Perry, who would later secure his place in history as the commander of an 1853 American diplomatic expedition to open up isolationist Japan, wrote a letter back to his Washington superiors that positively gushed with enthusiasm. Key West, he claimed, "possesses many advantages as a Naval Rendezvous," and he speculated that, during a time of war, "undisputed possession of the Florida Keys will be a matter of great importance as it will insure undisturbed Navigation" of the Florida Straits for U.S. merchant vessels.

Key West, then, was blessed with considerable strategic advantages, but in the short run, a combination of difficulties ensured that Simonton and Whitehead would benefit little from their purchase. Before Key West could be made a profitable American port, for instance, it would have to be swept clean of pirates, who from time to time frequented its many sheltered coves to collect water, weather storms, or lie in wait for passing merchantmen. Although the golden age of Caribbean piracy was already over by the nineteenth century, the years after 1812 saw a temporary revival of pirate predation since many sailors who had been employed during Napoleonic Wars and the War of 1812 suddenly found themselves out of work and unable to make an honest living. Key West was unlikely to turn much of a profit, Simonton and Whitehead realized, until these jackals of the sea were driven once and for all from the Florida Keys.

Furthermore, despite the formal transfer of the territory to U.S.

jurisdiction in 1821, the U.S. claim on the islands was by no means undisputed, and in particular, vessels flying the Bahamian flag had long relied on the shipwrecks and marine life of the Florida Keys for their livelihood. Although their activity as wreckers was largely benign and saved many lives, including that of John Whitehead himself, the Bahamian presence in the Florida Keys was a source of considerable annoyance to the fledgling U.S. government. As British citizens, these Bahamians often sympathized with the victims of U.S. government policy, and on more than one occasion they helped ferry runaway slaves and fugitive Seminole Indians out of Florida and into the havens of the British Caribbean. Furthermore, American wreckers and fishermen, who began to arrive on the scene in the aftermath of the War of 1812, were highly resentful of Bahamian competition along the Florida Reef.

The exploits of pirates and Bahamian wreckers eventually became so irritating to the U.S. government that it finally resolved, in 1823, to dispatch the quaintly named "Anti-Piratical West Indian Squadron," under the command of Commodore David Porter, with orders to eliminate the pirates and establish a credible U.S. military presence in this new and undeveloped corner of America. Porter and his men, including the future Civil War naval hero David "Damn-the-Torpedoes" Farragut, arrived in April with a small flotilla of ships, including the first steam-powered vessel ever to sail under the flag of the U.S. Navy. Like Perry, Porter brimmed over with enthusiasm concerning the naval advantages of Key West. The island, he said, "commands the outlet of all trade" in the Caribbean, it "protects the outlet and the inlet of the trade of the Gulf of Mexico." Furthermore, in case of war with Spain, ships stationed in Key West could "hold in subjection the trade of Cuba" and check the naval forces of Cuban ships.

To top it all off, Key West boasted one of the best natural harbors in the young nation, though this crowning virtue was not apparent at first glance to the casual visitor. Most harbors are defined by islands, capes, or other projections of the mainland that break the force of the ocean. In the case of Key West, however, the harbor is protected from the sea by a series of reefs, small islands, and shoal waters that combine to girdle the northwestern end of the island and create a wide basin of calm water. According to a visitor to the island in 1871, "these protecting arms of the reef, divided by the blue of the channels," could be seen from the lighthouse on calm days; when the north wind bellowed, on the other hand, the reefs were revealed only by the "falling crest, complete dispersion, and retreat" of the wind-blown waves as they dashed against the submerged coral breakwaters. Once inside the harbor, a ship-captain would discover its waters to be marvelously deep, even immediately adjacent to the shore. Commodore Porter, greatly impressed, would later write to his superiors that the island boasted the "best harbor, within the limits of the United States or its territories, south of the Chesapeake."

In the meantime, however, Porter proved to be more of a hindrance than a help to Key West's fortunes. To the dismay of Simonton and Whitehead, Porter treated the key as his own private property. Disregarding Simonton's claim of ownership, he built his naval installation on the choicest part of the island and relegated the actual owners of the territory to less commercially attractive locations. Worse yet, Porter and his sailors commandeered the resources of the island, including wood, sheep, and hogs, without any compensation for the owners. As the Florida historian John Viele has put it, Porter "in effect . . . declared martial law" during his tenure as Commodore of Key West. Eventually Porter's high-handed actions, including an unordered and illegal invasion of Puerto Rico, earned him a court-marshal in 1825, much to the delight of Simonton and his associates. With Porter removed from the picture, Simonton and Whitehead's investment finally paid off. Freed from piracy and Porter's interference, the merchants and property owners of Key West finally settled down to relative peace and prosperity.

Still, Porter left at least one enduring mark on the landscape at Key West: the naval station he built in 1823, which was long the southernmost such base belonging to the United States. As Porter predicted, the island's excellent harbor and marvelous location would make it crucial to U.S. coastal defense. In the early years, however, naval personnel sent to Key West were probably more impressed by the island's pestilent climate than the island's strategic advantages. At one point during the period between 1923 and 1928 no less than forty-eight of the island's garrison of 118 men were struck dead by yellow fever. Ironically, disease ultimately proved more deadly than pirates to Porter's "anti-piratical" squadron. But despite the threat to American servicemen, the naval base persisted, and the U.S. government has remained an important force in the history of Key West ever since.

Despite the presence of the naval station, however, Key West remained quite a humble town during the 1820s. As of 1827, Key West still had barely three hundred inhabitants, and the town would not even have a regular post office until 1829. Worse yet, the Key West postal station was visited by a mail steamship only once a month, so the presence of this far-flung postal service out-post did little to reduce Key West's profound isolation from the rest of the U.S. Despite this isolation, however, Key West boasted one of the most diverse and exotic populations in the United States. Thelma Strabel's vivid novel of Key West, *Reap the Wild Wind*, includes a memorable description of Key West's early inhabitants. On a given day, she wrote, one might see

> Cockney-speaking wreckers from the Bahamas; lean Connecticut fisherman . . . courtly silk-hatted gentlemen from Virginia and the Gulf States . . . Canary Islanders, Cuban lottery-ticket sellers, conch divers, swarthy Spaniards . . . Turtlers from the Tortugas, and Cuban eggers . . . a big Bahama Negress undulated down the street with a basket of crabs on her head, and a tall "Spanish Indian" [Seminole] passed, as silent as a shadow.

This motley cast of characters shared a small settlement on the northwest portion of the isle, and the rest of the key remained wild. Eaton Street defined the eastern border of habitation, and beyond it, "the woods crept up to the town. It was a low, lush, threatening jungle growth. You felt," wrote Strabel, "that one night it might steal up and claim the town again."

Key West's occupations were as varied as its inhabitants. As with most port cities of the day, a fair portion of its livelihood derived from watering, provisioning, and repairing passing ships. Still other Key West inhabitants worked as ship builders. In addition, Key West continued in the role it had served while an outpost of Spain, namely providing fish for Havana, which had great appetite for seafood thanks to the Catholic tradition of "meatless" Fridays. Another large group of Key West denizens were employed directly or indirectly by the naval base.

In addition to these standard port-city jobs, Key West sported a fair number of more exotic professions. The island, for instance, was called home by many "turtlers," who made a living capturing and

On land sea turtles could be captured by flipping them over on their backs, rendering them helpless and unable to escape. (USF Special Collections, Floridiana Collection)

slaughtering sea turtles. Although rare today, sea turtles once swarmed the south Florida shore: as late as 1890, in fact, after decades of harvesting, observers still reported that sea turtles were "so abundant in the waters of south Florida that a man could walk, if they were solid, from the back of one to the back of another for quite a distance." Seventy years earlier, when Key West was still young, the supply of turtles must have seemed inexhaustible.

Hunting these hapless creatures was ridiculously easy. Sea turtles traveled in large bands, which made it possible to harvest a great many at once, and they congregated in clear, shallow water, which made them easy to spot. Although some turtlers employed a harpoon of sorts in their hunts, and others used nets, even these tools were unnecessary; a competent hunter could catch a turtle using nothing more than skill at diving and a rope. The trick was to grab the turtle by the back of the neck and pull backwards, while simultaneously using the knees to press down on the turtle's back. This would angle the turtle's body upwards, and as a result, the turtle's desperate struggles to dive deep would instead bring it to the surface. All that remained was to hook a lasso around the turtle's neck, and the capture was completed. If, on the other hand, a turtler wished to remain dry while capturing his reptilian quarry, he needed only to wait until the June breeding season, when female turtles would heave their ponderous bulk onto the shoreline of the keys to lay their eggs. As one naturalist reported, during this vulnerable time, a turtler "had only to walk the beach and turn on their backs as many as [he] could use," since once flipped over with a wooden lever the turtles were helpless.

After they were captured, the turtles were placed into "kraals," or corrals, which at the time were common sights along the Florida Keys. Kraals were simple affairs, little more than wooden stakes driven into a muddy tidal flat. Here, the turtles would await slaughter, since their flesh was the base ingredient of a much-loved soup, highly prized in Northern cities. Depending on the type of turtle, the shell might be valuable as well; hawksbill turtles, for example, provided lovely shingle-like scales used in the manufacture of combs, snuff boxes, and other such ornamental bric-a-brac favored by the ladies of the North.

Other Key West inhabitants focused their efforts, not on the turtles, but on their eggs. Turtle eggs had a strong, salty flavor that could be rendered more palatable by careful preparation: they could be fried with butter, pepper, and salt, or else scrambled. Alternatively, the eggs could be used instead of hen's eggs when baking cakes and pastries; indeed, according to one observer, turtle eggs are "preferred for that purpose by some cooks who take a pride in their profession." Fresh turtle eggs, unfortunately, could not be stored for long. After a week, they lost their moisture, and were "little better in looks and taste than so many balls of white rags." Eggs pulled from the bodies of slaughtered turtles, however, could be preserved by a combination of pickling and sun-drying, and once so treated, they could be stored indefinitely. Today, because of continued harvesting of turtles and ongoing habitat destruction, sea turtles are on the edge of extinction. In the 1820s, however, turtles and their eggs were a much-loved staple of the south Florida diet, and a vital Key West industry.

๖ ๖ ๖

Despite the income derived from ships, fish, and turtles, Key West's population remained quite small up until the mid-1840s. In 1840, New York City claimed over 312,000 inhabitants, and even a second-ranked American city such as Charleston, South Carolina, could claim over 29,000 inhabitants. Nearer at hand, just ninety miles across the Florida Straits, the bustling Cuban city of Havana boasted an impressive total of 135,000 residents. Key West, in the meantime, could claim only 688 inhabitants in 1840; compared to the major cities of North America, then, Key West was barely a speck on the map. And this tiny hamlet, this bizarre outpost cut into the subtropical scrub, wanted a railroad? Hah! What Key West needed was not rails, but people, and many

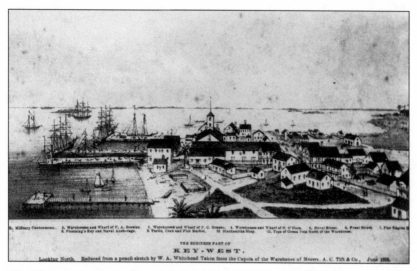

Key West in 1838 looking north. Large buildings along waterfront are merchants'
warehouses for storing salvaged cargoes. (from a sketch by W. A. Whitehead, courtesy of
Monroe County Public Library)

more of them. Unless Key West somehow managed to grow by a
factor of ten or more, it was unlikely even to be noticed by a railroad developer.

Key West rose to the challenge. In the period between 1840 and
1850, the population of Key West boomed, rising from 688 to
2,645, an increase of 280% over ten years. During the tumultuous
Civil War era, this upward trend was momentarily checked, but by
1870, Key West boasted 5,657 inhabitants, and by 1880 this number had risen to 9,890, which represents a fourteen-fold rise in population over four decades. From mid-century onwards, in fact, Key
West had become the largest city in Florida, and it remained so for
nearly fifty years.

What fueled this sudden spike in population? Several factors
played a role, but the most important was the development of several highly lucrative industries, some unique to Key West, that for a
while made the city one of the wealthiest in America.

One such industry was salt-making. In addition to the "threatening jungle growth" described by Strabel, the eastern portion of the

island was (and still is) graced with several large tidal flats, which could be blocked up, drained, and sun-dried to produce sea salt. The yield of these "salt ponds," as they were called, was small at first: in 1845 the ponds produced only 2,000 bushels of salt, and a year later, because of the ravages of the Great Hurricane of 1846, the ponds were washed out and produced no salt at all. In 1847, however, the production of the salt ponds jumped to 40,000 bushels, and eight years later, it topped 75,000, making Key West a significant exporter of salt. The prosperity brought by salt-making, incidentally, brought little comfort to those actually engaged in the labor of filling, draining, and harvesting the salt ponds; by and large, this toil was performed by black slaves who worked in atrocious conditions. Little surprise, then, that Key West salt-making was hurt badly by the emancipation of slaves following the Civil War. The year 1855, in fact, proved to be the apex of the industry, and in the aftermath of the Civil War, labor shortages led to years of sharply declined production. For a short while, however, the salt

A twentieth-century photograph of buyers examining sponges on the dock in Key West, relatively late in the sponge trade. (Florida State Archives)

industry brought very considerable wealth to Key West.

Salt-making came and went, but a second Key West industry, sponge harvesting, proved to be much more profitable over a far longer period of time. In the fifty-year period between the mid-1800s and the century's end, the Key West sponging industry provided nearly all of the nation's sponges, and the industry ranked as one of the state's most profitable maritime professions. Key West owed this prosperity to a number of favorable environmental factors. Out of the thirteen sponges which are commercially viable worldwide, eight could be found in waters off Florida. Furthermore, most of Key West's sponges could be found in relatively shallow reef waters no more than fifty feet in depth, allowing spongers to harvest them even with relatively primitive equipment. Wealth was there for the taking, then, as long as a man was willing to endure the hardships that sponge harvesting entailed.

And indeed, the hardships imposed by this most bizarre of industries were considerable. Early Key West spongers would spend weeks or months at sea in small, ill-provisioned vessels that provided little shelter against south Florida's scorching sun and sudden, unpredictable storms. To a certain degree, these difficulties were alleviated by the large freshwater springs that used to boil up in several places just off the Florida coast. While anchored inside one of these springs, which could be recognized by the "oily" appearance they gave to the water, a sponging boat was relatively safe from open swells of the sea, able, as south Florida sponging expert Kirk Munroe claimed, to "ride out the severest gale in safety." Munroe is perhaps overstating the case, but there can be no doubt that these upwelling springs far offshore provided welcome sources of fresh water for thirsty sponge boat crews.

Underwater springs, however, did little to alleviate a further hardship, namely the stench associated with dead sponges. Once brought to the surface, sponges immediately begin to decompose, and according to one observer, the rotting of the sponges beneath a tropical sun produced what Munroe described as "an odor so powerful and offensive that the presence of a sponge-boat can be detected a mile or more from the leeward." As if the stink of decomposition was not bad enough, spongers faced a further aerial menace in the form of mosquitoes, which infested the mangrove swamps and tormented all who dared make a living off of the south Florida shore.

South Florida sponging, at least as it was practiced at Key West, required two essential tools: a long pole equipped with a three-pronged hook, and a bucket with a glass bottom. The latter tool, dubbed a "water-glass," was an essential aid to spongers, since when half-submerged in the water, it allowed the spongers a clear and relatively undistorted view of the sea bottom. Once a valuable species of sponge was spotted, the sponger grabbed his sponge hook, which could be up to sixty feet in length, and used it to snatch the sponge from the rocks below. This was easier said than done; the pole was generally quite heavy, the sponges were far below, and a sponger's vision was confounded by a combination of dim light (some sponges were fifty feet under) and the refractive qualities of water, which were not entirely overcome by the water-glass. Despite the difficulties, skilled spongers could achieve remarkable results with these primitive tools, and few boats returned to Key West before they were filled to the brim with harvested sponges.

Next came the task of sponge cleaning. When taken out of the water, a living sponge bears little resemblance to the dry, pockmarked end product known to American consumers, who are probably used to synthetic sponges. Rather, a fresh sponge looked more like a "black, slimy mass," since mucuslike flesh still clung to the valuable skeleton. To remove it, spongers allowed the sponge to rot in the sun while on the boat, and when the boat was full, they would place the sponges in a "crawl," built with wooden stakes on a nearby key, where decomposition was allowed to continue. Once most of the flesh had rotted away, the spongers would beat the sponges with wooden bats until all animal matter had been dislodged from the sponge. Finally, the sponge (or more properly, its pliable and absorbent skeleton) would be compressed and stuffed into a cargo hold, and the process would begin anew, until the holds were full.

All that remained was to return to port and sell the sponges, but this too could prove a hardship on the spongers since they did not receive anything like a fixed price for their hard-earned harvest— quite the contrary, in fact. At three o'clock on each day, a sponge auction would be held at the Key West city wharf, and prospective buyers would make bids on each pile of sponges using small pieces of folded paper. As Munroe noted, the spongers awaited the closing of the bids impatiently, since "to them it represents all that is worth living for, and they will be passing rich or comparatively poor according to the price it brings." Even if the price was fair, however, half of the money from the sale immediately reverted to the owner of the sponge boat, so only half remained to be shared by the rest of the crew. The lion's share of wealth from sponging passed to the owners and merchants, then, and not to those poor "bronzed and brawny toilers who have torn it from the bottom of the sea."

Once sold, Key West sponges were clipped of coral residue, bleached, dried, and placed in specially designed baskets which could be flattened with powerful screws, so that they could be packed as tightly as possible before being shipped overseas. Then, depending on the type of sponge, it would be put to a number of different uses. The daintiest sponges generally found their way into ladies' toiletry kits, while rougher sponges were used to make roofing paper, and middle-grade sponges were employed by leather makers in the curing process. Other sponges, generally of the finest quality, were used in pot making, since they could be employed to impart a fine, smooth finish to delicate pottery.

Of all the Key West sponges, those of the "anclote grass" variety followed the most roundabout route to market. At the time, Mediterranean ear sponges were well known for their medicinal value, especially for their utility in staunching the flow of blood through large, open wounds. The anclote grass sponges, which were often harvested in Key West, had the same general size and absorbent properties as the Mediterranean sponge, but not the correct shape. This, however, did not deter enterprising sponge merchants, who purchased the anclote grass sponges in Key West and shipped them to Europe, where they were cut to resemble the elephant ear sponge and then "exported" to America as "Mediterranean ear sponges." Quite a testament to the selling power of a name brand!

In any case, by 1892, in the heyday of the sponging industry, good-quality sponges could command a price of over $60 a pound, or the equivalent of nearly $1000 in year 2000 U.S. currency. To put that value in perspective, pure silver was worth only about $16 per pound at the time. Good sponges, then, were worth almost four times their weight in silver. In the same year, the total income brought by Key West sponging topped a million dollars, and Key West had become the single most important sponge harvesting and distribution center in the world. Small wonder, then, that Key West's population grew so dramatically as the 1800s progressed.

Although of great importance to Key West's economy, however, sponging was never Key West's dominant industry. Nor did it define Key West's heart and soul. Rather, the industry which formed the core of Key West's identity—and provided the lion's share of its mid-nineteenth-century wealth—was wrecking.

On this point, all accounts of Key West history are in absolute agreement. As early as 1838, a Key West lawyer wrote that Key West derived its primary income "in, by, and through wrecks—if we are not directly interested in the business, our support wholly comes from it. Stop that," he claimed, "and we cease to live." In *Reap the Wild Wind*, Thelma Strabel concedes the existence of other industries in Key West, but she insisted that wrecking was "the real, the one business of the town," and that it made Key West's residents "gloriously proud." Even observers from outside Key West understood the importance of wrecking to the identity of the town; a columnist for the *New York Times*, for instance, stated bluntly in 1854 that "wrecking is the business of Key West."

This is not to say that the city of Key West invented the industry. Quite the contrary, in fact: the history of wrecking in Florida preceded the founding of Key West by hundreds of years. Within a few decades of Columbus' "discovery" of the Americas, Spanish treasure fleets began to sail from the Caribbean back to Europe, heavy-laden with gold and silver which had been extracted, either through war or through enslavement, from America's indigenous peoples. Before returning to Europe with their ill-gotten gains, however, these ships had first to navigate the treacherous Florida coastline, and this was no easy task. According to historians of the Spanish Caribbean, a Spanish galleon following the Gulf Stream back to Europe was obliged to "pass between Scylla and Charybdis," since the great Bahaman Bank would smash any ship who strayed too far to the south, and the Florida Reef, which runs roughly parallel to and five miles south of the Florida Keys, threatened any ship that wandered to the north. Even the "sounding leads," weighted lines which were used to determine the depth of the water, provided little protection, since both reefs consisted of coral ledges rising steeply from the deeps, and as a result it was rarely possible for a treasure galleon to anchor itself to the bottom before striking the reef.

The dangers of the Florida Straits were further compounded by the weather. In the late summer and fall, the Caribbean is vulnerable to hurricanes, which frequently splintered entire treasure fleets caught as they passed through the perilous Florida Straits. In winter or spring, on the other hand, Spanish ships might find themselves at the mercy of northeasters, which would rise up suddenly and lash passing vessels with furious gales before blowing themselves out, often in a matter of hours. Even when the weather grew calm, this might bring no safety. In the Florida Straits, lack of wind was just as dangerous as wind itself, since a becalmed vessel could find itself a helpless victim of the strait's strong currents, powerless to prevent itself from smashing up upon a reef. Given these dangers, it is little wonder that shipwrecks were a common occurrence during the great age of Spanish treasure fleets. D'Escalante Fontenada fell victim to a shipwreck of this sort, as did many others; in fact, as Fontenada's account vividly demonstrates, shipwrecks were so common that Spanish survivors formed a sort of expatriate community among Florida's Indian tribes.

Evidence suggests, in fact, that the first "wreckers" along the Florida shore were Native Americans. Fontenada, for instance, describes the Ais Indians north of the Miami River as being extremely wealthy, but "from the sea, not from the land"; over the years, this tribe had scavenged a fortune in bars of silver, gold, and Mexican jewelry from Spanish shipwrecks. Unlike later Key West wreckers, who saved crews as well as cargos, native wreckers generally killed or enslaved any Spaniards they found in the foundering ships, though as Native Americans gained greater knowledge of Spaniards (and greater respect for Spanish military might) they generally made it policy to spare the lives of Spanish-speaking captives.

Native American wrecking was, incidentally, no flash-in-the-pan phenomenon—tribes living on the Florida Keys apparently relied on shipwreck loot for their livelihood for as long as two hundred years. As late as 1722, a marooned French priest stranded on the Florida Keys found himself in the company of a band of native wreckers who, as far as he could tell, had no source of income other than European shipwrecks thrown upon the reefs by the sea.

The frequency of shipwrecks in the Florida Straits, combined with the less-than-welcome treatment the Indians generally afforded to Spanish survivors, prodded the Spanish into action, and by the middle of the 1500s the Spanish authorities had established a wrecking tradition of their own. Indeed, Spanish wrecking was quite sophisticated. Spanish authorities in the Americas created a total of four permanent wrecking stations in the Caribbean, including one at the Cuban metropolis of Havana. Each of these stations was equipped with both sturdy salvage vessels and a contingent of trained divers who were usually Bahamian Indians, Keys natives, or pearl divers borrowed from the oyster beds of the Caribbean isle of Margarita. In normal years, these wrecking crews might have to rescue several ships a year from the teeth of the reef, but when the hurricanes blew and entire flotillas of Spanish ships fell victim to the storm tides, these wreckers found themselves very busy indeed.

In 1622, for instance, a September hurricane followed a Spanish treasure fleet of twenty-eight vessels through the Florida channel and dashed at least six of them against the reefs, killing over five hundred Spanish crewmembers and passengers in the process. The wrecking operation that followed lasted over five years and ultimately led to the nearly complete recovery of all treasure from the *Rosario* and some of the treasure from the *Margarita;* a third treasure galleon, the *Atocha,* was not located and salvaged until the 1980s. Ironically, the Spanish wreckers were very nearly themselves wrecked; at one point during the 1622 salvage effort, a second hurricane roared through the Keys and nearly submerged the small key where the Spanish wreckers had sought safety.

Spanish wreckers faced an even more difficult task in 1715 when a treasure fleet of fifteen ships was all but destroyed by a ferocious early-season hurricane as it sailed along the east coast of Florida. Only a single vessel survived the tempest, and over seven hundred Spanish sailors perished in the storm. In the following spring, Spanish wreckers established a salvage camp at Sebastian Inlet, which is about fifty miles south of Cape Canaveral. By all accounts, the Spanish efforts were fruitful, and a great deal of the treasure was recovered from the sunken vessels. Still, quite a lot of gold and silver went unfound, much to the delight of modern scuba-equipped divers, who have been so successful in recovering gold and silver from wrecks that this entire portion of Florida has earned the nickname the "treasure coast."

Eighteen years later, yet another Spanish convoy was caught by a hurricane off the Florida coast, and this time no less than nineteen of the twenty-two ships in the fleet were wrecked along the Florida reef, including three treasure galleons. Unlike the 1715 hurricane, which took a heavy toll in Spanish lives, the 1733 hurricane killed relatively few people, and most of the sailors and passengers managed to reach the shore in the storm's aftermath. Many of these survivors, however, soon envied the dead, since the Spaniards found little water on the sun-scorched keys, and the parched survivors were tormented by thirst. The miserable condition of the castaways did not, however, prevent the Spanish government from employing them in the salvage operations, and within ten days of the storm, salvage camps were set up in the keys nearest to the sunken vessels.

To protect their 1733 salvage operation, the Spanish constructed two forts, each with four cannons, to protect the main wrecking camp. In addition, the Spanish conducted patrols of the nearby waters and stationed an armed sloop in the vicinity of the sunken treasure galleons. Why these elaborate precautions? In part, they reflected the sheer value of the recovered cargo; the wrecked 1733 fleet carried valuable bags of cochineal and indigo dyes as well as thousands of boxes of silver and hundreds of ingots of copper. To a greater degree, however, these military preparations were evidence that a group of interlopers had arrived on the scene, namely English-speaking wreckers from the Bahamas. These Bahamians called themselves the "Eleutheran Adventurers." The Spanish, who resented the intrusions of these unwelcome neighbors, called them pirates and turtle poachers. Under either designation, the Bahamians dominated wrecking in the Florida Keys for the next century.

These Bahamians, for the most part, were descendants of a group of Puritans who left Bermuda in 1648 in order to seek religious freedom on the Bahamian isle they called Eleuthera, which is Greek for "peace". Although their original plan was to live as farmers, they soon found themselves forced back to sea by the infertility of the land, and they became experts at salvaging shipwrecks, which were a common occurrence in the heavily traveled but treacherous Florida Straits.

Early Bahamian society was strongly communal in organization, in keeping with their Congregationalist religious beliefs. According to the Adventurer's *Articles and Orders,* which governed the disposition of shipwreck salvage, all guns and ammunition became property of the community as a whole, in order to ensure common defense, while all remaining salvage would be split between the wreckers, the public treasury, and the original settlers of the island. This early constitution, however, was undermined by successive waves of other would-be wreckers, who began to stream into the Bahamian isles in large numbers, lured by news of the ever-increasing number of ships splintered against the dangerous reefs of the Florida shore.

It is not entirely clear when these Bahamians began to frequent the Florida Keys, though the fact that the Spanish took such elaborate preparations against them during the 1733 wrecking operation suggests that they were already well-known Keys visitors by the 1730s. Visits by Bahamian wreckers became even more frequent after the Spanish withdrawal from the Keys in 1763; one year after the transfer of territory, in fact, a Spanish official passing from Havana to St. Augustine counted no less than fourteen Bahamian vessels in the Florida Keys. By the 1790s, the number of Bahamian ships to venture into the straits had climbed to at least thirty-seven a year. These Bahamians, it should be noted, did not depend entirely on wrecking for their subsistence. Indeed, most Bahamian vessels were also equipped for turtling, and nearly all Bahamian wreckers fished or hunted while in the Keys to stretch their limited shipboard food stocks. Still other Bahamians supplemented their income by cutting valuable hardwood timber from the Florida Keys. But wrecking was, and long remained, the main source of livelihood for the mariners of the Bahamas.

Contemporary observers had differing impressions of these Bahamians, or "Conchs" as they were often called, due to their fondness for the flesh of this large south Florida shellfish. Some considered the Conchs to be little better than pirates. Lieutenant Perry, who first planted the U.S. flag at Key West, called them "a Set of desperadoes who have paid but little regard to either Law or Honesty." Ten years earlier, however, another observer had claimed that "the *Natives of the Bahamas* have always as far as ever come into my knowledge, acted with Honor and Honesty to those unfortunate persons who wrecked among them." Still another observer wrote in 1892, with perhaps as much condescension as praise, that the Conchs were "the most simple-minded, honest, and inoffensive of seafaring men . . . he seldom swears, rarely drinks, [and] is as truthful as he is ignorant." On one matter, however, all observers were in agreement: Conchs had a curious way of talking. In Conch dialect, which resembled the English Cockney accent, v's became w's, and w's became v's, and the Conchs tacked an h sound onto the beginning of all words that started with a vowel.

Whatever their character, the Conchs had become permanent fixtures on the Florida shore by 1823, much to the dismay of American revenue collectors, who bemoaned that so much of the profit of the reefs was being reaped by ships sailing under the Bahamian flag. John DuBose, the U.S. inspector of customs at St. Augustine, noted that the Conchs considered wrecking the Florida shore "their right," and he complained that Bahamian wreckers, who took their salvage to Nassau rather than U.S. ports, were doing "very serious injury to the Revenue of the United States." In order to counter the activities of the Bahamian wrecking fleet, which DuBose estimated to be 120 vessels strong in 1823, DuBose advocated the "adoption of some energetick [sic] measures" to compel the withdrawal of the Bahamian wreckers. Two years later, DuBose got his wish, and the U.S. Congress passed a law requiring that all property salvaged in American waters must be brought to an American port of entry.

The purpose of this law was to exclude Bahamians from wrecking in the Florida Keys, and in the short run, it did precisely that. Within a decade, however, many of the Bahamian "Conchs" were back, having discovered a loophole: so long as they acquired U.S. citizenship, and operated out of American ports, they could wreck the Florida reef without restrictions. As a consequence, a large number of Conchs immigrated to Key West, and by the 1830s they had became the single largest group within Key West (or Key Vest, as they probably pronounced it). Indeed, the native-born citizens of Key West still call themselves "Conchs" today. In any case, this influx of Conchs meant that Key West soon became the unrivaled center of wrecking on the Florida shore.

Bolstered by the wealth of wrecking experience the Conchs brought with them to the city, the Key West wrecking industry expanded dramatically in the decades after 1830. In that year, there were still only about thirteen wrecking vessels based in Key West. Within five years, however, this number jumped to twenty, an increase of about a third. Key West wrecking suffered a temporary setback during the Great Hurricane of 1846, which either sank, dismasted, or beached nearly every wrecking vessel in Key West, and forced the wreckers into the bitterly ironic position of having to salvage their own wrecked vessels. By 1858, however, Key West wrecking had fully recovered, and no less than forty-seven vessels stationed in Key West boasted wrecking licenses.

Wreckers at work. (Florida State Archives)

This increase in the number of wrecking vessels reflects, to some degree, a gradual increase in the number of shipwrecks on the Florida shore. Although steamships were becoming more common in the period immediately before the American Civil War, the prewar years were also a golden age of large sailing vessels, which plied the Florida Straits in large numbers. As a result, wrecks became quite frequent; no less an authority than Stephen R. Mallory, Key West's custom collector, estimated in 1848 that a ship struck a reef along the Florida shore at a rate of nearly one per week. In the decade between 1849 and 1859, during which shipwrecks were at their height, there were at least 248 recorded wrecks, in addition to an unknown number of ships which either freed themselves from the reefs without assistance or vanished without a trace.

Wrecks along the Florida shore occurred so regularly, in fact, that the Atlantic coastline became littered with the battered residue of sailing ships. One observer, writing in 1871, wrote that "everywhere along the beach were fragments of wrecks . . . old hulks are seen on the shoals, and at high-water mark winrows [low ridges] of wood lined the shore." To a wrecker, this debris meant food on the table and money in the pocket. Misfortune in the Florida Straits, the wreckers knew, could mean fortunes made in Key West.

Wrecking could be a source of great profit, but it was no life of ease. Far from it, in fact: wrecking required both constant vigilance and backbreaking effort. Each wrecker's first task was to locate a wreck, and this meant days or weeks spent at sea either patrolling the shore or anchored near particularly dangerous reefs. As every wrecker knew, it was absolutely essential to be in the right place at the right time, since the captain of the first wrecking ship to arrive on the scene earned himself the much-coveted title of wreck master.

In theory, the wreck master received no more money for his labors than any other wrecker, since compensation was prescribed by law and custom, and the wreck master received no extra shares. In practice, however, being first on the scene was crucial to a profitable voyage. The wreckmaster was in charge of the entire salvage operation, and had the right to decide how many other wrecking vessels, if any, would share the job (and the resulting profits). In addition, the wreck master was able to negotiate with the captain of the foundering ship for a better rate of pay, and since conditions on the wrecked ship were often desperate, in many cases the wreck master's offer was accepted. Some wrecking captains, in fact, were willing to risk their own deaths and the deaths of their crews to be the first on the scene. One captain in particular, John H. Geiger of wrecking schooner *Champion,* was famous for braving shallow waters and gale force winds in his determination to be the first man to board a wreck. Geiger was well rewarded for his efforts: he ultimately participated in thirty-seven recorded salvage operations, amassed a large fortune, and sired eleven children before his death in 1885.

After having successfully reached the site of a shipwreck ahead of his many competitors, a wreck master's highest duty was to save the lives of the passengers and crew of the imperiled vessel. In some cases, this proved to be a difficult task, especially when the passengers were numerous and the wreck occurred far from a friendly port. In nearly all cases, the rescue of passengers and crew brought no profits to the wreckers. Established law and custom dictated that all rescue efforts, however timely or heroic, were simply one of the obligations imposed upon the wreckers by their chosen profession. In 1837, for instance, when a certain Captain Benners of the wrecking ship the *James Webb* rescued sixteen desperate and half-dead shipwreck survivors clinging to the bow of their almost submerged vessel, he received many thanks but no money for his efforts. Captain Benners did eventually get $500 in payment, but only after his crafty lawyers convinced the Key West wrecking court that two of the survivors were black slaves, and thus were properly classified as cargo, not passengers, for the purposes of salvage. Benners was no doubt delighted by the decision of the court, though one imagines the two items of "cargo" in question were less than flattered by the judge's ruling.

Once the passengers were safe, the wreckers began the laborious and often perilous task of rescuing the vessel or, failing that, salvaging the cargo it contained. In the case of the latter, it was generally necessary to begin unloading as soon as possible, since most wrecked ships were under enormous strain from winds and tides and could break apart almost without warning. As a result, wreckers often found themselves contending with the same heavy seas that had caused the wreck in the first place. The decks of the boat would lurch underfoot—indeed, more than a few wreckers were bruised and battered by the heaving waves. Sometimes the wrecked ship would lie on her side, or at a bizarre angle, and in nearly all cases, most of the ship would be under water, forcing the wreckers to dive into dark, crowded ship holds to retrieve the cargo. Despite these dangers, there is not a single known case of a wrecker being killed while working a shipwreck, though history does record numerous injuries. The wreckers' vessels, too, rarely escaped unscathed, and it was common for wrecking craft to suffer split sails, cracked masts, lost anchors, and stove-in hulls while wrecking the Florida Straits.

In addition to the perils of the sea, wreckers faced an unexpected danger by land between 1836 and 1840: attacks by the Seminole Indians. The Seminoles were by no means a constant threat to the inhabitants of the Keys, and for the most part the Seminoles and settlers left each other alone. After 1836, however, the Seminole Indians became so enraged by years of betrayed trust and deception by federal agents that they struck back hard against white men in Florida. The first victims of the Seminoles were the regular army forces of Major Francis Dade, who had led his men on a march through Indian territory in transit between two forts; out of the 108 men in the company, only three survived to tell the tale of the so-called Dade Massacre. Once the Seminoles were stirred into action, the inhabitants of the Keys did not escape their wrath, and no group in the Keys were more vulnerable than the wreckers, who traveled in small, widely separated parties along the wild coast of the Florida shore.

In October of 1836, a small wrecking vessel was unexpectedly attacked and destroyed by a war party of thirty Indians, and the wreckers barely escaped with their lives in the ship's rowboats. Evidence suggests that a second wrecking vessel and its crew may have barely escaped a planned Seminole ambush in 1839. A year later, the Seminoles struck again, this time targeting the prosperous wrecking settlement which had been established on Indian Key, about seventy-five miles east of Key West. The Seminoles attacked at the light of dawn on August 7th, 1840, and by the end of the raid, five settlers were dead, including the noted naturalist Dr. Perrine, who was conducting botanical experiments on the key at the time of the attack. In the aftermath of the Indian Key massacre, panicked white settlers all but abandoned every island in the Florida Keys outside of Key West.

If they managed to survive the Seminoles, the wreckers still had to contend with a far more hostile tribe once they returned to Key West—the lawyers hired by the shipping companies. Before a wrecker could realize any profit for his hard labor, he generally had to await the ruling of the wrecking court at Key West, which determined what percentage of the value of the vessel and the cargo the wreckers would receive. In the early days of wrecking, when awards were determined by local juries, wreckers might receive as much as ninety-five percent of the value of the salvage, leaving only five percent to its owners. To ship owners and insurance companies, however, awards on this scale were little better than piracy, and they successfully pushed for the creation of an admiralty court authorized to determine the fair rate of compensation received by wreckers. Within a month of the court's creation in 1828, the first seven lawyers arrived in Key West, and within two decades, at least twelve major court cases involving wrecking settlements were passing through the wrecking court each year, in addition to an unknown number settled by out-of-court arbitration.

Once a wrecking case came to court, litigation generally revolved around the amount of compensation the wreckers would receive for their salvage operations, and since this was determined largely by the difficulty of the conditions in which the wreckers worked, the lawyers of the wreckers and those of the shipping companies generally painted vastly different pictures of the same event. The wrecker's lawyers would describe cresting, white-capped swells, while the shipper's lawyers would claim the weather was calm and mild. What looked like backbreaking exertion to a wrecking lawyer might, when described by an insurance attorney, seem like an easy day's labor. In the words of the Keys historian John Viele, "often the differences between the two stories made the judge wonder if they were describing the same incident." After weighing the rival claims of the contending lawyers, the judge would award the wreckers a percentage of the cargo's value; this percentage generally hovered at about twenty-five percent, though in some extreme cases, such as instances where most of the cargo had to be retrieved by diving underwater, the wrecker's share might be as high as sixty percent. In other cases, if the judge determined the wreckers had acted dishonestly, he might award them nothing, or even take away their wrecking licenses entirely. In 1836, for instance, three caffeine-loving captains lost their shares of the reward for the salvage of the *Dorothea Foster* after the court learned they had pilfered small amounts of coffee and sugar from the wreck—which just goes to show the price people are willing to pay for their beloved cup of joe.

Assuming a wrecker managed to successfully navigate the perils of the sea, the shore, and the courtroom, he would finally receive payment for his labors. As is the case in nearly all human industries, however, compensation for working men was far from equitable. Instead of receiving wages, crew members were paid in shares of the salvage award. Before the crew received anything, however, half of the proceeds of the wreck were claimed by the owner of the salvage vessel, and the captain was given three shares of the remaining half. Since the owner and captain were often one and the same, this meant that the rest of the crew had to make do with less than half of the profit of the voyage. As a result, the common crewmen generally received little for his labors, even if the voyage as a whole was lucrative. If the salvage operations were unprofitable, on the other hand, the crew might receive a pittance, or nothing at all. As one contemporary observer of the wreckers noted, "his profession is that of taking a share in a lottery. He may draw a prize, but he is more likely to receive a blank."

As a general rule, the only members of the crew who were well paid for their exertions were the divers, who did the worst and most terrifying labor of the entire wrecking team. Divers would be obliged to swim as deep as thirty feet, make their way into the ship's holds, and then attach rope lines to cargo containers before rushing to the surface to gasp desperately for air. Quite often, the ship's holds were pitch black, and the diver would have to work by his sense of touch alone. Worse yet, in some cases the water of the holds was polluted with dye, paints, patent medicines, lamp fuel, and other caustic materials, and more than one diver lost his eyesight while salvaging the holds of a sunken ship. Small wonder, then, that divers could make as much as ten times as much as a common crewman. They earned every penny.

The divers notwithstanding, most of the income derived from wrecking made its way into the pockets of a few rich families who provided the vessels, captained the boats, and owned the warehouses in which the salvage was stored. Loxi Claiborne, the heroine of Thelma Strabel's *Reap the Wild Wind,* belonged to such a family, and her household epitomized the wealth and opulence that wrecking could bring. Her mansion, described as the largest in Key West, was graced with brocaded curtains made of silk, cane-bottomed chairs, four-poster beds, mahogany chests, and a pianoforte draped with a blue-green Chinese scarf (the latter, recovered from a wreck, was slightly stained by salt water). The Claibornes themselves were veritable royalty in Key West, and were welcomed as equals by the rice aristocrats of Charleston, the whalers of New Bedford, and the sugar planters of Havana. Although fictional, Loxi and her family were quite representative of the glittering upper crust of Key West society.

However unequally distributed, wrecking brought real wealth

to Key West. By the 1830s, Key West had become the wealthiest city per capita in the American South, and perhaps even the North as well. In the prosperous 1850s, $16 million worth of salvage from five hundred wrecks passed through Key West, and the greatest years were still to come; in 1873 alone, seven hundred ships struck the reefs of the Florida Straits. Key West was turning splintered wood into gold, growing fat reaping the harvest of the stormy seas.

◎ ◎ ◎

By mid-century, then, Key West had come a long way from its humble start as a fishing village on the Isle of Bones. Its population was surging, its port was thriving, and its coffers were swollen with sponges and wrecks. Furthermore, it had become a major American naval base, recognized in Washington as the "Gibraltar of the Caribbean." Given this dramatic change of fortunes, then, perhaps the idea of a Key West railroad was not so ridiculous after all. Even without a rail connection to the mainland, Key West was becoming a thriving town. Once linked to the land, who knew what heights the city might achieve? So Key West should have a railroad, every Conch agreed. It *would* have a railroad, they insisted, in the fullness of time—assuming, of course, that the hurricanes cooperated.

2

Salvage, Starch, and Seminoles

In order to better acquaint you with the unique geography of the south Florida shore, which will serve as our setting for the rest of this book, I would like to send you on an eastward journey by sailboat from Key West. The year is 1850, and you have just finished a pleasant week's visit with the quaint inhabitants of this most curious of American cities. The time has finally come to depart, but before heaving off, you consult the crude navigational charts you purchased in Key West and consider your possible routes.

One option is Florida Bay, the triangle-shaped wedge of water separating the Keys from the mainland. In the end, though, you decide against it; according to the Conchs of Key West, Florida Bay is a trackless tangle of underwater shoals and small mangrove islets, and you feel no inclination to put Conch expertise to the test. Well, then, how about the Florida Straits? This is the most well-traveled route, of course, and you are curious to see the midnight-blue waters of the famous Gulf Stream with your own eyes. After much thought, however, you reject this route as well. You are not eager to take your small vessel out into the choppy waters of the open sea—and in any case, you are looking forward to encountering the sights and sounds of natural Florida, which would be concealed by the northern horizon if you followed the Gulf Stream through the Florida Straits. As a result, you opt for the third route—the narrow but calm avenue of water, called Hawks Channel, which lies between the Florida Reef and the Keys proper. Although large boats rarely brave it, Hawks Channel is the perfect route for a small sailboat like your own: it averages over ten feet deep in most places, and is sheltered by the reef from the swells of the open sea.

Your decision made, you bid farewell to your hosts on the island and set out to sea. After leaving the thriving city of wreckers behind, you find yourself tracing the southern coast of the Florida Keys, a mismatched collection of swampy sandbars, mangrove thickets, rocky outcroppings, and dense wooded keys. A well-spoken Key West Conch of your acquaintance, you remember, had described Florida Keys as "the sweepings and debris which the Creator hurled out to sea after He had finished shaping the Florida Peninsula," and you cannot help but agree. The wild and nearly uninhabited Florida Keys appear in your eyes to be little more than a hasty afterthought tacked onto God's master plan.

As you travel eastwards, you spot the top of an occasional sail in the distance to the south: most likely a merchant vessel passing through the Florida Straits, you decide. Now and again you pass near small but sturdy boats, much like your own shallow-draft sloop, patrolling Hawks Channel. Wreckers, you tell yourself, and you hope you will not require their services before the trip is over. While in Key West, you heard countless stories of wrecked ships and imperiled passengers, and you have no desire to become a wrecker's legend yourself. Eventually, after eighty-odd miles and dozens of low-lying islands, you pass by Indian Key, and you shiver, remembering stories you have heard about the Indian attack that ravaged the island only ten years before. For the next twenty miles, you imagine that every log or piece of driftwood beached upon the shore is a Seminole canoe, and in your mind, every bird cry sounds as sinister as a war whoop.

Finally, at about the hundred-and-twenty-mile mark, the wall of keys on the port side of your vessel opens up and reveals a wide expanse of water, about five or six miles across and forty miles long. The water here, you soon realize, is quite shallow, and several times your small craft leaves chalky streaks in the water behind you as your keel scrapes against an underwater sandbar or mud bank. You have entered Biscayne Bay, and according to the wreckers of Key West, even seasoned Conch sailors have trouble navigating its many shoals. Dangerous or not, however, you have little choice but to proceed, since your water supplies are running low, and Biscayne Bay, you know, is the best place to refill your nearly empty casks.

After half a day of sailing, the Bay begins to narrow, and soon the Cape Florida Lighthouse approaches on the starboard side. It

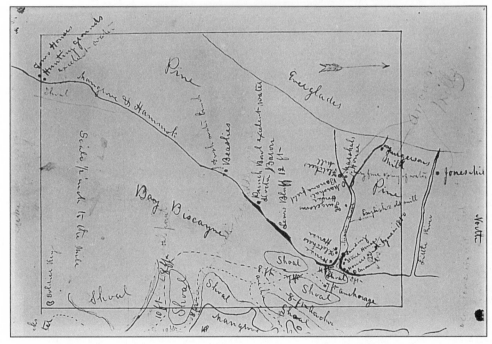

An early sketch map of Biscayne Bay, drawn during the 1800s by an American military officer. (Florida State Archives)

looks newly built, as indeed it should. During the Second Seminole War, you were told, Indians attacked the lighthouse and, in an effort to smoke out the lightkeepers who sought refuge at the top of the lamp tower, set the interior of the structure on fire; the lighthouse was not finally rebuilt until 1846. During the Civil War, the lighthouse would be attacked again, this time by Florida Confederates who smashed the lenses of the light in order to wreck havoc on Union shipping. But that is still ten years into the future. In the 1850 present, the sight of the Cape Florida Lighthouse fills you with a great sense of comfort and relief, since it is the first human-built structure, outside of the occasional turtle or sponge crawl, that you have seen in days of sailing the lonely Florida shore.

As you continue north, and leave the Cape Florida light behind, Biscayne Bay becomes narrower and narrower, until less than two miles separates the mainland from the new line of keys to the east. If what the wreckers told you is correct, a stream of fresh water from the Everglades flows into the northern end of Biscayne Bay. But where is it? Doubt begins to gnaw your mind. Could you have possibly missed the entrance to the inlet? Finally, however, after rounding one last cape, you spy it in the distance: a shining highway of water, lined with coconut palms and mangrove thickets, leading into the Florida main.

With a sigh of relief, you turn your small boat westwards towards the shore. Anchoring your boat as close to land as you dare, you descend into the ship's launch and row your way into the mouth of the river. Since you are eager to explore this isolated cor-

"Bay Buisquine." (*Harper's Magazine*, 1871. University of Miami Archives and Special Collections, Otto G. Richter Library)

ner of the country, you follow the winding stream for several miles, past a ruined plantation and a handful of homesteads, until the current picks up and you hear the distant sound of rushing rapids ahead. Time to stop. Exhausted and thirsty from your exertions, you dip your cup into the stream, and drink deeply of the sparkling waters of the Miami River.

You are, of course, far from the first traveler to seek fresh water in Biscayne Bay. For centuries, Spanish explorers, pirates, Bahamian mariners, and wreckers all visited the area, in their time, seeking to replenish their water supplies. Biscayne Bay's history, in fact, is defined to a remarkable degree on the confluence of salt and fresh water.

In geographic terms, the Bay consists primarily of a long ridge of limestone rock, blanketed in tropical vegetation, which separates the fresh water of the Everglades in the west from the salt waters of the Atlantic to the east. This limestone dike, however, is far from impregnable. Beyond the obvious breach of the Miami River, fresh water escapes from the Everglades by flowing beneath the limestone through numerous underwater channels. Some of these underground veins of water erupt to the surface at the very edge of Biscayne Bay; one such spring, called the Devil's Punch Bowl, was a favorite stopping-off point for mariners traveling the Florida shore. Other such underground rivers do not discharge their water until they are far out to sea and form bubbling springs of fresh water in the middle of the bay. During the 1880s, the yachtsmen who would make the Bay their seasonal home managed to cap one such spring with a wooden platform and a pipe, much in the manner of an oil well, enabling sailors to secure fresh water without even leaving the comfort of their vessels. As one observer commented, this freshwater fountain surrounded by the salty sea was "a great convenience to yachts."

Despite the availability of fresh water, Biscayne Bay remained one of the most isolated locations in North America for centuries, due again to its precarious position as a boundary between fresh and salty water. To the east of Biscayne Bay lay the Everglades, dense and trackless, and inhabited by Seminole Indians with a fearsome reputation. Even if a voyager into the Glades survived an encounter with the Seminoles, he might run afoul of the legendary "Big Snake" of the Everglades, a huge creature with the horns of a great owl and eyes of fire that purportedly dwelled in the perilous marshland to the east. Between the Seminoles and the "Big Snake," few white men were willing to brave the waterlogged wilds inland of Biscayne Bay.

Although it contained no "Big Snakes," the ocean to the south and the west of the Bay was no less dangerous and had an equally treacherous reputation. Although the Florida Straits was a well-traveled waterway, few deep-draft ships ventured into the bay since they would have a difficult time negotiating the bay's shallow waters. Furthermore, the seventy or so miles of coastline above Biscayne Bay offered few harbors for ships, and this could spell disaster for sea travelers caught in the violent and unpredictable "northers" that occasionally rage along the Florida shore. As late as 1873, the crew of a storm-smashed vessel nearly starved to death after being wrecked on the uninhabited Florida shore only twenty miles north of the settlements of Biscayne Bay.

The only land route into Biscayne Bay was from the north, but this was in most ways the most difficult route of all. Since no roads had yet been cut into the dense palmetto scrub north of the bay, a traveler's only land-based option was to follow the beach northwards to the relative "civilization" of distant Lake Worth, and as the coast was low and swampy, neither horse nor wagon could be used. Most voyagers, in fact, opted to go barefoot along the muck of the coast rather than ruin good pairs of shoes during the seventy-mile walk. Even though technically part of the mainland, Biscayne Bay was as profoundly isolated as Key West. Perhaps even more so—Key West, after all, boasted a world-class deep-water harbor.

Given all of these geographical impediments, it is not surprising that Biscayne Bay's population remained quite low up until the twentieth century. True, in the centuries before the European conquest, the Miami area did boast a healthy population of Tequesta Indians, as evidenced by the numerous shell middens they left behind. One particularly large midden near the mouth of the Miami River, in fact, covered 750 square feet and stood over twenty feet high; when workmen tore it down during the construction of the Royal Palm Hotel, they discovered between fifty and sixty Indian skulls buried inside. Little is known about these Indians, however, and in any case, they were not able to withstand the disease and dislocation that accompanied Spanish incursions into Florida. Following the disappearance of the Tequesta, the Spanish themselves made two attempts to create a settlement on the site, once from 1567 to 1574 and then again in the 1740s, but both proved unsuccessful, in part because they made few friends amongst the few remaining natives, whom the Spanish claimed were prone to "rootless and unadulterated fickleness" and accustomed to "migrate as do the birds."

Following the failed Spanish attempt at colonization, Biscayne Bay's population remained small and intermittent for over a century. A few Bahamian mariners did come to the area in the early 1800s, including a fair number of black Bahamians, who created a small settlement a few miles south of the Miami River. During their tenure near the Bay, the Bahamians brought with them West Indian food crops, such as soursops, Barbados cherries, and sugar apples, which gave the foliage of the Bay a distinct West Indian character. For all practical purposes, then, Biscayne Bay was a fringe colony of Bahamian civilization for over a hundred years after the Spanish withdrawal from the area; as Miami historian Helen Muir put it, until almost the turn of the twentieth century, "south Florida might as well have been an island joined to the Bahamas by sailboat and custom." The Bahamian population remained quite low, however, and during the Second Seminole War, most of the few settlers in the area evacuated for safer havens.

By mid-century, a few settlers had returned. One ambitious early pioneer named William Fitzpatrick erected a large plantation at the river mouth in 1835, but it was destroyed only a year later in the Second Seminole War. The land then, belatedly, became an army base against the Seminoles, though with Fitzpatrick's plantation in ruins it was unclear what remained for the army to guard. In any case, after the end of the war, the mouth of the Miami River fell into disuse once more.

Interest in the property was revived once again a few years later, when the same land was purchased by William English, a South Carolinian who shared Fitzpatrick's ambition to transplant plantation slavery to the banks of the Miami River. Borrowing a large number of slaves from his mother in the Carolinas, English cut a sizable plantation into the scrub north of the Miami River and planted it with cotton, sugar cane, and limes. In addition, he ordered his slaves to build two large stone structures on the site: a barracks-like slave quarters, and a two-story structure that he intended to make his home. But English's plantation, a modest farmstead on a remote river, did not satisfy him. Like many Florida promoters to come, English dreamed of creating a paradise on Biscayne Bay. In his mind's eye, the Bay was transformed into a resort city, manned by slaves, where the upper crust of Southern society could luxuriate under swaying palms. To realize this dream, English needed cash, and since the year was 1849, he imagined he could get it in California, where the gold rush was in full swing. Not a man to dally, English sped himself to California by way of the Isthmus of Panama, but he found no gold, and his adventure eventually came to an ignoble end when he accidentally shot himself in Grass Valley, California, while dismounting from a horse. As we will see in later chapters, however, the idea of a resort city on Biscayne Bay did not die with him.

In any case, the two stone structures William English left behind near the mouth of the Miami River also survived their builder's death, and their eventual fate is nearly as colorful as English's own. In the first five years following the abrupt end of English's California dreaming, the two stone buildings were abandoned to the fast-growing tropical foliage, which rapidly reclaimed the site. In 1855, however, in the midst of the Third Seminole War, the U.S. Army reestablished an outpost at the mouth of the Miami River, and they chose English's old plantation as their base. The first visitors were unimpressed—the troop commander described the plantation ruins as "a two-story stone building without a roof, the first-story wall of a long structure and a small frame building"—but the military soon improved the site into a respectable little army base named Fort Dallas. Army laborers transformed the two-story structure into an officers' quarters and the small frame building into a hospital; the ruins of the slave quarters, in turn, were improved and renovated, and eventually served as a barracks for the common soldiers. Whether the soldiers were amused or angered at the prospect of being housed in a former slave's quarters, history does not record.

Much like the Spanish missions built earlier near the same site, Fort Dallas was destined to be short-lived. In 1858, the army abandoned the site, and returned the land to the ownership of the English family. During the years of the Civil War, the site of Fort Dallas became inhabited by what one Miami historian has called a band of a "dubious characters"—Confederate and Union deserters, blockade runners, and the odd Union spy. That these rough-and-tumble characters would agglomerate at Biscayne Bay is no surprise; frontier settlements far from government control almost always become havens for the human flotsam and jetsam set adrift by war. More surprising is the fact that two of the Confederacy's most notable leaders, John C. Breckinridge and Judah P. Benjamin, both former Confederate secretaries of war, graced Biscayne Bay with their presence near the war's end. They did not stay long to enjoy the tropical delights, however, and quickly boarded a blockade-running vessel bound for Cuba. Ultimately the Rebel pair would make their way to Europe, and several years of political exile.

Not long after these unrepentant Rebs escaped for Cuba, ambitious Northern opportunists called "carpetbaggers" began to make their way into the American South, and a few ventured all the way down to Biscayne Bay. One such gentleman was the unscrupulous William H. Gleason, who tried to take control of the potentially valuable Fort Dallas land tract through an ingenious, though sinister, courtroom maneuver. Decades before the 1860s, the land upon which Fort Dallas stood had been owned by a certain James Eagan, who had attempted to establish a coconut plantation on the Miami shore in the 1820s. Eagan, who hailed from the Bahamas and shared the same odd accent of his fellow Bahamians, apparently pronounced his name "Hagan." Since all the records of ownership reflected Mr. Eagan's pronounced rather than written name, Gleason made an unsuccessful attempt to convince the courts that a man of his own acquaintance, Mr. James Hagan, was the rightful owner of the property. Not surprisingly, given this past history of crooked dealings, Gleason also tried his hand at politics, and he even held the office of lieutenant governor of Florida for a time. His political career came to a crashing halt in 1876, however, when he was defeated in the Dade County election of 1876 by John J. "Pig" Brown, a Democrat and local pig farmer, who won the vote by a count of 27 to 24.

This same Gleason was also involved in a second great misadventure, one with national rather than merely regional implications. Immediately after the 1876 election that had removed him from power, Gleason went for a week-long hunting trip into the wild Florida scrub with the federal election returns for Dade County still in his pocket. As a result, the 1876 electoral contest remained in limbo, since the 1876 election battle was decided by a razor-thin margin, and the handful of voters in Dade County had the potential to decide the outcome of both the state and, with it, the federal election. As all of those who lived through the sorry spectacle of the 2000 presidential election know all too well, this would not be the last time that electoral irregularities in the Miami area would cloud the outcome of a national election!

In any case, following the sordid incident with Gleason, Fort Dallas' misadventures continued. By 1871, Fort Dallas was occupied by two gentlemen with a particularly strange scheme; according to one contemporary account, these men claimed to have received a land grant from the state authorizing them to create a colony in the area, which they apparently intended to fill with Swedish immigrants. This project failed miserably, however. By 1879, a certain J. W. Ewan, called locally the "Duke of Dade" since he served as Dade County's treasurer, surveyor, notary, and customs officer, had made the building his own, and was reportedly running an Indian trading post out of a room in the fort. At about the same time, the old Fort Dallas slave quarters/barracks was selected as the courthouse for Dade County, though given the miniscule population of Dade County at the time, very little actual legal business was conducted there. Still, the courthouse was a source of great pride for the inhabitants of Biscayne Bay, and when the town of Juno to the north managed to claim the title of county seat in 1889, Bay residents were unwilling give up the court records to the Juno upstarts. Eventually, the citizens of Juno were forced to recruit the help of a Seminole Indian to sneak the court records out of Fort Dallas in the dead of the night.

Fort Dallas, then, seemed to be the focus of those early settlers who harbored ambitions for Biscayne Bay, both the dreamers and the schemers. Most inhabitants of the Bay, however, were cut from

The mouth of the Miami River c. 1894. Fort Dallas is on the left-hand side; the other bank was the domain of the Brickell clan. (Florida State Archives)

more practical cloth. Indeed, given the area's few natural resources, just earning a living in early Biscayne Bay could be a considerable challenge. One of the few local products that turned a modest profit was Florida arrowroot, made from a native plant called locally "coontie" or "compte." Coontie is a relatively small plant, rarely more than a foot and a half in height, consisting of a large, rutabaga-size root topped with fronds of palm-shaped foliage, and it grows well in the rocky soil of the pineland covering Biscayne Bay's limestone ridge. Although the arrowroot was poisonous in its crude state, it could be rendered safe by careful preparation. First, the tubers were placed in a large wooden mortar or trough and beaten until they were reduced to a pulp. This pulp was thrown into water, which dissolved the starch in the root, creating a sort of "milky liquor." After being run through a course cloth sieve, this fluid was allowed to settle and the water was drained off, leaving only a white mass of pure starch. Finally, the starch was dried and packaged, and then sold to biscuit companies, or used locally to make what one contemporary described as an "exceedingly nice white bread."

For a while, the people of Biscayne Bay were able to turn a tidy profit on arrowroot. One historian of the Bay reports that a family of three or four with a grinding mill and a horse or mule could manufacture about one barrel, or 250 pounds, of starch per week. Since this amount of flour brought an average of $12.50 at the market in Key West, arrowroot starch was a potentially lucrative industry. Perhaps the only drawback to the industry was the smell; decomposing arrowroot, observers reported, could be quite pungent. Ultimately, however, what doomed this industry was not the stink, but scarcity. Coontie could be gathered, but since it grew wild in crevices in the limestone under pinewood forests, it was difficult to cultivate or replace once harvested. By the 1890s, the industry had all but died out, and as one Bay resident explained regretfully to the visiting explorer James Ingraham, "there is no money in starch making from compte."

The end of the arrowroot industry also meant the end of a

means of acquiring cash money, but no matter; historians of early Florida tell us that early Biscayne Bay residents did not necessarily need cash to survive. Most families had a few chickens, which provided both meat and eggs, at least so long as the chickens could be kept safe from the ravages of local raccoons and wildcats. If you had a gun, and most people did, you could hunt wild ducks and quails in the hammocks (hardwood stands) scattered through the pine uplands and the swamps bordering the Bay. Other meats were available, too: deer and wild hogs from the pinewoods and Everglades, plus turtles, fish, and manatees from Biscayne Bay. If all else failed, there was always fruit, including such exotics as the hog plum, coco plum, sea grape, and custard apple as well as better-known fruits like sapodillas, guavas, limes, and a few pomegranates. Though cash poor, Biscayne Bay's residents were so few in number that they rarely exceeded the natural food supplies of the Bay, and as a result, Bay dwellers almost never went hungry.

For other supplies, Biscayne Bay dwellers turned to wrecking, though not in the same sense as the inhabitants of Key West. True, some in Biscayne Bay had wrecking licenses, and participated in salvage operations when ships foundered on the reefs. Most inhabitants of the Bay, however, were wreckers of the beach-combing variety. Whenever supplies were low, the inhabitants of Biscayne Bay took their launches across the Bay to Cape Florida to salvage whatever treasures the sea might have washed up on the Atlantic shore. Since all sorts of ship traffic passed through the Florida Straits, nearly anything might turn up; in the words of Helen Muir, a historian of Miami, beachcombers might find anything from "a grand piano to silk shawls and a fancy carriage."

The early settlers of the Bay had little use for such finery, but the sea tossed up more practical items as well. Cheese, candles, soap, bags of flour, wines and liquors, canned goods, and household furniture all made an occasional appearance on the Atlantic shore. According to one Biscayne Bay legend, so many bottles of champagne washed up in the Bay after one shipwreck that a certain creaky-boned old Bay dweller filled a metal tub with champagne and then bathed in the bubbly concoction, in hopes that it would relieve his rheumatism. According to a still less credible legend, a Biscayne Bay mother with a newborn child once told her husband, "I wish you'd go over to the Cape and see if you can find a cradle." He did as he was asked, and sure enough, he found a child's cradle washed up on the beach. No doubt these stories are largely apocryphal, but they do highlight the importance of shipwreck salvage to Biscayne Bay's early inhabitants.

By far the most common piece of flotsam to wash up on the beach was timber, which could be either the splintered remnants of packing crates, or in the case of a truly catastrophic wreck, fragments of a shipwreck itself. Whenever the inhabitants of the Bay set their minds to constructing a new home, they would organize a timber-gathering expedition to Cape Florida, and would build rafts out of the driftwood logs before using the Bay currents to float them back to the mainland at the next high tide. The only construction materials the Bay residents generally lacked were nails and roof shingles, and only the former were a true necessity, since straw or palm thatch could be substituted for the latter. Indeed, the white residents of the Bay may have learned this technique from the Seminoles, who constructed thatched-roof huts of their own in their remote Everglades settlements.

Shipwreck timber was also put to other uses, such as coffin making, with occasionally regrettable results. One early Biscayne Bay legend concerns a newly-departed Bay woman who was placed in a locally built coffin for shipment to her relatives in the north. As the story goes, right before the vessel was to sail from Biscayne Bay, her neighbors noticed that one of the planks which made up her coffin had once been part of a packing crate, and bore the following inscription: "Mumm's Extra Dry." Realizing that such a label was a mite on the insensitive side, the people of the Bay quickly procured some white paint and covered over the unfortunate lettering.

※ ※ ※

Life in Biscayne Bay, then, was an uncomplicated affair, at least so long as a man was satisfied with a driftwood shack and a bellyful of coontie bread. For the more ambitious residents of the Bay, however, there was one possible avenue of self-enrichment: trade with the Seminole Indians of the Everglades. Indeed, for a period of over half a century, most of the Bay's wealth (such as it was) came from that source.

Many modern-day visitors to Florida assume that the Seminole Indians have always been in the Everglades, and that their intimate knowledge of this unique submerged grassland was born out of centuries, if not millennia, of lived experience. In fact, however, the Seminoles were relative newcomers to the Everglades, which they entered, not out of choice, but out of desperation. Florida's Seminole people owe their origins to the tribes of the Creek Confederacy, a powerful association of related Indian peoples centered in modern-day Alabama and Georgia. In the period after 1700, these Creeks began to penetrate Florida, at first in order to raid tribes friendly to the Spanish, and later as settlers in the northern portion of the state, which greatly resembled Alabama and Georgia in its vegetation and climate. Although slow at first, the Creek settlement of Florida increased dramatically in the period after 1812, largely due to the ever-growing pressure exerted on the Creek nation by the expanding United States. Since the Spanish crown was also worried about rising U.S. power, they made common cause with their former opponents, and actively invited Seminole tribes into north Florida. As a result, by 1800, an estimated thirty-six large villages of Seminole Indians had been established in Florida south of the U.S.–Spanish border.

The presence of so many Indian tribesmen near lands coveted by the whites, however, eventually caused friction with the U.S. government, especially since these Florida Creeks made a practice of offering shelter to slaves escaping the brutality of America's most peculiar institution. Indeed, the name Seminole is probably derived from the Spanish word *cimmaron,* which is in turn related to the

English word maroon, or "runaway slave." Whatever the origin of the term, hostilities between white Americans and the Seminoles, as the Florida Creeks were generally called, came to a head in 1817. After several months of raids and counter-raids across the Spanish–U.S. border, the U.S. general Andrew Jackson was given permission by President Monroe to launch a large-scale expedition against the Seminole tribesmen and their black allies, despite the fact that the expedition, which would have to pass through Spanish territory, was an egregious violation of international law.

The unlawfulness of the American invasion of Spanish territory was, truth be told, quite intentional. Part of Jackson's mission was to scare the Spanish out of Florida by demonstrating to the rapidly declining Spanish Empire that, should America chose to flex its growing muscles, Spain was powerless to protect its legal claim to Florida in the case of war with the United States. The Spanish seem to have gotten the message—only four years later, Spain agreed to sell Florida in its entirety to the U.S. government. As for the Seminoles, they saw which way the wind was blowing as well and withdrew deeper into the Florida Peninsula out of respect for the military power of the expanding United States. By the mid 1820s, the surviving 5,000 or so Seminoles had settled in a swath of territory ranging from the Apalachicola River in the Florida panhandle all the way to the Manatee River and modern-day Sarasota County.

In the decade that followed, the Seminoles accustomed themselves quite well to their new surroundings, and they even took advantage of their new-found proximity to the sea to establish trading contacts with the outside world. The best evidence for this comes from the writings of William Whitehead, the cofounder of the modern city of Key West, who discovered in 1831 the existence of a remarkable joint Spanish-Seminole settlement on Charlotte Harbor. According to Whitehead, the Spanish and Seminoles had joined together to create a fishing village of 134 Indian and white men, 30 Seminole women, and between 50 and 100 mixed-blood children. Some Seminole men, Whitehead reported, worked on the Spanish fishing vessels as crewmen, while others were involved in catching Florida birds for resale in the distant markets of Havana. These Charlotte Harbor Seminoles, however, were an exceptional group: the majority of Seminoles settled down to a more traditional hunting and farming existence much like they had enjoyed in Georgia and northern Florida.

The Seminoles were barely established in their new domains, however, before the land-hungry United States provoked a second war with the Seminoles. Really, the two conflicts were a continuation of the same basic struggle: the American whites wanted Seminole land and were angry that the Seminoles harbored escaped black slaves, while the Seminoles were deeply resentful of the depredations of white frontiersmen who had already begun homesteading in Florida. In 1834–1835, a series of talks took place between the U.S. government and the Seminoles over these outstanding issues. U.S. government policy, in these discussions, was to convince the Seminoles of the wisdom of removal to the west, and eventually about an eighth of the Seminoles agreed to accept money and land in Oklahoma in exchange for abandoning central Florida. Those who agreed to the government's demands, however, were making a fool's bargain: they would be deposited in the windy plains of Oklahoma, which bore little relation to southern pinelands they were accustomed to, with few supplies and very little food. For many, exile from Florida proved to be a death sentence.

Even though they could not possibly have known about the horrors of Oklahoma, most Seminoles had no intention of leaving Florida, and they demonstrated this quite forcefully to the whites in the so-called Dade Massacre of 1835, in which a Seminole raiding party of about 130 members wiped out almost an entire detachment of nearly one hundred American soldiers as it traversed a pine woodland near present-day Ocala. The massacre also made a martyr of Major Francis Dade, the force commander, and in tribute to the slain "hero" who had led his men to slaughter, south Floridians voted one year later to name the area between Indian Key and the Jupiter Inlet "Dade County" in memory of his death.

For the next seven years, the forces of the United States government tried to answer the Dade Massacre with a decisive blow of their own, but with little success. The Seminoles knew central Florida well, and since their encampments could be moved quickly when threatened, American armies sent into Indian country found themselves striking blindly against a dangerous but elusive enemy, capable of inflicting serious casualties upon the white forces before slipping away into the pine forests or the muck of the Everglades. The American forces were further hindered by their motley character. When General Winfield Scott, the future hero of the Mexican-American War, took command of Florida's forces in 1836, his army consisted of regular troops, volunteer soldiers, militiamen recruited by the state, and Indian allies hostile to the Seminole tribes. Scott attempted to use this pieced-together army in the grand style of the Napoleonic wars and marched it in great columns towards known Indian settlements, only to find them long abandoned. In the meantime, small bands of Seminoles launched devastating raids on American border settlements, including the infamous massacre at Indian Key and the assault on the Cape Florida lighthouse.

One of the few American commanders able to coax the Seminoles into fighting a field battle was Colonel Zachary Taylor, who located a large force of Seminoles north of Lake Okeechobee on Christmas Day of 1837. In the engagement, Taylor's 1,032 troops assaulted a well-prepared Indian position defended by 480 Seminoles, and suffered 26 killed and 112 wounded in the process. Seminole losses were only 11 and 14, respectively. Despite the lopsided casualty figures, Taylor held the field after the firefight, which made him the victor of the engagement, at least according to white rules of war. In reality, of course, the battle earned the American forces nothing, since the territory they seized was of no importance, and it failed to reduce Seminole fighting effectiveness in any significant way. Still, the resulting notoriety would serve Taylor well; in the aftermath, Taylor was promoted to command of the Seminole campaign, and he later earned the U.S. presidency in 1848, in part on the strength of his reputation as a stalwart soldier and Indian fighter.

Despite his later success in politics, Taylor was no more effective than his predecessors in bringing the Second Seminole War to a close. Ultimately, the Seminoles were overcome not by field battles, but by starvation, treachery, and stealth. Even before the war began, the Seminoles were low on food, largely because the U.S. government had reneged on the food supplies it had promised the tribesmen. During the war, the situation worsened, since the nomadic life the Seminoles were obliged to adopt during the conflict made it difficult for the Seminoles to grow much in the way of crops. The Seminoles also suffered from a lack of leaders after the first few years of the conflict, since the frustrated white commanders, unable to best the Seminoles in the field, resorted to the odious stratagem of seizing chiefs while under the flag of truce. The most notable victim of this practice was Osceola, victor of the Dade Massacre, who was seized in 1837 while negotiating with commander Thomas Jesup, and who ended his days imprisoned at Fort Moultrie in Charleston, South Carolina. Even his death in 1838 did not protect Osceola from one final outrage; the presiding surgeon at Moultrie cut off Osceola's head after he died and brought it with him to his home in St. Augustine, Florida. According to one account, the good doctor employed this grisly trophy to terrorize his children.

In the meantime, while Osceola's head was being put to ghoulish use in a north Florida nursery, Osceola's people in south Florida were steadily succumbing to starvation or hopelessness, and one group after another was captured or else grudgingly accepted the white man's offer of Indian territory in the west. In 1838 alone, General Jesup managed to dispatch nearly 2,000 Seminoles to the west, in addition to another 400 or so he sent to their graves. Taylor, who succeeded Jesup, exiled another 1,200 Indians and black allies, and his successor managed to capture another 700. By the time Colonel Worth took command of Indian operations in 1841, so few Seminoles were left that he was forced to resort to guerilla-style operations to track them down. By breaking his command into detachments of no more than twenty men, Worth was able to surprise the remaining encampments of Seminoles deep within the forests and swamps where they sought refuge. Consciously or unconsciously, Worth was using against the Seminoles the same strategy that the Seminoles themselves had long employed against the whites. Faced with the depredations of small, mobile groups of well-armed invaders, most remaining Seminoles were forced to surrender.

The Second Seminole War did not end—rather, it petered out. Eventually, so few Seminoles were left in Florida that Colonel Worth decided that he had broken the back of Indian resistance in Florida, and at the Worth Conference of 1842, he declared that all Indians remaining in Florida who did not wish to accept land in the West had the option of joining an Indian reservation near Charlotte Harbor. According to Seminole historian James W. Covington, the Worth Conference really signaled a victory of sorts for the Seminoles, since unlike so many other Indian tribes, some Seminoles were allowed to remain in their adopted lands rather than transplant themselves to an alien land and alien way of life in barren western Indian reservations. Covington also cites the extraordinary efforts required of the U.S. army to defeat the Seminoles as evidence of their success; at one point, nearly 50,000 men, including every division of the U.S. regular army, saw action in Florida, and over 1,400 were lost to combat or disease. In addition to this high human price tag, the war was an enormous drain on American finances, and it cost the government of the U.S. an estimated $40 million dollars, or the modern-day equivalent of nearly $670 million. Still, given their greatly depleted numbers and massive loss of territory, it is doubtful that many Seminoles considered themselves to be victorious in 1842.

Some Seminoles, in fact, were so discouraged by the Worth Conference provisions, and the meager lands set aside by the government near Charlotte Harbor, that they abandoned the reservation for the trackless wetlands of the Everglades. The government responded by sending expeditions against these intractable Indians, at great expense, but to little effect. Indeed, any rational observer might wonder why they didn't just leave these Seminoles alone; after all, why risk lives and waste government dollars to depopulate a remote and mosquito-infested swampland? In answer to this argument, Florida legislators would likely have pointed to the federal Swamp Lands Act of 1850, which made all submerged territories within the United States property of the state governments. Since Tallahassee was chronically short of cash, some Florida state legislators began to see greenbacks in the Glades; the sale of the Everglades, they reasoned, was an easy way to refill the state's empty coffers. Before the Everglades could be sold, however, they had to be surveyed and drained, and as a consequence, the state government encouraged surveyors and homesteaders to penetrate Seminole lands in southwest Florida.

Not surprisingly, the Everglades Seminoles were deeply troubled by these latest incursions, and clashes between the Indians and the white intruders became increasingly frequent. Well aware that they had already come out on the losing end in two previous clashes with the whites, however, the Seminoles tried to placate the American government, even to the point of surrendering Seminole warriors who had killed white settlers to state authorities for punishment.

Eventually, though, the patience of the Seminoles ran out. In December of 1855, a party of U.S. Army Engineers, who were running a survey line south of Fort Myers, entered an Indian camp occupied by Chief Billy Bowlegs of the Seminoles, and while there, they destroyed a stand of banana trees belonging to the chief. When an outraged Billy Bowlegs confronted the soldiers, they refused to make compensation and did not even apologize for their actions, which has led at least one historian to speculate that the survey party was attempting to deliberately provoke a confrontation in order to stir up public sentiment against the Seminoles. If so, the ploy worked: the enraged Seminoles attacked and killed four soldiers, and the Third Seminole War had begun.

Truth be told, this "war" barely deserved the name; rather, it resembled a guerilla action, in which approximately a hundred Seminole warriors played a game of hide-and-seek with over fourteen hundred American soldiers. At the start of the war, the Seminoles held the initiative and managed to stage fifteen successful raids against white settlements in South Florida, killing twenty-eight people in the process. By 1857, however, the vastly superior American numbers had begun to take their toll on Billy Bowlegs' men, and the remaining Seminoles, unable to hunt due to patrols of white troops, were nearing starvation. Finally, in November of that year, Billy Bowlegs finally accepted the American terms of surrender, and another 170 or so Seminoles were dispatched to Oklahoma territory. Following Billy's departure, the commander of the Florida forces, Colonel Loomis, declared unilaterally that the Third Seminole War was over.

Loomis' self-proclaimed victory notwithstanding, the Third Seminole War had not succeeded in its primary objective, which was to completely empty Florida of Seminole Indians. Indeed, the military commanders of the third war were well aware that a few bands of Seminoles remained in the Everglades, including one relatively large group of seventeen men and probably double that number of women and children under the leadership of the ancient Seminole chief Sam Jones, who was reputedly over one hundred years of age. Army scouts ordered to locate the Seminoles were unable to make any contact with these fugitive bands, though they did find recently abandoned camps in the Everglades. In 1859, Billy Bowlegs was brought back to Florida in an attempt to convince the survivors to remove themselves to parts west, and he did persuade another seventy-five men, women, and children to return with him to Oklahoma. This was destined to be the last official attempt at ethnic cleansing in Florida; in the following years, the eruption of the Civil War consumed America's attention, and the Seminoles were forgotten.

Between 1817 and 1859, then, the Seminole people were

reduced from a powerful confederation of thirty-six towns to a mere handful of left-over families. One observer, writing in 1869, dubbed the three hundred–odd remaining Seminoles in Florida a "remnant of a remnant." Be that as it may, this ragtag remnant showed surprising resiliency in adapting to life in southern Florida. Abandoning the settled agricultural ways of their Creek ancestors, who had raised cattle and cultivated large communal farms, the remaining Seminoles adopted a mixture of hunting, fishing, and small-scale agriculture perfectly suited to the Everglades. At the same time, the Seminoles ceased building the large cabinlike structures favored by the Creeks in Georgia, and began to construct "chickees," small thatched-roof structures open to the subtropical breezes of south Florida. For transportation, the Everglades Seminoles perfected the cypress log canoe, whereas their ancestors had mainly traveled on foot. The Seminoles also changed their appearance, abandoning the buckskins they had worn in northern lands in favor of loose-fitting tunics and turbanlike head dresses better suited to the subtropics. The Seminoles even adopted American technology, if it suited their needs; one visitor to the Seminoles in 1879 was surprised to find that the Indians possessed a well-constructed sugarcane mill.

These changes in lifestyle allowed the Seminoles to adjust quite well to their new abodes in a subtropical marshland, but they required the Seminoles to continue trading with the whites for items they could not themselves produce, such as guns, gunpowder, ammunition, cotton cloth, and metal tools. White traders, in turn, were happy to supply these needs in exchange for alligator skins, otter pelts, bird plumes, and other exotic animal products found in the Everglades. To this end, white merchants founded a number of trading posts along the fringes of Seminole territory, including establishments on the New River near modern Ft. Lauderdale, in the Big Cypress Swamp near Immokalee, at Everglades City, and at old Fort Dallas near the mouth of the Miami River.

Even before the Third Seminole War, white traders on Biscayne Bay had conducted trade with the Seminole Indians, and there is evidence that a store existed on the Miami River as early as 1844. The golden age of Miami Indian trading, however, began in 1870, when William Barnwell Brickell arrived at Biscayne Bay. By all accounts, Brickell was a fascinating man. A native of Ohio, Brickell was apparently afflicted with a restless soul, which drew him to California at about the same time as William English. Unlike English, however, Brickell did apparently manage to acquire a sizable fortune. Soon after, Brickell left for a tour of the Orient, where later he claimed (rather implausibly) to have met the emperor of Japan. At some point, Brickell found himself in Australia, where he met his future wife, an Englishwoman from Yorkshire. Brickell then returned to Ohio and established a grocery business there, or so he claimed: historians disagree as to whether Brickell's past as a successful grocer is a matter of actual fact or a product Brickell's overactive imagination.

Whatever the truth of Brickell's background, it is indisputable that Brickell and his family arrived in Biscayne Bay in 1870, and within a year of his arrival on the Bay, Brickell had constructed a two-story wooden home and a trading post on a low bluff overlooking Biscayne Bay and the Miami River. Brickell's post rapidly became a center of both white and Indian life. In addition to being the main grocery establishment on the Bay, the Brickell's store served as a post office as well as the center of Bay transportation; the Brickell's sloop *Ada* made regular trips to and from Key West in the period between 1870 and 1890. By controlling the lion's share of both transportation and trade, the Brickells soon became the biggest fish in the small pond that was Biscayne Bay.

Bay residents became so dependent on the Brickells for supplies, news, and transportation, in fact, that they grew to tolerate the rather poor customer service the Brickell family provided. Alice Brickell, the eldest of the Brickell children, was particularly infamous in this regard. Although she held the official title of postmistress of the Biscayne Bay mail station, Alice made little effort to actually distribute the mail, which she often dumped on a table and neglected for days at a time. Alice was no more considerate to shoppers at the Brickell family trading post. According to one early Miami tale, a customer once went into the Brickell's store and demanded size ten shoes, and Alice refused to sell them, claiming to have none in stock. The customer then pointed to a high shelf, upon which sat a box of shoes clearly marked size ten. Rather than backing down, however, Alice looked the customer in the eye and said, "Who's running this place, you or me?" Alice was, obviously, and the customer settled for size eight shoes.

Why was Alice so disdainful of her white customers? Quite possibly her actions represented nothing more than her own personal manifestation of the Brickell family tendency towards bizarre behavior. It is more likely, however, that Alice's behavior is a reflection upon the relative unimportance of white customers to the Brickell family business. Ultimately, the bulk of the Brickell family's fortune was derived, not from white men, but from the Indians left over from the Third Seminole War. The portion of the Everglades near the mouth of the Miami River boasted a relatively large clan of Seminoles, about seventy strong, and these Indians regularly descended below the rapids on the Miami River to trade at the Brickell's store. During the heyday of the Indian trade, the dugout canoes of the Indians brought the Brickells a number of trade goods, including alligator hides and teeth, buckskins, egret plumes, vegetables, and coontie starch. The Brickells, in turn, would sell the Indians salt, guns, ammunition, canned goods, sewing machines, and various decorative items, especially colored glass beads, which the Seminoles purchased by the hundreds. These beads, generally blue in color, were strung together to form countless necklaces, which would lie so thickly on a Seminole woman that they might cover her upper torso from the tips of her shoulders to her ears, and might weigh as much as twenty-five pounds.

According to most accounts, the Brickells treated the Seminoles fairly. One observer, it is true, claimed that the Brickells sold the Seminoles a pair of worthless binoculars fitted with ordinary glass instead of proper lenses. For the most part, however, the evidence suggests that the Brickells enjoyed quite good relations with the Seminoles. Indians were frequent guests at the Brickell's home and may have even attended Sunday religious services there. When friction arose between the Bay whites and the Seminoles, the Brickells usually supported the latter, even to the extent of writing Washington to complain of local mistreatment of the Seminoles.

The Seminoles clearly benefitted from the friendship, but there can be no doubt that the Brickell clan profited greatly from their relations with the Seminole Indians. One observer, writing in the 1880s, estimated the value of the Miami Indian trade at $2,000 annually, and this represents only purchases made by the Indians. The Brickells earned even greater profits on Everglades products that they bought from the Seminoles and then resold to other traders. A barrel of coontie starch purchased from the Seminoles for five cents a pound, for example, might earn twice that amount in Key West. The same held true for alligator hides, which the Brickells purchased from the Seminoles for a few dollars each before reselling them for a tidy profit to Key West merchants. During the heyday of the southern Florida Indian trade, Seminole hunters were harvesting thousands of dollars' worth of furs and hides from the Everglades every week, and the Brickells, who controlled a significant share of that trade from their base on the Miami River, grew wealthy from the profits.

The Seminole trade, however, did have one potential drawback. The value of many of the trade goods brought by the Indians, especially the hides, plums and skins, could fluctuate wildly according to the dictates of fashion in distant metropolitan markets, which meant that a good that was profitable one year might have little worth the next. Florida bird plume hats, for instance, were quite popular in northern cities until 1917, when they were adopted by prostitutes and soon disappeared from the wardrobes of fashionable ladies. Diamond terrapin turtle shells, on the other hand, were potentially worth two dollars each in New York City, but demand for them was spotty at best, and it often took weeks for a Miami Indian trader to find a buyer. The Indians, however, were not interested in the workings of far-away markets, and insisted on being paid a fixed price for their goods. As a result, Indian traders like the Brickells occasionally had to purchase pelts and hides at a net loss rather than alienate the Seminole hunters, on whose goodwill the entire industry depended.

Although the Brickell clan was more closely intertwined with the Seminoles than other Biscayne Bay families, they by no means enjoyed a monopoly on the Indian trade. Other Indian traders, such as the "Duke of Dade," sold wares to the Seminoles, and a great number of more informal relationships existed binding Seminoles to whites. Barter trade between the two groups was also very common, especially for food staples; settlers living along the coast, for instance, frequently traded fruits or vegetables to Indian hunters from the Everglades in return for fresh meat. In addition to selling goods to the whites, the Seminoles sometimes sold their own labor as well and frequently served as guides for hunting parties and surveying teams. The Seminole hunter Billy Bowlegs III was particularly sought after as a guide in the period after the 1880s, perhaps in part because of his blood relationship with the Third Seminole War chief who shared his name. By all accounts, then, the Seminoles were an important, if not indispensable, part of Bay Biscayne life in the late eighteenth and early nineteenth centuries.

It would be perhaps be too strong to call the 1880s and 1890s a "golden age" of the Seminoles—after all, the three hundred–odd Seminoles who remained in the swamps of south Florida after the three Seminole wars cannot compare to the powerful Seminole tribesmen who held sway over northern Florida seventy years earlier. Still, by all accounts, the remaining Seminoles were doing surprisingly well in the two decades before the turn of the century. Clay MacCauley, an agent of the government who visited every known settlement of the Seminoles in 1880–1881, was quite impressed by the Indians: "If judged by comparison with other American aborigines," he declared, "I believe they easily enter the first class."

This is not to say that MacCauley was blind to the weaknesses of the Seminoles. The Seminoles lacked a clear political organization, MacCauley noted, and they were a mite too fond of alcohol for their own good—a tendency, unfortunately, which grew over time. Nonetheless, MacCauley wrote favorably about the degree to which the Seminoles had been able to adapt to their new existence in the Florida swamps. MacCauley also commented favorably about the homes and the costumes of the Seminoles, which he felt were excellently suited to the realities of south Florida. He was even impressed by the physical appearance of the Seminoles, and described their menfolk as tall, handsome, and well-built, with square-shaped heads and copper-colored skin. The women, he noted appreciatively, had dark good looks, augmented by a simple two-piece outfit consisting of a long calico or gingham skirt and a low-cut shirt that barely covered their breasts.

Although impressed by his observations, Clay MacCauley foresaw trouble on the horizon for these attractive and versatile dwellers of the Everglades. Florida, he well knew, was beginning to change. The American frontier, which at one time seemed so vast and untamable, was beginning to be settled and domesticated by the 1880s, and white settlers seeking cheap land were becoming increasingly interested in the blank spaces on the map of south Florida. MacCauley was also well aware of the fact that the first wave of new settlers had already arrived in Florida, drawn by the promise of cheap land created by swamp drainage schemes north of Lake Okeechobee. As white pressure inevitably mounted on Indian land in coming decades, MacCauley feared, the Seminoles would be thrown into conflict with whites yet again, only this time, the geographic realities of the Florida peninsula left them no refuge, no room for retreat. Sooner or later, MacCauley predicted ominously, "a great and rapid change must take place . . . the Seminole is about to enter a future unlike any past he has known."

Time would prove MacCauley's prophesy correct. Within fifty years, William English's dream would be realized, and tiny Fort Dallas on the Miami River would balloon from a provincial Indian trading post into a vast resort city with seemingly unlimited prospects and ambitions. In the process, speculators and land developers would manage to do what the U.S. army had never been able to accomplish: strip the Seminole Indians of their independence and dignity. By the 1920s, the Seminoles would face two unenviable choices, obliged either to eke out a miserable existence as hunters in a vanishing wilderness they had fought three wars to keep, or else play the role of tourist attractions and golf course caddies in the fairyland of Miami. As we shall see, the Seminoles would be far from the last victims of unbridled human ambition on the south Florida shore.

3

Sails and Rails

Ralph Middleton Munroe was a mechanical engi-
neer by trade, but sailboats were his passion, and whenever the
opportunity presented itself, he set out to explore the bays and
waterways near his home in New York City. During one of these
many trips, while he was sailing in the vicinity of Staten Island,
Munroe helped rescue a small sloop belonging to a Florida Indian
trader. In an effusion of gratitude, the trader offered Munroe free
farmland in southern Florida, if Munroe ever happened to find
himself in such distant parts. It was the mid-1870s, and the Indian
trader was none other than William Brickell of Biscayne Bay.

Intrigued by Brickell's stories of life on the wild edge of America,
Munroe looked for a chance to visit, and in 1877, just such an
opportunity presented itself. In that year, an acquaintance of Munroe
named John Demarest fell ill, and his doctor suggested that a visit to
the healthful climate of Florida might alleviate Demarest's condition.
Munroe offered to tag along, but only on the condition that

Demarest visit Biscayne Bay rather than St. Augustine, the favorite Florida destination for invalids at the time. Demarest agreed, but getting to the bay in the 1870s was no easy task. Since boats did not sail directly to Biscayne Bay from the north, and would not do so on a regular basis for at least another decade, the two companions sailed first to the growing metropolis of Key West, in hopes of finding passage to Biscayne Bay from there.

As it turned out, Munroe and Demarest did not have long to wait. Soon after reaching the island city, they ran into William Brickell himself, who offered to take them to the Bay on his trading sloop, though (to Munroe's dismay) Brickell made no mention of the farmland he had offered to give Munroe several years before. Although disappointed by Brickell's failure to live up to his earlier promises, Munroe was in no way displeased by Biscayne Bay itself, which in Munroe's mind was even lovelier than old man Brickell had led him to believe. When he first arrived, Munroe later wrote, the Miami River was "a beautiful clear water stream, its banks lined with towering coco-palms and mangroves," and he was favorably impressed by Brickell's plain but substantial home built on a bluff at the river's edge. Other than Brickell's establishment, Munroe wrote, the works of man on the Bay were represented "only by a few primitive houses and small sailboats," and wildlife teemed in every direction. Munroe was absolutely enchanted. Although he and Demarest would spend only a few weeks at Biscayne Bay, Munroe's heart belonged to the Bay from that day forward.

In 1881, Munroe returned again, in the company of another invalid—this time it was his wife, who had contracted tuberculosis. Munroe hoped that the tropical breezes would restore his wife to health, but it was not to be; she perished soon after their arrival. Despite or perhaps because of her death, Munroe was determined to make the Bay his permanent home. For the next four years, Munroe labored in the north as a boat builder and designer, but always with the intention of returning to the Bay as soon as possible. He even hired a Biscayne Bay settler to construct a house for him; not surprisingly, it was built out of salvaged shipwreck timbers. Finally, in 1885, Munroe finally managed to extricate himself from his Northern commitments, and he moved to Biscayne Bay for good.

Munroe's move to the Bay was by no means unique. During this period, a number of middle- or upper-class Northerners transplanted themselves to Biscayne Bay, either as seasonal visitors or as full-time inhabitants. The fact that Biscayne Bay was remote and unproductive did not dissuade these intrepid Northerners; in fact, the very remoteness and poverty of the Bay appealed to a certain breed of American citizens. Biscayne Bay, wild and undeveloped, was the antithesis of the American North, which had entered what Mark Twain called the "gilded age," a period of rapid industrialization, urban expansion, and social dislocation. In his autobiography, Munroe seems almost gleeful when he declares that, in 1877, "no more isolated region was to be found in the country [than Biscayne Bay], and scarcely any less productive." Munroe and his fellow Bay-dwellers had found a diamond in the rough, and they reveled in the isolation of the Bay, which seemed frozen in time, and quite immune to the swift changes occurring elsewhere in the United States.

Although Munroe was probably the most vocal member of Biscayne Bay's small community of self-exiled Northerners, he was by no means the first. That honor probably belongs to Charles Peacock, an Englishman who ran a "ham and beef warehouse" in London during the early 1870s. Charles was persuaded to visit the Bay by his brother, "Jolly Jack" Peacock, who had secured a job running the "House of Refuge" for shipwrecked sailors on what is today Miami Beach, and who wrote effusive letters back to his brother in dreary London praising the Bay's tropical delights. Charles eventually gave in to temptation, and in 1875, he moved himself and his wife to the Bay.

It was rough going at first. Charles and his wife Isabella were initially shocked by the utter isolation of Biscayne Bay, which must have seemed light-years away from the bustle of London, still the world's most powerful and cosmopolitan city in the 1870s. In addition, they were likely somewhat intimidated by the shady characters who still haunted Fort Dallas in the aftermath of the Civil War; during the 1870s, in fact, Biscayne Bay still had a reputation for harboring renegades and runaway criminals, and according to one historian, post-war political tensions between Democrats and Republicans still ran so high that most local people did not dare attend the meetings of the county commissioners unless they were "armed to the teeth."

But Peacock and his wife stayed nonetheless, and in 1882 they built a hotel, which they called Peacock Inn, a few miles south of Fort Dallas in the town of Coconut Grove. Like all local houses, it was constructed of salvaged driftwood timbers, though its roof was fancier than most; it was made of honest-to-goodness shingles, each of which had been painstakingly cut from the white pine mast of a wrecked merchant vessel. Business was good from the first, due largely to a steady flow of shipwreck survivors, and soon became better, as their small hotel gained a reputation for warm hospitality and superb food. In order to accommodate visiting guests, who were drawn by word of the excellent hunting and fishing grounds located near Biscayne Bay, the Peacocks were forced to expand their hotel twice, each time adding a two-story annex to the main structure.

As the Peacock Inn's reputation grew, more and more lodgers began to sail into the Bay in their private pleasure boats, and this soon became a growing trend. Isolated Biscayne Bay was becoming a fashionable wintering spot for aristocratic members of the yachting set. One of the first to visit the Bay was former Confederate General Jubal A. Early, a Virginian who had voted against secession but who loyally supported his native state during the Civil War years. By 1887, so many yachts entered Biscayne Bay annually that the local residents established the "Biscayne Bay Yacht Club," with Munroe as its first "commodore," a title which he treasured for the rest of his life. For an emblem, the Biscayne Bay club adopted a

Sailing across the becalmed bay, Kirk Munroe approches Coconut Grove anchorage. Key Biscayne in background. (Ralph M. Munroe, Historical Association of Southern Florida)

large N superimposed upon the number twenty-five, which was supposed to signify that the Biscayne Bay Club was located near the twenty-fifth degree of north latitude, making it the southernmost yacht club in the entire United States.

Munroe's appointment as commodore of the yacht club came as no surprise to anyone in Biscayne Bay. Ralph Munroe was involved in the project from the very beginning: he and the other founding members supposedly came up with the idea over a pot of coffee, and divvied up the high offices of the club on the spot. Even if a formal election had been held, however, it is likely that Munroe would have earned the honor, since in 1885 Munroe had designed a new type of schooner, a "round-bilged sharpie," which rapidly became indispensable to life on Biscayne Bay. Munroe's sharpie was stable enough to risk the open seas, and could sail from New York City to Cape Florida in less than seven days, but also boasted an extremely shallow draft of only twenty-seven inches, making it perfect for the Bay's shoal waters. In the period after 1885, Munroe's design rapidly became a fixture on the Florida shore, and Munroe began to earn a busy living as a boat-builder. Munroe also dabbled in a number of other professions: he was a harbor guide, a turtler, a sponge cultivator, and even owned a wrecking license.

Other early Bay Biscayne residents earned their living, not with the sweat of their brow, but with the nibs of their pens. In fact, a number of Biscayne Bay residents earned a living with the nibs of their pens. Probably the most well-known such author was Kirk Munroe, a celebrated author of adventure stories for boys. Inspired in part by the wonders of Biscayne Bay, Kirk proved to be a prodigious writer during his lifetime, but his career still pales before that of his own mother-in-law, Amilia Barr, who eventually wrote an astounding eighty-eight novels, including the hugely popular *Remember the Alamo*. Although Kirk was not a blood relative of the Commodore, he was certainly a kindred spirit, and he shared both the Commodore's love of Biscayne Bay and his love for sailboats. It was Kirk, in fact, who appointed Ralph Munroe commodore of the Biscayne Bay Yacht Club, and the Commodore returned the favor by making Kirk the club's secretary.

Still others boasted even more colorful backgrounds then the two unrelated Munroes; indeed more than a few Coconut Grove residents seem to have walked directly out of Jimmy Buffet songs. Take Count James L. Nugent and Count Jean d'Hedouville, for example. Both of these esteemed gentlemen were of French descent, though the latter also claimed some Irish blood: his Irish-born grandfather, in fact, had served as a general in Napoleon Bonaparte's army. Nugent was well known for his odd clothing choices; he was famous for his loud plaid shirts, and he once attended a wedding in full dress attire, but barefoot, since he decided at the last moment that it seemed ostentatious to wear shoes to a Biscayne Bay wedding. D'Hedouville, on the other hand, reportedly collected pirate treasure maps and kept them hidden under his dining room tablecloth. According to Coconut Grove legend, he eventually did manage to find a trove of pirate loot and used it to purchase enough land to restore the fortunes of his aristocratic French family.

And then there was Richard Carney. Dick, as he was usually called, arrived in Biscayne Bay sometime around 1887 as a hired hand in the employ of an entrepreneur named Henry R. Lum, who intended to turn the Biscayne Bay shoreline into a vast coconut plantation. Lum's scheme was to purchase land for a pittance on the Biscayne Bay shoreline, clear the shore of underbrush and mangroves, plant it with coconuts, and then reap huge profits on the proceeds. Unfortunately, the men Lum hired were mostly employees from Northern naval life-saving stations who knew next to nothing about mangrove clearance and pretty much botched the job. In any case, it is unlikely the plan would have worked even if the vegetation had been properly cleared, since Florida's subtropical foliage regrows at an astonishing rate; as it is, the coconuts inexpertly planted by Lum's men quickly fell prey to the ravages of rats, rabbits, strangler figs, and mangrove roots.

Most of the would-be coconut farmers eventually returned to the North, but Dick Carney stayed and quickly became an intimate

Earliest yacht club members, Commodore Ralph M. Munroe and Edward A. Hine (right), are joined by Richard Carney. (Ralph M. Munroe, Historical Association of Southern Florida)

of the two Munroes, with whom he shared a passion for sailboats. Dick also harbored a seemingly limitless enthusiasm for practical jokes, some of which became Bay Biscayne legends. On one occasion, Dick spied a boat containing the sleeping body of J. B. Hammond, the famed typewriter tycoon of the age, and he towed it for a mile or two to a different location, leaving Mr. Hammond in a state of great confusion upon his awakening. On another night, during a Coconut Grove community "hop," Dick sneaked into the "nursery" building where the infants were sleeping and shuffled both their locations and their clothing. Since the mothers did not notice Dick's switcheroo until the next morning, "daylight brought scenes of consternation and wrath, all over the Bay, that are better imagined than described." On still another occasion, Dick applied zebra stripes to an old gray mule with shoe polish, so that its owner, who did not recognize his own mule, hunted for it high and low while the poor zebra-striped mule waited patiently near home for its master. According to the Commodore, who wrote approvingly of Dick's exploits in his autobiography, "a shotgun is said to have figured in this story" after the hoax was discovered, but "Dick laid low until he was forgiven."

If this peculiar ensemble of engineers, writers, pranksters, and Frenchmen shared anything, it was a deep-rooted love of sailing, and indeed, Biscayne Bay was a yachtsman's paradise until at least the turn of the century. The Bay was wide enough to accommodate any number of yachts at once, and its shallowness kept the water pleasantly calm, while the Bay's constant gentle breezes made for fine sailing. In 1887, Munroe and his fellow yachtsmen organized a large yacht race to celebrate Washington's Birthday, and this soon became an annual tradition. If a visitor did not have a sailboat, yet wanted to participate in the lively Bay yachting scene, he was welcome to do so. Sailboats were available for two dollars a day, and ocean-going sloops, many of which were of Munroe's own design and manufacture, could be hired for fifty dollars a month.

In addition to this cast of regular characters, the Bay also received a fair number of distinguished seasonal visitors, who were generally called the "swells" by the long-time inhabitants of the Bay, since (as the joke went) they flowed in with the tide. In addition to poor mistreated Mr. Hammond of typewriter fame, the Bay was also graced by occasional visits from Charles Stowe, son of Harriet Beecher Stowe, best known for penning the anti-slavery classic *Uncle Tom's Cabin*. What is more, Mrs. Andrew Carnegie, the wife of the ultra-rich Pittsburgh steel baron, is known to have made at least one appearance in Biscayne Bay.

For the most part, these winter visitors stayed at the Peacock Inn, which by all accounts boasted a lively social scene well into the 1890s. Charles Richard Dodge, who visited Biscayne Bay in 1894, noted that the Peacock Inn was "a very fair hostelry," and added that "in the winter months the society of the settlement is delightful," since the "cultivated people" of the locality would mingle with strangers from the North, "who come down here to lead a *dolce-far-niente* existence in this dreamland, all unmindful of the blizzards which are sweeping over the wintry north." Conditions in Coconut Grove, the author admitted, could be a trifle primitive, but "one soon becomes accustomed to the absence of fresh beef and ice." In any case, "venison and sea-turtle more than makes up for the lack of the former, and the necessity for the latter is soon overlooked." It is worth mentioning that Dodge sailed to Biscayne Bay in a thirteen-ton "sharpie" named *Micco,* built and formerly owned by none other than Commodore Ralph Middleton Munroe.

Despite the Peacock Inn's considerable success attracting sportsmen and invalids, the population of Biscayne Bay remained quite small, at least through the 1880s. As late as 1887, Ralph Munroe wrote, the "points of interest" of the Bay were "almost entirely natural features," other than a few crudely built driftwood businesses and homes. The Bay's largest industry at that time was still the Indian trade, and the mouth of the Miami River, which would shortly become the nucleus of the surging metropolis of Miami, sported only the two houses belonging to the eccentric Brickell clan.

Taken together, the permanent white population of the Bay probably did not exceed a few hundred souls, and the Bay still had a wild character; indeed, as late as 1891, a ten-foot-long Florida panther played its own joke on Dick Carney, assaulting him unexpectedly and ripping his clothing to tatters. Carney had the last laugh, however. Soon after the attack, a friendly Seminole Indian tracked down the huge cat and presented its carcass to Dick as a trophy. Given the fact that the Florida panther is now at the brink of extinction, one cannot help but wish today that Carney had accepted the panther's "prank" in good humor rather than seeking revenge.

Although the Commodore didn't know it in 1887, Biscayne Bay's splendid isolation from the rest of the United States was about to vanish. In 1890, the Bay was finally connected by land to the rest of the country for the first time by a mule stagecoach line, which linked Lake Worth with Lemon City, the northernmost settlement on Biscayne Bay. Even before the coming of the stage line, rumors began to fly that Henry Flagler's railroad was coming to the Bay, and real estate prices began to rise during the 1880s: a piece of land which was offered to the Commodore for $350 in 1881 had risen to about $800 in value by 1886. By 1890, a veritable land boom had begun, and settlers rushed in, eager to snatch up available land for a low price before the first train steamed into town. During his 1895 visit to the Bay, Charles Dodge noted that "this portion of Florida has been filling up very rapidly in the past three or four years, and now there are few, if any, homestead lands on the four-mile strip not occupied."

This is not to say that Biscayne Bay had in any way assumed an urban appearance by the mid-1890s. Indeed, the site of the future city of Miami still could claim "not more than half a dozen houses" in 1895. Still, the Bay was filling up, and what is more, it was filling up with precisely the wrong sort of people. According to Munroe, as the 1890s progressed, the old-time residents of Biscayne Bay "found the pleasant solidarity of the old Bay community broken by the influx of settlers and speculators, the former too many to absorb, the latter always and increasingly objectionable."

Complain though he might, Munroe was powerless against this invasion from the north, which would soon transform the character of Biscayne Bay forever. The rumors were correct; the railroad *was* coming, and it would bring in its wake many of the ills of Gilded Age America that the inhabitants of Coconut Grove had sailed southward to avoid.

ⓖ ⓖ ⓖ

In 1895, a hunter and explorer by the name of Hugh Willoughby set his sights on the Everglades, which were still an almost unknown piece of real estate on the eve of the twentieth century. True, earlier expeditions had crossed the Everglades, but in Willoughby's judgment, they had crossed the northern portion of the swamp, where the Everglades were easiest to traverse. Willoughby was determined to penetrate the dense sawgrass marshes of the south, which earlier explorers had sought to avoid, and with good reason! The razor-sharp grass could bite deeply into hands and feet, or even split the sides of a canoe, if not treated with utmost caution. In order to ensure his success, Willoughby actually launched two expeditions into the Glades three years apart: a preliminary reconnaissance of the area east of the Miami River in 1895, and a full trek from Everglades City to Biscayne Bay in 1898. As Willoughby's memoirs make clear, although only three years separated the two expeditions, those three years witnessed a quantum leap in the settlement and development of Biscayne Bay.

When Willoughby emerged from the sawgrass in 1898 and visited Biscayne Bay for the second time, scarcely three years after his first preliminary visit, he was dumbfounded by the changes that had been wrought over such a short period of time. In the published accounts of his expedition, Willoughby claimed that the mouth of the Miami had been utterly transformed: "from two houses [in 1895] it has been made a town of two thousand inhabitants." Although impressed by Miami's growth, Willoughby had little good to say about the burgeoning Biscayne Bay metropolis. The Seminole Indians, he noted, were struck hard by Miami's headlong expansion. One island near Miami that had hosted an Indian encampment in 1895 was now occupied by a white settler, who had run off the Indians and erected a crude homesteader's hut on the site of the former Seminole village. In addition to the damage wrought upon the Seminole people, Willoughby complained bitterly about the injuries the growing city had inflicted on the environment. "The picturesqueness [of the Bay] seemed to have gone," Willoughby lamented, "its wildness had been rudely marred by the hand of civilization."

The man most responsible for bringing "civilization" of this type to Biscayne Bay was Henry Morrison Flagler, one of the most famous men of his age, and almost certainly the most important single man in the history of Florida. Walt Disney, it is true, left an

Henry Flagler, the man who developed St. Augustine, Palm Beach, and Miami, then put his considerable fortune and energy into his railway to Key West. (Florida State Archives)

indelible imprint of his own on Florida, but he was a mere follower in Flagler's footsteps. Flagler found Florida a nearly uninhabited wilderness, bent it to his will, and all but created the modern state of Florida in the process. For good or for ill, Florida as we know it today is largely Flagler's creation.

One of the ironies of Florida history is that Flagler, who would eventually have such a dramatic impact on the peninsula's people and landscape, seems to have been scarcely even aware of Florida for most of his life. Flagler was already forty-eight years old when he visited Jacksonville, Florida, during the 1878–1879 winter season; like Ralph Munroe, Flagler came to expose his ailing wife to the healthy tropical breezes, in hopes of alleviating her tuberculosis. Unfortunately, the tropical winds seem to have had the opposite effect on Flagler, who returned from vacation so ill that he was unable to work for over a month. His wife Mary apparently received no long-term benefit either, and she died of her illness four years later, in May of 1881.

Despite the apparent failure of his first Florida adventure, Flagler returned to the state during the winter of 1883–1884, this time to visit St. Augustine rather than Jacksonville. Accompanying Flagler on this occasion was his scandalous new thirty-five-year-old wife Alice, a fiery, attractive redhead who had served as a nurse for Flagler's dearly departed first spouse. Contemporary accounts about Flagler's second visit to Florida suggest that the honeymooning couple left with mixed feelings about their Florida adventure. True, the climate was lovely; Flagler and his wife revelled in the mild subtropical weather, happy to be avoiding the blizzards and ice storms sweeping through the American North. They were also charmed by St. Augustine's old-world sensibilities, borne out of the city's long history as a Spanish provincial capital. On the other hand, Flagler and his wife were not impressed by the available accommodations; the hospitality offered by local hotels was not up to Flagler's normal five-star standards. Almost on the spot, Flagler resolved to build a fabulous modern hotel in St.

Augustine, worthy of visits from America's moneyed elite.

Once committed to the project, Flagler threw himself into it heart and soul. When he visited St. Augustine again a year later, Flagler snatched up so much property in the ancient city that he set into motion a full-blown land boom; by late 1885 and 1886, property that was assessed at only $6,000 was being sold for $30,000 on the real estate market, at five times its original value. By 1886, the construction of the $2.5 million hotel had begun, and it was opened for business on January 10, 1888, which represents an impressive rate of work, given the massive scale of Flagler's ambitions.

Once completed, Flagler's Ponce de Leon Hotel boasted both vast proportions and a nearly unprecedented level of opulence. The main building, which consisted of three stories constructed in an ambiguous "Mediterranean" architectural style, measured 380 by 520 feet, and occupied four and a half acres of land, plus another acre and a half for a dining hall and assorted other buildings. From the top of the hotel rose two imposing minaret-like towers, which were practical as well as ornamental, as tanks in the two towers contained sixteen thousand gallons of water for protection against fire.

The interior of the hotel could boast superlatives of its own. The front door opened into a three-story rotunda that served as a lobby, from which guests were shown to one of the hotel's 540 rooms, each of which reportedly cost over $1000 to decorate. The entire hotel was fitted with electric lighting, still a rarity at the time, and the hotel's water was sulfur water, which doctors of the 1880s claimed had medicinal value. For the first season, Flagler imported both a military band and a twenty-piece orchestra from the New York City music scene for the entertainment of his rich Northern guests. Once fully complete and operational, the Ponce de Leon rivaled Chicago's Palmer House and San Francisco's Palace, widely seen as the leading hotels of the day, in both size and splendor.

Who was this Henry Morrison Flagler, who had the resources, not to mention the audacity, to build a monumental five-star hotel on the Florida frontier on a honeymoon whim?

Although not well known to most modern Americans, even those who inhabit the Sunshine State, Flagler enjoyed celebrity status by the 1880s, and was mentioned in the same breath as such industry kingpins as Andrew Carnegie and John D. Rockefeller. Indeed, Flagler was a long-time confidant and business partner of the latter, with whom he created the "Rockefeller, Andrews & Flagler" business partnership in the late 1860s. The goal of the RA&F was to secure as great a share of the Cleveland market as possible, but their efforts were repeatedly foiled by the extreme volatility of oil prices. Over time, Flagler and Rockefeller came to realize that the key to staying ahead in the oil industry was favorable transportation arrangements. Since most of their business consisted of selling oil to European markets, and since their New York and Pennsylvania competitors were better positioned to sell oil to Europe through the Eastern Seaboard ports, Flagler and Rockefeller became convinced that they could never compete effectively unless they secured preferential transportation arrangements with the railroad companies. As the RA&F's chief transportation negotiator, it was Flagler's job to court the railroad conglomerates for suitable transportation contracts.

Flagler soon proved that he was ideally suited to this role. By playing the canal companies against the railroad companies, Flagler managed to secure quite favorable shipping rates, and he even managed to get many railroads to offer the RA&F a "drawback"—in other words, a sum of money given to RA&F every time a railroad transported a competing oil company's product. "Drawbacks" of this sort gave RA&F a crucial advantage against its competitors and allowed the company to expand by leaps and bounds in the coming years. Flagler also started a policy of promising railroads large, guaranteed shipments of oil, which drastically reduced the freight rates those shippers charged Flagler's company. As a result of these measures, the volume of traffic controlled by RA&F skyrocketed, from 770 thousand barrels in 1868 to 1.6 million barrels in 1871, an increase of over 111% in three years. Purchasing enough oil to fulfill these commitments, however, proved to be a serious strain on the RA&F, and as a result, Flagler and Rockefeller were forced to reincorporate and recapitalize their firm in 1870. The resulting corporation, Standard Oil, was destined to become a legend in the annals of American business history.

The Standard Oil Company already controlled ten percent of the nation's refining capacity in 1870, but this was just the beginning. In the 1870s, Flagler and Standard Oil took advantage of freight wars between railroad carriers to secure even lower shipping rates for its oil, further swelling Standard Oil's profits. By 1872, Standard Oil was the leading refiner of petroleum in America, and Cleveland contained the single largest concentration of refineries in the country. Making effective use of Standard Oil's strong Cleveland power base, and using a combination of clever negotiation and ruthless intimidation, Flagler soon managed to leverage Standard Oil into the position of "evener" of the oil industry, giving it the right to dictate what percentage of the oil freight would be controlled by each railroad. The point of "evening" the industry was, in theory, to avoid costly rate wars between refiners or transporters, which might reduce profits for everyone involved. In actual practice, however, Standard Oil's position as "evener" made it fabulously wealthy, since Standard Oil received a ten percent commission on all oil freight revenues through the "evened" lines. Because of these arrangements, Standard Oil all but controlled the American oil industry by 1877.

Flagler was well rewarded for his diligence on behalf of Standard Oil, and the soaring value of his Standard Oil stock made him one of the richest men in America: his estimated net worth in the mid-1880s was nearly $20 million, or nearly $300 million in today's dollars. Still, Flagler was not content. Standard Oil's meteoric rise was accompanied by furious public outcries, and the company was increasingly regarded as a villainous monopoly by the American public; the progressive era muckraker Ida M. Tarbell, for instance, later labeled the Standard Oil conglomerate an "unholy alliance."

After 1878, an increasing number of lawsuits, both civil and criminal, were hurled against the Standard Oil Company, and Flagler spent more and more of his time during the 1880s in courtrooms defending his company against charges of malfeasance. Flagler's discouragement over the treatment of Standard Oil serves to explain, in part, his seemingly whimsical desire to build a luxury hotel in St. Augustine. The Ponce de Leon, Flagler hoped, would be as much of a subject of popular adulation as Standard Oil was a target of popular ire.

At the same time, however, Flagler never lost sight of practical considerations, and he realized early on that success in the tourist industry, just like success in the oil industry, depended heavily on favorable transportation agreements. The challenge in Florida, though, was not securing beneficial shipping rates, but in providing the rapid and pleasant transportation facilities that tourists desired, and, as Flagler quickly realized, the existing facilities in Florida were far too primitive for the elite guests he intended to entice to St. Augustine. Up until 1870, travelers to St. Augustine had to take a steamship up the St. Johns River, disembark at the tiny town of Tocoi, and travel the rest of the way in slow-moving railway carriages pulled by mules, which had the habit of lying down on the job, so that the fifteen-mile trip could take as long as five hours to negotiate. After 1870, the Tocoi line did finally acquire a steam locomotive, but this purchase did little to modernize the line: all the owners could afford was a jury-rigged engine car consisting of a second-hand coffee mill engine fitted with wheels.

By 1883, when Flagler began his Florida adventures, the trip had been improved still further by the completion of the Jacksonville, St. Augustine & Halifax River Railway, but although this rail line offered a direct connection, it was hardly a substantial improvement over what came before. First of all, since no railroad bridges had yet been built to span the St. Johns River, passengers from the north were forced to detrain, cross the river by ferry, and then board a different train in the town of South Jacksonville. In addition, the thin rails of this crude line weighed only thirty pounds to the yard, as compared to the ninety-pound rails which were the industry standard, and they were a mere three feet apart, which made it impossible for most American train cars to operate south of the St. Johns. Furthermore, the locomotives were old wood-burning engines, slow and smoky, and the equipment on the train cars was years out of date. If Flagler was going to draw guests of the highest caliber to St. Augustine, clearly, he was going to have to make vast improvements in the quality of the available transportation.

Flagler rose to the challenge. In December of 1885, Flagler purchased a substantial portion of the shares of the Jacksonville, St. Augustine & Halifax River Rail Line, and had himself elected president of the railroad company. Within three years, Flagler had begun construction of a bridge across the St. Johns River, and a year after that, Flagler paid to convert the old three-foot narrow-gauge rail line to a standard gauge, four-foot-eight-and-a-half-inch road. The latter improvement was of particular importance, since at the time it was common for the nation's wealthiest citizens to travel in their own custom-built Pullman train carriages, and these carriages were generally built to run on standard-gauge track. By 1889, Flagler and his allies in Florida had constructed a network of standard-gauge railways, called the East Coast Lines, which dominated rail traffic in northeast Florida. In the process, Flagler added "rail baron" to his already impressive resumé of lifetime accomplishments, which comes as little surprise to anyone well acquainted with his Standard Oil past; indeed, Flagler's past experience with railroads while transportation negotiator gave him excellent qualifications for his new career as a Florida railroad tycoon.

Flagler hoped that the Ponce de Leon would prove popular, and he was not disappointed. The Ponce de Leon, in fact, was so successful that Flagler soon began construction of a sister hotel on an adjacent plot of land. Called the Alcazar, Flagler's second hotel boasted three hundred guest rooms, a first-floor shopping arcade, and a mid-priced restaurant, designed for the use of the hotel's primarily middle-class clientele. In the meantime, Flagler expanded his Florida railway system, which he eventually renamed the Florida East Coast Railway, and pushed it farther to the south. Flagler had solid financial reasons for doing so: by virtue of a law that had been specially passed for Flagler, each mile of track Flagler built entitled him to up to eight thousand acres of public domain land. As Flagler extended southward, he sprinkled that land with small hotels and resorts. One such small resort town was Ormond Beach, located about forty-odd miles south of Jacksonville, which was to become a favorite holiday getaway of Flagler's former Standard Oil partner John D. Rockefeller.

By 1893, Flagler's line was nearing Lake Worth, which boasted hundreds of coconut palms and a lovely beach, but no more than a few score full-time inhabitants. Flagler, who had long recognized the potential of the area, arrived to purchase real estate in April of 1893, though in secret; Flagler knew from his St. Augustine experience that an open visit on his part would set up a frenzy of land speculation, inflating the prices of land that Flagler might want to purchase down the line. As subsequent events would prove, Flagler's clandestine trip to Lake Worth was an act of great prudence. Once the cat was out of the bag, and Flagler's intention to come to Lake Worth was confirmed, land values in Lake Worth mushroomed, and the price of some lots jumped to as high as $1,000 an acre. Flagler was not harmed by the sudden land boom, however, since he had already purchased much of the property he wanted, including a two-hundred-acre plot of nearly pristine wilderness on the west shore of Lake Worth. "In a few years," Flagler confided to a local resident in 1893, "there'll be a town over there as big as Jacksonville."

As events soon proved, this was no idle boast. Within a month of his surreptitious trip to Lake Worth, laborers began to flood into the area, and construction was begun on Flagler's next hotel, the Royal Poinciana, on the east shore of Lake Worth. By all accounts, the Poinciana was a huge undertaking. Once fully completed, the six-story hotel could boast of two superlatives: not only could it claim to be the largest hotel in the world, it also had the distinction of being the world's single largest wooden structure. Like the Ponce de Leon, the Royal Poinciana was electrified throughout; indeed, the hotel used so much power that the hotel's generator consumed twenty-five tons of coal every day in an effort to produce sufficient electricity. Guests might have taken the electricity for granted, but few failed to be impressed by the Poinciana's 125 private bathrooms, which were still a rarity at the time. In addition to these peerless accommodations, guests at the Royal Poinciana enjoyed rides in one of the hotel's two hundred "Afromobiles," rickshaws pedaled by uniformed black men, which allowed guests to tour Palm Beach's splendors in comfort.

From the first, visitors to the Royal Poinciana included many of the so-called "Four Hundred," the glittering topmost crust of the late-nineteenth-century American social register. Flagler was so eager to cater to these illustrious guests that he constructed a spur

A birds-eye view of Flagler's Royal Poinciana Hotel on the east shore of Lake Worth. (Florida State Archives)

line in 1896 that ran from the main East Coast Line to the very gates of the Royal Poinciana. As a result, some of Flagler's guests, such as his friend and fellow railway-baron Cornelius Vanderbilt, were able to arrive at the Royal Poinciana at the helm of their own private trains.

In the meantime, Flagler was true to his word, and he set about laying the foundations of a new city in the "wilderness" of the western edge of Lake Worth. Like Walt Disney, another Florida entertainment entrepreneur who would seek to shelter his fantastical dreamlands from the real world most men inhabited, Flagler deliberately separated the "commercial" city of West Palm Beach from his hotel wonderland on the coastal island of Palm Beach. Lake Worth, in fact, served as a moat separating the haves and have-nots, the guests who played at the Poinciana and the employees who merely worked there. Under Flagler's direction, West Palm Beach became a vast company town inhabited primarily by black employees of the hotel. Until the railway spur was completed in 1896, Flagler's employees had to row across Lake Worth to Palm Beach in small boats every morning, and then back to West Palm Beach by dusk; after 1896, Flagler allowed the employees to walk to work on the railway bridge, but only after paying a toll. The class divisions that Flagler created between Palm Beach and West Palm Beach still linger today: the median family income of Palm Beach in 2002 was over $56,000, while median family income of some communities on the West Palm Beach side of Lake Worth is as low as $23,000.

By the 1890s, then, Flagler had become the most powerful man in Florida, able to create entire cities and people the wilds of Florida at the stroke of his pen. During this same period, in fact, Flagler ruled Florida as a virtual dictator. Flagler himself bragged about his ownership of the state, and told friends that "my domain begins at Jacksonville." Others joked that "Fla.," the abbreviation for Florida of the day, was actually short for "Flagler." So secure was Flagler in his dominion that he flagrantly disregarded any Florida law which stood in the way of his goals, such as the state's prohibition of gambling, which flourished unhindered at Flagler's hotels. When Flagler's second wife Alice began to slip into madness—she saw images of Jesus in pebbles and became convinced that she was the bride of the Russian czar—he was able to intimidate or bribe the Florida legislature into changing Florida's divorce law to allow separation on the grounds of insanity. This high-handed action by Flagler caused a mild stir in Florida, but the reaction was muted by the fact that Flagler, like all dictators, controlled most of the organs of the press. Flagler founded newspapers throughout the state to promote his interests, and generally purchased outright any paper which criticized his Florida regime.

Although Flagler wielded great power over Florida's landscape and peoples, he could not control the climate, and during the mid-1890s the weather dealt a harsh blow to Flagler's eastern Florida "domain." In the winter of 1894–1895, uncommonly cold air blasted into northern Florida, and much of the state suffered several nights of below-freezing temperatures. The severity of the 1894–1895 freeze can be seen most clearly in the dramatic drop of Florida citrus fruit production: the Florida citrus industry, which shipped five million boxes of fruit north in 1893, managed to produce only 147,000 boxes in 1895, which represents a staggering ninety-seven percent drop in a single year. Two years later, in the winter of 1896–97, bitterly cold temperatures again came to northern and central Florida and killed most citrus trees that had survived first freeze. Since most of the destroyed orange crops would have made their way north through Flagler's East Coast Line, these two freezes cost Flagler millions in lost railroad revenue. Flagler's chain of hotels fared no better. For years, Flagler had exploited Florida's mild winter climate to draw visitors to his vacation wonderland. News of the freezes, however, shattered the image of a mild, frost-free Florida that Flagler had worked long and hard to construct.

What happened next is an often-told Florida legend. Immediately after the first freeze, an agent of Flagler's named James Ingraham arrived at Flagler's estate in St. Augustine bearing a box of still-blooming orange branches, clearly untouched by the killing frosts that had ravaged the rest of the state. These blossoms, Ingraham supposedly informed Flagler, came from Biscayne Bay, virtually the only part of Florida to have escaped the horrible freeze. Ingraham also produced a written proposal, signed by a certain Mrs. Tuttle, Mrs. Brickell, and Mr. Brickell, offering Flagler extensive land grants along the Miami River, if only he would build his rail line to the Bay. Intrigued by the offer, Flagler agreed to visit the future city of Miami, and was so enchanted by what he saw that he resolved to extend the East Coast Line to the Bay on the spot. Thus was born the magical city of Miami.

Although it is pleasant to imagine that a major American city could be born out of a box of flowering orange branches, this charming tale misleads the reader on several points. For one thing, this story downplays Flagler's own initiative and fails to mention the fact that Flagler had ordered Ingraham to Biscayne Bay in the first place, with the express mission of determining how far south the freeze had penetrated. In addition, plenty of evidence exists that Flagler was well aware of the possibilities offered by Biscayne Bay and had already been mulling over the idea of extending his rail line to Miami for years. Until the freeze, however, Flagler failed to see the logic in extending his line to Miami; according to one historian, Flagler believed that creating a town in Miami while simultaneously building one in Palm Beach "would be a duplication of effort," since the two towns would presumably offer identical services and would thus be forced to compete with each other for paying customers. After the freeze, however, the move to Miami became far more appealing; any hotel built on Biscayne Bay was virtually guaranteed to be frost-free.

In addition, the orange blossom story makes it appear that Flagler was a stranger to Tuttle and the Brickells before the '94–'95 freeze, and this is simply not true. In actual fact, the Tuttles and Brickells had been in correspondence with Flagler for years in an unsuccessful attempt to persuade Flagler to extend his empire southwards to the Bay. What is more, contacts among Mrs. Tuttle, the Brickells, and Flagler began long before any of them arrived in Florida, and they serve to demonstrate how small a country America still was at the end of the nineteenth century.

At one point in his long business career, Flagler had been a grain merchant in Cleveland, and during that time, Brickell came to know Flagler quite well since Brickell's grocery concern put him in contact with Flagler on almost a daily basis. Mrs. Julia Tuttle's ties with Flagler were even more extensive, if somewhat more indirect. She was the daughter of Ephraim T. Sturtevant, William Brickell's one-time business partner and later bitter rival. It is quite likely that Julia Tuttle first met with Flagler in the company of her father, who had dealings with Flagler in Cleveland, though this cannot be proven. What is certain, however, is that Julia Tuttle was on good terms with Flagler's business associate John D. Rockefeller, who was a fellow member of Cleveland's Euclid Baptist Church. In addition, Tuttle's father-in-law had offered the young Rockefeller his first job, way back in the 1850s. Julia had repeatedly made use of her ties with Rockefeller to curry favor with Flagler and even tried to use Rockefeller's influence to secure herself a management position at Flagler's Ponce de Leon hotel during the late 1880s, but to no avail.

What is more, Tuttle had a close business relationship with James Ingraham, the man who had borne the blooming orange boughs to Flagler. Indeed, the evidence suggests that Tuttle and Ingraham had been conspiring to bring a railroad to Miami for many years, even before Ingraham signed on as a land agent with Flagler's East Coast Line. Ingraham and Tuttle first met in Cleveland in 1890, while Ingraham was still in the employ of Henry Plant, a rival to Flagler who was engaged in building his own railway and entertainment empire down the west coast of Florida. Julia Tuttle, who was about to move permanently to the Fort Dallas tract on the Miami River for the sake of her daughter's health, convinced Ingraham to look into the possibility of extending Plant's lines to Biscayne Bay. In order to assess the feasibility of the idea, Ingraham led a large expedition of twenty-two men into the Everglades in the early spring of 1892.

When Hugh Willoughby claimed in 1898 that all earlier expeditions into the Everglades had traversed the more easily passable northern portion of the swamp, he had Ingraham's 1892 expedition specifically in mind. As Ingraham's journal makes clear, however, the northern route presented would-be explorers with almost insurmountable obstacles. Tormented by mosquitoes, stung by vicious swamp fleas, and lacerated by the sawgrass, Ingraham's men alternatively paddled and slogged through the Everglades for a full weary month, and by the time they shot the rapids of the Miami River and left the Everglades, they had nearly exhausted their provisions. When they finally arrived at Tuttle's estate on the Miami River on the 5th of April, and saw the U.S. flag that Julia Tuttle had hoisted to honor their accomplishment, Ingraham's men were so overcome with relief and gratitude that, according to Ingraham's account of the expedition, they "exploded a dynamite cartridge in her honor." Still, these fireworks could not conceal the fact that the expedition was a failure; it became clear to both Ingraham and Tuttle that, if Biscayne Bay was going to get a railway, it would have to come from the north rather than the waterlogged west, and from Flagler's rail system rather than Plant's. Three years later, after the horrific freeze of 1894–1895, Flagler was all too happy to oblige.

Before beginning construction of the next leg of Flagler's railway empire, however, Flagler insisted that Tuttle and the Brickells make it worth his while, and the deal Flagler ultimately cut with Tuttle and the Brickells put important tracts of Florida acreage into Flagler's possession. As payment for bringing his railroad to the Bay, Tuttle granted Flagler a hundred-acre block of land on the north side of the river for construction of a new hotel and railroad terminal, plus one-half of her remaining north-bank acreage, which amounted to another 270 acres of land. The Brickells, in turn, agreed to provide Flagler with one half of their 640 acres on the south side of the river. All told, then, Flagler's railroad to Miami netted him only 690 acres of land, but since these land tracts were soon to become the central core of a bustling city, Flagler had no cause for complaint.

Indeed, Flagler was probably quite pleased to have acquired the land he needed in one fell swoop, thus outflanking the land speculators who hounded him all up and down the east coast of Florida, offering him small plots of land for outrageous sums in hopes of siphoning off some of Flagler's Standard Oil millions. One particularly aggressive group of property owners in the coastal town of Juno, which was still the county seat of Dade County at the time, pooled their land in an attempt to force Flagler to pay them through the nose for railroad-building rights through their territory. Rather than give in to their demands, Flagler boldly chose to cut inland and bypass the troublesome town of Juno altogether, a decision that condemned the formerly prosperous town of Juno to obscurity and oblivion. Flagler's fateful decision to route his railway around the grasping citizens of Juno has left a lasting imprint on eastern Florida even to the present day: as of the year 2002, the modern town of Juno Beach had little over 2,000 full-time residents, a far cry from the 70,000 citizens inhabiting the nearby city of West Palm Beach.

In any case, once Flagler made up his mind to build to Miami, events unfolded quickly. In order to secure enough labor to ensure the rapid construction of the West Palm Beach–Miami line, Flagler leased a large number of convicts from the state to bolster his own company's construction crews, which was a common (albeit inhumane) practice in Florida at the time. As a result, the entire sixty-four-mile rail line took only ten months to complete, despite the fact that it cut through some of the most empty patches of wilderness remaining in America; in one forty-mile stretch, for instance, Flagler's rail builders found only a single isolated homestead. Even before the railway was completed, Flagler dispatched work crews to Miami to begin clearing the way for his next great hotel, which he dubbed the Royal Palm, and to start construction of a temporary railroad station. On April 21, 1896, Flagler's rail line finally opened for business, and Biscayne Bay's long isolation from the rest of America ended forever.

Flagler probably never intended the city of Miami to be much more than an annex to his new Royal Palm hotel; indeed, Flagler is said to have told Julia Tuttle and the Brickells that "the town [of Miami] will never be more than a fishing village for my hotel guests." The course of events, however, would soon prove Flagler wrong. Because of the unquenchable ambition of the "settlers and speculators" that Commodore Munroe so despised, the city of Miami would grow at an astounding rate over the next three decades. Unprecedented fortunes would be made, then lost virtually overnight. A natural paradise would be destroyed by the hands of man, and a man-made paradise would be set in its place. Finally, as if in revenge, nature itself would expend its fury upon Miami, and the city of sunshine, which owed its very existence to a favorable climate, would fall prey to one of the most destructive storms ever to strike American soil. And so it goes: great dreams, after all, entail great risks, and ambition is often little more than a throw of the dice.

4

Dusty Old Town

Assuming you do not mind getting your feet wet for a second time, I would like to send you once again on an imaginary sailboat journey along the Florida shore. This time around, you are a well-to-do member of the Northern yachting set, and it is the late summer of the year 1894. You have sailed south to Biscayne Bay in hopes of partaking of the fabled hospitality of Peacock Inn and of enjoying the lush pleasures of this subtropical paradise, upon which your compatriots up north have heaped effusive praise. To your great disappointment, however, you find that Biscayne Bay of 1894 is no longer the wilderness Eden that it was in the mid-1800s. The once-lovely shore, which used to be lined with splendid hardwood hammocks, is now swarming with settlers, who have cut down much of the native timber, erected crude driftwood huts along the water's edge, and ruined the rustic beauty which used to be the talk of the town in Northern sailing society. Even the warm welcome provided by Commodore Munroe of the Biscayne Bay Yachting

Club does not comfort you. Far from it, in fact: Munroe himself seems uneasy about the changes that the newcomers from the north have brought with them to his beloved Biscayne Bay.

So you decide to move on. Wishing the Commodore and his fellow Bay yachtsmen luck in their struggle against settlers and speculators, you set your sails for Key West, that city of burly spongers and surly wreckers that you remember fondly from the sailing expeditions of your childhood. After passing the old Cape Florida Lighthouse, now disappointingly abandoned and unlit, you head into the open water of the Bay, which is so broad that it might resemble the open sea except for the telltale signs of shallow water all around you. After about a dozen miles of steady southward travel, you shift your course to the west and sail to the westward side of the tiny Ragged Keys. These humble isles, you know, are just the first vanguard of the Florida Keys, the island archipelago that you will follow for the remainder of your voyage.

At first, truth be told, you find the Keys rather dull. The malaise befalling Biscayne Bay, you tell yourself, seems to be spreading— most of the Upper Keys have been deforested, and several bear the scars left behind by years of pineapple, tomato, sisal, and sweet potato cultivation. At one point, you spy a shallow channel cutting through the wall of keys and you realize that you have reached Caesar Creek, a saltwater gut named in honor of a black pirate of south Florida legend. Through this break in the keys, you can see the glimmer of open waters of the southern end of Biscayne Bay. With regret, you bid the Bay farewell, and wish that you could have seen its natural splendors before they were sullied by the grasping hand of civilization.

Ah well, nothing to be done. You sail onwards, and soon you are passing south of Key Largo, the largest and, outside of Key West, the most densely populated of the Florida Keys. After several shouted ship-to-ship conversations with the local "Conch" inhabitants, who seem to spend as much time at sea as on land, you learn that this is prime land for pineapples—called "pines" in local parlance—

and you happily accept a few thorny examples of the industry as gifts. So touched are you by the hospitality of these frontier settlers that you accept their offer to spend the night at one of their rough cabins. It would be pleasant, you decide, to spend at least one night on dry land.

By the next morning, however, you bitterly regret your choice. Since the Keys have no natural source of fresh water, virtually all the drinking water comes from brackish wells, or from rain-fed tin cisterns, which give the stagnant water a horrible metallic aftertaste. While your tongue protests the foul water, your nose struggles with the putrid smell of decaying sponges, which fill the air near the Conch homesteads with a most pungent aroma. Worst of all, though, are the mosquitoes, or the "skeeters" as the Conchs call them, which swarm in such huge numbers that they paint the sides of buildings black with their bodies. In order to deal with these buzzing blood-suckers, the Conchs burn smudge pots, but in your opinion, the acrid smoke produced by these pots creates miseries all its own, while offering little relief from the tormenting insects. At first light of dawn, you arise, share a metallic-tasting coffee with the Conchs for politeness' sake, and make your hasty exit from the discomforts of Key Largo, vowing never to return.

The middle portion of the voyage proves more interesting. After a day or so of leisurely travel away from Key Largo's many irritations, you pass by Indian Key and note that a few homesteaders have returned to its shores, apparently unconcerned by the fact that they inhabit the scene of an infamous Indian attack. Past Indian Key, the islands of the archipelago become more infrequent, yet far more beautiful. The keys here are draped with hardwood hammocks and dense mangrove thickets, and host healthy populations of pelicans, cormorants, and gulls, along with an occasional white heron and spoonbill. You cannot help but note that some of these birds sport the same striking plumes which you have seen adorning the hats of well-dressed ladies in the fashion-conscious cities of the north.

On one occasion, while scanning Big Pine Key with your spyglass, you are astounded to behold a tiny deer, about half the size of its northern counterpart, grazing near the water's edge. You later learn that you have spotted one of the dwarf deer of Big Pine Key, which are closely related to the northern whitetail, although they only achieve a small fraction of the whitetail's size. As you are a good Christian, and thus an opponent of Darwin's new-fangled theories of natural selection, you can only speculate as to what part these diminutive deer must play in God's inscrutable plan.

Finally, after several days of travel, you find yourself approaching Key West, and none too soon! Over the course of the day, you have been worried by the appearance of high, scudding clouds, which usually herald the coming of a storm. Other signs also hint at the approach of foul weather: although the air is quite humid, it is strikingly clear, and the setting sun throws vibrant, almost unearthly, colors into the sky. Could these be portents of a coming tropical hurricane? Concerned, you consult the ship's barometer, and sure enough, you find that the air pressure is considerably lower than normal. Worse yet, the column of mercury in your barometer keeps dropping steadily as the hours pass. There can be very little doubt that a hurricane is lurking somewhere in the vicinity of the Florida Straits, and it is getting closer by the minute.

As a result, you are in a state of near-panic as you approach Key West. Will you reach the harbor in time to save your vessel, and your life? And even if you arrive in time, how will you gain entrance to the harbor? Key West's port, you know, is one of the best in North America, but it is also perilous, since the same reefs that break the ocean waves could splinter your hull if you approach from the wrong direction. Still, you remember the advice which Commodore Munroe gave you back at the Biscayne Bay Yacht Club: "If entering Key West at night," he had said, "remember, 'Key West lights under the north star.'" Despite the rising winds, you manage to follow Munroe's directions, and after a tense passage, you find yourself within the relative safety of Key West's protected harbor. Since the weather is already too rough for an attempt to reach land in the ship's launch, you drop anchor, lower your sails, stow your gear, and prepare for the coming of the hurricane.

The storm soon arrives. For most of the next day, the 25th of September, your small vessel is battered by blinding rain and buffeting winds. You fear for your safety, and with good reason: you later learn that this storm was accompanied by gusts as high as 104 miles per hour, and it dropped over twelve inches of rain upon some unfortunate parts of the Florida peninsula. As it is, you spend most of the day working the boat's pump in a desperate effort to keep afloat. By the morning of the 26th, however, the weather finally relents, and you are able to row your boat's dinghy through the still-heaving seas to the thriving metropolis of Key West. To your great surprise, you find that the city seems almost untouched by the storm. Only a few lost shingles, and a few piles of wind-blown debris on the streets, offer testimony to the hurricane's tropical fury.

Still, it soon becomes clear to you that the passage of time has changed Key West far more than the passage of the hurricane. The Key West of your childhood memory, of legend and story, was a Key West of Conch wreckers and bronze-skinned spongers. And certainly, many of Key West's eighteen thousand–odd inhabitants still fit these molds. But the prevailing language on the streets of Key West, you quickly discover, is now Spanish, and huge multi-story wooden factories now loom over both the old sponge market and the dockside warehouses of the wreckers. This is not at all what you expected. Intrigued, you make your way down Duval Street, through the heat of a Florida summer day and through the bustle of the Spanish-speaking crowd, hoping to find the secret to Key West's remarkable transformation.

ⓖ ⓖ ⓖ

Indeed, many people acquainted with Key West of old would have found the 1894 version of the city greatly changed, and in some ways, almost unrecognizable. Key West's population,

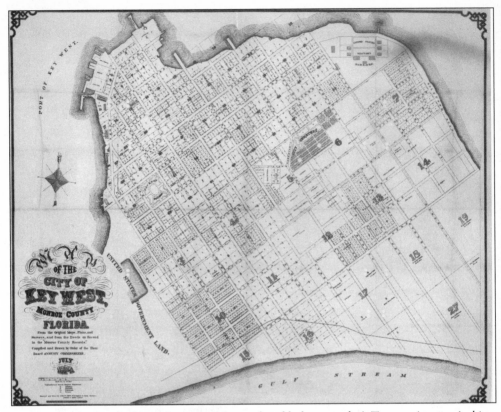

By 1874 development had spread to United Street, three blocks past today's Truman Avenue. And in the 1880s it would spread even further as the population grew rapidly. (P.K. Yonge Library of Florida History)

you may recall, had swelled to nearly ten thousand inhabitants by 1880, which represents an almost sixteen-fold increase over forty years. Although impressive, this rate of growth cannot compare with Key West's population spike during the 1880s. Over the course of only ten years, the city's population mushroomed to over eighteen thousand inhabitants, which represents an increase of nearly one hundred percent and an average net increase of nearly one thousand new inhabitants a year over the course of the decade. Such a high rate of growth was not unprecedented in the burgeoning United States—the population of the city of Denver, for instance, nearly tripled during the same period—but it nonetheless represents a rate of expansion well above the national average.

Why did so many people flood the tiny island of Key West during the 1880s? The answer to this question, strangely enough, lies ninety miles to the south of Key West in the Spanish-controlled island of Cuba. In the period before the Napoleonic wars, Spain controlled a vast empire in the Americas, and Spanish dominion stretched from Mexico to Chile. A series of post-Napoleonic wars of independence brought liberation and autonomy to all of Spain's continental possessions, but Spain's Caribbean island colonies, of which Cuba was by far the most important, remained under firm Spanish dominion. Spain was so determined to retain its sovereignty over Cuba, in fact, that it ruled over the last remaining vestiges of its American empire with an uncompromising iron hand, fearing that any steps towards reforms, however reasonable, would only serve to encourage the birth of an independence movement. Indeed, African slavery was not outlawed in Cuba until 1886, over twenty years after slave emancipation in the United States.

Ruthless oppression, however, inspired stubborn resistance, and by the middle of the nineteenth century, the history of Cuba becomes the story of one attempt after another to liberate the island from Spanish domination. Many American citizens were involved in these efforts, and since Key West is by far the closest American port to Cuba, Key West played an important role in the struggles of independence from the very beginning.

The close alliance between the people of Key West and the cause of Cuban revolution was demonstrated most dramatically in the events of May 1850. Weeks earlier, a small military party headed by former Spanish colonel Narcisso Lopez had landed in Cuba and had attempted to rouse the oppressed population into open rebellion against its Spanish masters. Finding little support, Lopez and his expedition were forced to flee Cuba in their steamship, the *Creole,* in an attempt to reach sanctuary in American territory. Escape soon became pursuit, and by the time the *Creole* reached Key West, the Spanish gunboat *Pizarro* was hot on its tail; the *Creole,* in fact, managed to outrun its pursuer only by throwing any and all loose wood-

"Cuba Libre" *served as a rallying cry for expatriate Cubans in Key West, Tampa, and Martí City. This late-nineteenth-century cigar label illustrates the popularity of the expression.* (USF Special Collections)

en items, including boxes of bacon and parts of the woodwork of the vessel, into the *Creole's* boiler. The citizens of the city were enthralled by Lopez's narrow escape, and during his stay in the old Island of Bones, star-struck residents gave him a royal welcome.

Key West's sympathy for Lopez, incidentally, probably arose as much from Southern slave-holding sentiment as from a real desire for the liberation of Cuba. If Cuba was made independent, many in the Southern states reasoned, it could join the Union as a slave state, and thus tip the balance of power towards the slave-holding South. Indeed, it is revealing that all of Lopez's compatriots on board the *Creole,* outside of five real Cubans, were riflemen from the slave state of Kentucky. On the whole, then, Lopez should probably be labeled a "filibuster"—that is, a private military adventurer—rather than a true revolutionary. If so, he joins some interesting company, including filibuster extraordinaire William Walker, a native of Tennessee, who once invaded Nicaragua with fifty-eight men and had himself elected president of the country, before he was removed from power by foreign pressure in 1857.

Whatever Lopez's motives, his attempts to liberate Cuba were ultimately fruitless, and following another failed expedition in 1851, Lopez met his untimely end at the hands of a Spanish executioner. His death, however, did not end American attempts to annex Cuba. In 1854, for instance, Southern-sympathizing President Franklin Pierce of the United States tried to purchase Cuba from the Spanish empire for a sum of $130 million, but met with no success. Seeing Cuba as both a valuable ally against the Northern states, and as an arena of unlimited expansion for slave-based agriculture, pro-slavery interests in the United States continued to call for the annexation of Cuba right up to the very eve of the American Civil War.

After the defeat of the Confederacy, Key West's ardor for the cause of independent Cuba waned somewhat, but only for the time being, since events in the late 1860s would soon restore this enthusiasm to fever pitch. In 1867, the Spanish colonial government imposed harsh new taxes upon Cuban incomes, real estate, and business transactions, which infuriated a Cuban public already discontented with the high customs duties imposed by the mother country. When Cuban notables complained, they were declared outlaws by the government, and this triggered the outbreak of what would later be called the First Cuban Revolution in 1868. During the conflict, which would ultimately drag on for more than ten years, the armies of Spain employed draconian tactics in an attempt to put down the resistance, including (but certainly not limited to) sentencing those who spoke in favor of the rebels to as much as six years of hard labor. One Cuban to be so imprisoned was seventeen-year-old José Martí, a future founding father of Cuban independence from Spain. As we shall see later, Martí never forgave the Spanish for his mistreatment.

In the face of such severe repression, Cubans like Martí began to leave their island in droves, especially those Cubans most sympathetic to the cause of independence. Since Key West was a mere ninety miles away from Cuba, and since many Cuban revolutionaries regarded the United States as the model of democracy in the western hemisphere, it was only natural that the city of Key West would absorb a considerable portion of these political refugees. By 1870, there were already enough Cubans in Key West to support a Spanish-language newspaper. A year later, the swelling Cuban community in Key West was strong enough to support a Cuban civic center, called San Carlos Hall, named after Carlos M. de Cespedes, one of the founding leaders of the first Cuban revolution. Within five more years, Cubans had become so powerful in city politics that the son of the self-same Carlos M. de Cespedes, who bore his father's name, was elected mayor of the city of Key West.

After 1876, in fact, the Cubans more or less controlled Key West's politics, as illustrated by the election results for Monroe County in 1892. In that year, two seats were open in the state legislature, and in an attempt to attract the votes of the powerful Key West Cuban community, the equally-divided Republican and Democratic parties each nominated one English-speaking and one Cuban candidate for the offices. When the votes were tallied, pollsters found that most English-speaking Republicans had voted the party ticket, as had the majority of English-speaking Democrats. Key West's Cuban expatriates, however, tended to vote on cultural rather than party lines, favoring candidates of their own ethnicity. As a result, Monroe County sent one Democrat and one Republican to the Tallahassee legislature in 1892, and both were Cuban. As Key West historian Jefferson B. Browne observed, the Cubans of Key West "were not only good revolutionists but keen politicians."

Good politicians or not, it is unlikely that many Cubans would have come to Key West, or would have stayed long after arriving, if they had been unable to make a living in this city of wreckers. Luckily for the Cuban political exiles, work was to be had in the growing Key West cigar-making industry, which flourished during the 1870s, '80s, and '90s. Cigar-making, it should be said, had already enjoyed some minor success in Key West before these years; indeed, the earliest such establishment in Key West dates back as far as 1831, the same year that Key West first announced its grandiose railroad ambitions. Unfortunately, this 1831 cigar factory, along with the other small-scale enterprises that joined it over the next decade, was never particularly profitable, largely because of the lack of regular, reliable transportation between Key West and northern markets.

By the 1860s, however, the city of Key West had become a major American port, and transportation to and from the north was no longer a significant problem. Key West now had the opportunity to become a major cigar-producing city, and the Cuban revolution of 1868, which led to an influx of Cuban labor, soon gave Key West the means. Key West also benefited greatly from U.S. importation duties, which slapped heavy taxes on cigars imported from Cuba, but which levied no taxes whatsoever on imports of tobacco leaves; as a result, the infant Key West cigar industry was shielded from possible competition by a sheltering wall of protective tariffs.

By virtue of these advantages, the Key West cigar-making industry had already reached what one chronicler of Florida history called "gratifying proportions" by 1876; in that year, Key West boasted twenty-nine factories, employing 2,100 people, and produced 62.5 million cigars annually. Within another fourteen years, Key West cigar-making had reached its height, and as many as one hundred million cigars were rolled each year by a population of six thousand mostly Cuban cigar-makers. By this time, the Key West cigar industry was unquestionably the single greatest source of income on the island, and massive cigar factories dominated the cityscape. The city of wreckers, it seems, had become the city of cigars.

Key West's cigar-makers worked hard, and their life was far from idyllic, but their profession did provide them with certain advantages. Key West's cigar "factories," which rose as many as four stories over the dusty streets of the town, were not really factories at all, but more properly craft shops in which highly skilled laborers would work together to produce a high-quality, handmade finished product. Within the factory, individual workers were assigned highly specialized jobs. "Strippers" selected and stripped the tobacco leaves, and carried them to cigar rollers for assembly. The cigar rollers then assembled a package of leaves, which in industry slang was termed a "bunch," and wrapped it carefully inside a large, well-cured tobacco leaf wrapper. Probably the most delicate part of the entire enterprise was the assembly of the bunch: if well prepared by a competent professional, the cigar would burn evenly and hold its ash properly, but an incompetently prepared bunch would either burn too fast, or not at all.

Once the bunch was assembled, the cigar was sealed using a dab of tragacanth gum imported from distant Persia, and handed over to another specialist, the "picker," who collected groups of cigars with a similar size, shape, and color so that they would look uniform when finally placed together in a cigar box. All the while, the factory workers were entertained by yet another specialist, the *lector* or "reader," an articulate and well-informed orator who read novels, poetry, and newspapers to the workers in the factory, in an attempt to stave off the inevitable boredom inherent in the mindless monotony of a cigar-maker's labors.

On the whole, Key West cigar-makers lived well. True, their living quarters were less than impressive. Visitors from the north, such as Charles Richard Dodge, found their houses to be "small and cheap," due in part to the absence of chimneys, an essential feature which only the most squalid of northern homes would be without. But chimneys would have been of little use in tropical Key West, where temperatures never dropped below freezing, and most cooking was done outside. Furthermore, given Key West's marvelous climate, who would want to stay indoors for long in any case?

With the exception of their humble homes, the living standard of a Key West cigar-making family was actually quite comfortable. At a time in which the average annual income of an American family of four was $380 per year, the average Key West cigar-maker

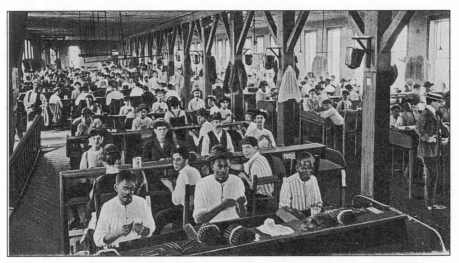

Cigar-makers plying their craft in a late-nineteenth-century cigar factory in Tampa. The factories in Key West would have been similar. (USF Special Collections)

earned the respectable annual salary of about $500, and since they were paid by piece, and not by the hour, Key West cigar-makers had the enviable ability to decide for themselves how many hours they would work. Furthermore, once they had been paid for their labors, a Key West cigar-worker could spend it at one of America's greatest trading emporiums. By 1897, the thriving harbor of Key West was the twelfth busiest port in America, at least as judged by the revenue from customs receipts, and Key West's markets bubbled with activity. The only item in short supply was good quality beef; meat could be obtained from Florida cattle herders, but according to Charles Richard Dodge, if a Northern tourist were forced to choose between stringy scrub-cattle steaks and semi-starvation, "I fear there would be no doubt whatever about his choice." But the cigar rollers didn't mind; as anyone who has ever dined with Cuban-Americans knows, *Cubanos* prefer pork.

◊ ◊ ◊

Cigar-making gave the city of Key West an aura of great prosperity, and to a large degree, this reputation was well deserved: the cigar-making inhabitants of Key West received the respectable sum of $3 million in 1894 as compensation for their labors. Still, a keen observer might have noticed that cracks were forming in Key West's mighty economic edifice by the end of the 1890s. The success of cigars could not conceal the fact that Key West's older industries, which had once made the city one of the richest in the American South, were slowly beginning to fail.

Take turtling, for example. The harvesting of these unfortunate creatures, as we have already seen, was one of the most venerable industries practiced along the Florida shore, and Key West had long been a center of the trade. By the 1890s, however, turtle populations near Key West had begun to plummet. In part, this decline can be ascribed to Key West's insatiable and growing appetite for turtle eggs and turtle flesh. During the 1840s, when Key West was still little more than a tiny hamlet, the number of turtles which had to be slaughtered to satisfy local demand was relatively small. By the 1880s, however, the city had expanded more than forty-fold, and the pressure on sea turtle populations increased correspondingly. The result of this burgeoning hunger was depressingly predictable. When the small settlement of Key West nibbled on turtle populations in the 1840s, the turtles still had a chance to replace their numbers; by the 1880s, however, Key West and its eighteen thousand hungry mouths had begun to gorge, and turtles began to disappear from Florida's waters.

The gluttonous population of Key West cannot shoulder the blame alone, however, for the coming of steamships to the Florida Straits in large numbers also played a crucial role in driving turtles to the edge of extinction. Before the steam-powered vessels came to the Keys, the sea turtle's own biology had made exporting turtle flesh to Northern markets a dicey proposition. Since turtle meat spoiled rapidly, it was nearly impossible for a sailing ship to carry meat to Northern markets before it rotted in the holds. Transporting still-living turtles was no easier, since the normally plant-eating turtles tended to become carnivorous, and quite cannibalistic, while held in captivity. Worst yet, once they had begun to feast on their own kind, sea turtles lost the delicate flavor which made them so prized. A sailing ship captain who docked at a New York wharf after a two-week journey from Key West, therefore, might find that the turtles in his hold had become both fewer and less valuable while in transit.

The fast-moving, dependable steamship, however, greatly reduced transportation times to Northern ports, and mass harvesting of sea turtle flesh now became possible for the first time. As a result, commercial turtle hunters, using large nets, began to extract vast numbers of sea turtles from Florida waters. In the year 1890, when the turtling industry was nearing its height, turtle fishermen managed to pull over 468,000 pounds of turtles from the seas around Key West, and seven years later, the total harvest weighed over 634,000 pounds. Turtle catches on this scale, however, were utterly unsustainable, and the Florida shore's turtle population soon began a rapid decline. By 1898, the turtle catch had fallen to a mere 72,000 pounds, and within a few decades, the Florida turtling industry had ceased to be of any real importance.

The decimation of the sea turtle was hastened considerably by continued local demand for sea turtle eggs, which many in the Keys considered a sublime delicacy. There is some reason to believe that, if these eggs had been cared for rather than consumed, the decline of Florida turtle stocks could have taken far longer, or been avoided altogether. Commodore Munroe, for one, was convinced that if the turtle nests of Biscayne Bay had been protected from predators rather than plundered by hungry Floridians, and if the young turtles of the nests had been assisted in their often dangerous journey down the beach and into the surf, then the Biscayne Bay turtle industry might have been able to continue indefinitely. By the time that Munroe conceived of this plan, however, turtle populations in the Bay were already so low that Munroe was unable to purchase the eggs he needed at any price. In any case, it is unlikely that Munroe's plan could have worked in the long run, since the growth of Miami in subsequent decades would have doomed the turtles of Biscayne Bay despite the Commodore's tender ministrations. Just-hatched turtles instinctively head towards the brightest lights, a primal instinct which should bring the turtles to the ocean, but which would likely have caused the baby turtles to flop their way inland instead, towards the electric glitter of downtown Miami.

The decline of the Key West turtling industry deprived Key West of one of its favorite foods, but since relatively few Conchs were employed by this industry, its failure was hardly a knockout blow to the island's prosperity. The downfall of the Key West sponging industry, however, was far more serious, since sponging had become crucial to Key West's prosperity. In the early 1890s, Key West sponging employed over 1,300 men and 350 boats, and sponge fishing was second only to cigars in overall importance to the economy of Key West. Each year, spongers plucked an average of 165 tons of sponges from the ocean, and the industry brought in an annual revenue of approximately a million dollars.

By the turn of the century, however, Key West sponging was in serious trouble. As early as 1875, spongers began to notice ominous green streaks in the water, which, as they soon discovered, left a wake of dead fish, sharks, and sponges in their path; only porpoises, curiously enough, seemed to be unaffected by this emerald plague. These green streaks, which were later proven to be a form of fungus, bedeviled the industry for years, and caused occasional sharp drops in sponge production, but they did not destroy the Key West sponge industry. Ultimately, Key West sponging was obliterated not by fungus, but by human competition—more specifically, competition from the Tampa-area town of Tarpon Springs.

Tarpon Springs' growing dominance over Key West in the sponge diving industry can be attributed to two main factors: the quality of the sponges and the techniques used to collect them. In early Florida history, Key West enjoyed a nearly insurmountable advantage over Tarpon Springs insofar as the Keys sponges were generally found in relatively shallow water, which made them far easier to harvest using the pole and water-glass technology that the Conchs had brought with them from the Bahamas. Over time, however, the inhabitants of Tarpon Springs became increasingly adept at diving for deeper-water "bay" sponges, as they were then called, and since these sponges tended to be of higher quality than the shallow-water sponges of the Keys, Tarpon Springs began to gain ground on its southern rival. By 1895, in fact, the value of Tarpon Springs' sponges exceeded that of Key West's, and the island city would never regain its former dominance.

The industry probably could have continued profitably in Key West for years, however, if not for the arrival of Greek spongers in Tarpon Springs in 1905. Unlike Conch spongers, who collected their squishy prizes using boats and extraordinarily long poles, the Greek spongers were expert divers, able to pluck sponges directly from the seafloor where they grew. Many Greek spongers, in fact, used "hard hat" diving suits equipped with air hoses, allowing them to remain on the seafloor for minutes or even hours at a time. A Greek sponge diver, thus equipped, enjoyed enormous advantages over his Conch counterpart. Not only was he able to bring up deep-water sponges of the highest quality, he could bring them up in one piece, whereas spongers using hooks tended to damage their quarry in the process. Furthermore, sponge divers could strip clean the entire seafloor before returning to the surface, a feat which Conch spongers could rarely accomplish. As a result, diving for sponges replaced the pole-and-hook technique in Tarpon Springs with stunning rapidity; indeed, between the 1905 and 1906 alone, the number of sponges acquired using these traditional Conch methods declined from 97% to 39%.

Thanks to the exertions of Greek sponge divers, who flooded the market with cheaper and higher-quality sponges, the price of sponges began to drop, and the Conch spongers of Key West proved unable to compete. Desperate to defend their livelihood, Key West spongers tried to pass legislation against sponge diving, and hotheads even took potshots with their rifles at the boats of Greek spongers who entered their domain, but to no avail. Some tried to copy Greek techniques, but by this point, the shallow waters which had once assured the success of Key West sponging now cemented its downfall. Compared to the deep-water "bay" sponges of Tarpon Springs, the shallow "reef" sponges of Key West were of a decidedly lower quality and could not fetch a comparable market price. As a result, by 1912, sponging in Key West had declined to such a low level that Jefferson B. Browne's history of Key West, published that year, makes no mention of sponging at all. Despite Browne's oversight, Key West sponging was not yet dead; indeed, 1918 saw a temporary revival, and over fifty tons of sponges were harvested in Key West that year. Nonetheless, competition from Tarpon Springs, continued fungal blooms, and the invention of synthetic sponges conspired to ensure that Key West's sponging industry remained only a ghost of its former glory.

The decline of sponging was a double tragedy to Key West, since its downfall cost the island city not only a considerable source of income, but also an important element of the city's unique identity. The same is true, to an even greater extent, for the Key West wrecking industry. Although the city never entirely abandoned wrecking as an occupation, forces beyond Key West's control soon made the salvaging of shipwrecks an occasional occurrence, where once it had been the foundation of a thriving Key West economy.

Although several factors contributed to the decline of wrecking as the nineteenth century progressed, the most obvious change was the construction of a chain of modern lighthouses on the Florida Reef after 1850. One of the first advocates of such lighthouses was Lt. Matthew Perry, who wrote in 1821 to his government superiors to encourage the construction of lighthouses, arguing that this would be "an act of justice on the part of our Government," and that "humanity and a regard to the safety of the lives and fortunes of our citizens seriously demand so desirable a measure." Persuaded by Perry's eloquence, the government developed a chain of lighthouses and lightships along the Florida Reef, but these early attempts at warding ships off the reefs met with little success. Dimly lit and prone to outages, these early lights did little to warn voyagers off of the reef.

Of all the early attempts to light the Florida Reef, the most ambitious, and the most unsuccessful, was the plan to station a lightship atop Carysfort Reef, one of the most dangerous along the Florida shore. The first lightship was supposed to have been stationed on the reef in 1825, but ironically, a storm drove this ship aground while it was on route to the reef, delaying its arrival for a year. When it did finally arrive, it lasted only five years before succumbing to the dry rot and fungus common to poorly maintained ships in Florida's subtropical air. A second lightship was designed to replace her, and although this ship survived the climate, it barely survived the Seminoles: the captain of the ship and one of his crewmen were killed in an Indian ambush in 1836 during the Second Seminole War.

It would be comforting to say that these men did not die in vain, but all the evidence suggests the contrary; in fact, the Carysfort light was widely regarded as worse than useless. One sea captain of the period went so far as to demand that it be either improved or dismantled, since "the navigator is apt to run ashore looking for it." Other sea captains claimed that Carysfort lightkeepers were in league with the wreckers, and that the lightkeepers purposefully dimmed the lights in order to provide more spoils for the wrecking pirates of Key West. The government finally gave up on the lightship in 1848 and ordered that a more powerful lighthouse be driven directly into the submerged reef. The engineer who was charged to build it, interestingly enough, was Lt. George Gordon Meade of Civil War fame, who would later defeat Robert E. Lee at the battle of Gettysburg.

The new Carysfort Lighthouse was the first of a new breed of lighthouses, taller and more powerful than before, which the government gradually strung along the Florida Reef between 1852 and 1880. These new lighthouses doubtless prevented many wrecks, though the evidence suggests that they caused some as well. In his excellent book about the wrecking industry in Key West, historian John Viele recounts three separate incidents where boats ran aground after confusing one light for another; the French ship *Jeune Ida,* for instance, ran aground after mistaking the Sombrero light off Key Vaca for the Salt Cay light, which was sixty miles away! Confusion on this scale was exceptional, however, and on the whole these new lights probably helped to reduce the frequency of shipwrecks along the Florida Reef.

Still, at least until the 1870s or so, enough shipwrecks occurred along the reef to gratify all but the most ambitious Key West wrecker, due to the greatly expanded volume of maritime traffic following the conclusion of the Civil War. By 1880, however, the number of wrecks began to decline rapidly. Three more powerful new lighthouses had been placed by this time on the Florida Reef, and new, more accurate, navigational charts had become available to ship

Carysfort Reef Lighthouse, the first of the new lighthouses to be built on the Florida Reef. (Ronald Foster)

captains. Furthermore, as steamships began to replace sailing vessels, the number of wrecks was reduced further, since steamships could fight winds and current more effectively than their wind-driven counterparts, and thus were more able to avoid the dangers of the Straits. Land-based steam engines, surprisingly enough, also contributed to the reduction of wrecks on the Florida shore. By the 1880s, America had entered the golden age of railways, and the gradual rise in the volume of railroad freight across the United States led to a steady decline in the number of ships that were forced to risk the perils of the Florida Straits.

As a result, wrecks along the Florida shore became increasingly rare, and profitable wrecks rarer yet. Perhaps the last wreck of note was that of the *Alicia,* bound from Havana to Europe, which struck Ajax Reef in 1905. The *Alicia* was loaded with luxury merchandise, including fine silks, linens, furniture, pianos, and spirits, much of which had to be extracted from underwater holds by divers working in pitch dark in water fouled with potash and rotting food. Keys residents still alive in the 1960s remembered how yards of brilliant white lace were strung on mangrove limbs to dry after that wreck, as if the city were being decorated for some sort of marvelous holiday. And perhaps it was a holiday of sorts, a celebration of remembrance for Key West's wrecking past. But even though the wreck brought a modest profit to Key West, the salvage of the *Alicia* ultimately proved to be little more than a tribute to a bygone age, a reminder of lost glory. By 1921, wrecking had become so infrequent an occupation along the Florida shore that the wrecking register, which had handed out licenses to would-be wrecking captains for nearly a century, was closed for good.

๑ ๑ ๑

By the turn of the century, Key West had lost several of the industries that had both filled its coffers and given the city its unique character. Still, what did this matter? In the meantime, the fast-growing city of Key West had gained a new identity as the queen city of American cigar-rolling, and its prospects seemed limitless. Key West had found its road into the twentieth century, and it was paved with Cuban cigars. Or so it must have seemed. As events soon proved, however, cigars were destined to be a dead-end street, and would soon join turtles, sponges, and shipwrecks in the dustbin of Key West history.

The first blow struck against the Key West cigar industry landed in 1886. Early in the morning on the first of April, a devastating and deadly fire swept through downtown Key West. By the time the fire played itself out, eighteen cigar factories had been destroyed, and four lives had been lost, including those of three firefighters who were killed while attempting to check the ferocious blaze. The origin of the fire is unclear, but interestingly enough, some evidence points to Spanish involvement. According to the cigar historian Loy Glenn Westfall, some suspicious-looking characters were seen shortly before the fire carrying sawdust and kerosene in the area of the cigar factories. Furthermore, news of the Key West fire was reported in a Havana newspaper several days *before* it actually occurred, which suggests that the authorities in Havana might have had foreknowledge that a fire was expected shortly in Key West.

Responsible or not, the Spanish colonial government certainly had ample reason to seek vengeance against the meddling inhabitants of Key West. Despite, or perhaps because of, the ultimate failure of the 1868–1878 revolution in Cuba, the Cuban population of Key West remained fervently anti-Spanish and had organized itself into a number of revolutionary societies dedicated to the liberation of Cuba from Spanish rule. Would-be rebels against the Spanish regime in Cuba found Key West a fertile recruiting ground for both men and money, and although no filibustering expeditions were launched directly from Key West, nearly all revolutionaries depended heavily on Key West for support of their plans.

Key West's intimate involvement in the cause of Cuban revolution is illustrated most vividly by the example of Carlos Aguerro, a would-be liberator of the Cuban people. Following an abortive

1884 attempt to raise rebellion in the island colony, Carlos fled to Key West, where, despite his defeat, he was treated with the same hero's welcome that had been lavished on Narcisso Lopez nearly three decades earlier. The Cuban population of Key West pooled their money to outfit Aguerro for a second expedition to Cuba, and representatives from both political parties contributed money as well, in an attempt to court the all-important Key West Cuban vote.

Anxious to prevent a second expedition from getting off the ground, the Spanish authorities in Havana charged Aguerro with "rapine, arson, highway robbery, and murder," and demanded his extradition to Cuba. Aguerro was soon cleared by an American federal court, however, since the judges determined that his supposed crimes were committed in furtherance of a revolutionary movement and were thus not properly crimes at all. Following this verdict, thousands of cheering Key West Cubans paraded Aguerro through the streets in celebration; it was, as Jefferson B. Browne noted, "a scene long to be remembered." Key West's money and enthusiasm, however, were not sufficient to save Aguerro's life, and like Lopez, he and his followers were killed during a second expedition to Cuba almost immediately after his trial.

Aguerro perished at the hands of the Spanish, but the dream of independence did not die with him, and it perhaps burned most brightly in the breast of José Martí, who we last met as a young man on his way to a Cuban prison following his denunciation of the Spanish colonial government. Following several years of life as a dissident in Cuba, Martí was exiled to the United States in 1880, where he maintained a network of contacts with other exiled Cuban rebels for a number of years. By 1892, Martí judged that the time was ripe for Cuban independence, and he founded the Cuban Revolutionary Party, which created networks of communication between potential rebels within Cuba and active rebels working outside the island. Among Martí's co-conspirators were Máximo Gómez and José Maceo, both veterans of the first revolution in 1868, and both seasoned and stubborn field commanders; Maceo, for instance, managed to survive an astonishing twenty-four wounds while combating Spanish forces.

Martí, on the other hand, proved unable to survive even a single wound, and he was killed upon his first appearance on the battlefield during the Cuban War of Independence of 1895. Gómez and Maceo fought on, however, and inflicted impressive defeats upon the numerically superior Spanish forces. All the while, the United States watched greedily from the sidelines, hoping to expand its own influence in the area at Spain's expense. Some in the government still clung to the antebellum South's old dream of absorbing Cuba; indeed, Undersecretary of War J. C. Breckenridge advocated the outright annexation of Cuba to the United States and expressed his hopes that this would end America's "internal race conflict," since he assumed, without any apparent justification, that the cur-

A nineteenth-century portrait of José Martí, the Apostle of Cuban Liberty. (USF Special Collections)

rent "overflow" of blacks within America would naturally gravitate south towards tropical Cuba. Before this could happen, Breckenridge conceded, the island would have to be purged of its current "immoral," "apathetic," and "indolent" inhabitants, even if doing so would require "using the methods Divine Providence used on the cities of Sodom and Gomorrah."

Thankfully, calmer heads prevailed, and American officials such as Breckenridge were not allowed play out their dreams of genocide on Cuban soil. Indeed, quite a few American legislators were genuinely behind the cause of Cuban independence, and opposed Breckenridge's brand of imperialist arrogance. Still others advocated a policy of complete non-involvement in Cuba's affairs or favored continued Spanish occupation of Cuba, believing that the Spanish could best defend American business interests on the island. In the meantime, however, nearly everyone agreed that the turmoil in Cuba ought to be watched, and Spain should be reminded of U.S. power in the western hemisphere. To that end, the U.S. Navy dispatched the battleship *Maine* to Havana harbor. It arrived on January 24, 1898. Within three weeks, on February 15, the *Maine* exploded. Outraged by what they thought was an underhanded Spanish attack on a U.S. vessel—though no proof has ever been uncovered to support this contention—the United States declared war on Spain exactly two months later.

The resulting conflict was short, decisive, and filled with absurdities. Intimidated by the reputed size of the Spanish fleet, American politicians prevented the admiral commanding the American Atlantic fleet from sailing to Cuba with his full force until after he had called some Civil War–era Monitor-class gunboats into service to guard the Eastern Seaboard ports; although this decision made for good politics, it made no military sense whatsoever, since no ammunition could be secured to fit the outmoded guns of these aging relics. Luckily for the Americans, the main Spanish fleet was even more decrepit than the American battleships, and it took only two battles—one in Manila Bay and the other at Santiago de

Cuba—for the smaller but more modern American fleet to sink the fourteen Spanish vessels which were ship-shape enough to reach the theaters of war. Indeed, the casualty figures for these battles seem to suggest that the Spanish never stood a chance: a total of 483 Spanish crewmen died at their posts, compared with only a single American.

Ultimately, these sea battles decided the war, since they left Spain's large Cuban and Philippine armies stranded on remote island possessions, far from the mother country, surrounded by hostile rebel groups, and without any possibility of resupply. In the meantime, before this became apparent, Teddy Roosevelt put on a little sideshow in Cuba for the benefit of the American press. Eager for action, Roosevelt abandoned his desk job as the assistant secretary for the Navy and joined the First Volunteer Cavalry, which later became known as the "Rough Riders." This unit, which Roosevelt eventually rose to command, consisted of a bizarre mix of Western frontiersmen, Indian warriors, amateur sportsmen, and Ivy-League athletes; in other words, an uneasy amalgam of hardened warriors and politically connected men of leisure.

Although his Rough Riders were technically cavalrymen, they landed on Cuba on the 20th of June along with the rest of the American expeditionary force without any steeds, but no matter— Roosevelt and his lads could do without horses. They could not, however, do without publicity, and Roosevelt ensured that his Rough Riders would get good press by the simple expedient of dragging newsreel photographer Alfred Smith along on his campaigns. Roosevelt's men fought in several minor skirmishes, including the battle of San Juan Hill, all of which had a negligible effect on the outcome of the war, but a meteoric effect on Roosevelt's fortunes. By the war's end, the relentlessly self-promoting Roosevelt had become a household name, and Roosevelt was catapulted into the White House three years later.

Helpless against the victorious American forces, the Spanish gave in and surrendered their colonial empire to America in December of 1898. Ironically, the peace settlement which concluded the Spanish-American war ultimately killed more Americans than the war itself. The American conquest of the Philippines had occurred almost by accident—indeed, if the American Pacific squadron had not been on the way to Hong Kong at the war's start, it probably would not have occurred at all—but Americans were loathe to part with the colonial treasure that had so fortuitously fallen into their grasping hands. Reasoning that the Philippines were America's gateway to the vast markets of China, and that this gate would be slammed shut by one European power or another if America proved too weak to hold it open, the McKinley administration resolved to annex the islands. This decision, however, came as a rude shock to the Philippine revolutionary movement, which had fought in support of U.S. forces during the war, and as a result the Philippine rebels soon turned their guns against the occupying Americans. By the time the rebellion was finally quashed in 1902, it had cost 4,200 American soldiers their lives, in addition to an estimated 20,000 Filipino insurgents and 200,000 civilians, who perished due to a combination of hunger, disease, and the brutal pacification tactics of the U.S. Army.

The end of the war brought misery to the Philippines, therefore, but transports of joy to the Cubans, who were released from four centuries of Spanish domination. True, independence from Spain did not transform Cuba into a functioning autonomous state overnight; the U.S. military more or less ruled the island for the next decade, and the Cuban economy continued to suffer under the strong thumb of Spanish merchants and American sugar planters. Still, the collapse of the Spanish empire seemed to signal the dawn of a new day in Cuba, alive with possibilities.

So what does all of this have to do with Key West? Simply put, the withdrawal of the Spanish from Cuba more or less removed the entire *raison d'être* of the Key West Cuban exile community. For twenty years, the Cubans of Key West had held aloft the torch of independence, and had done everything in their power to free their homeland from Spanish oppression. Now that the deed was accomplished, many Cubans opted to return to Cuba, and as a result, the total population of the city actually declined by nearly 1,000 people between 1890 and 1900, from just over 18,000 to 17,114 inhabitants. Given the fact that the city had gained 9,000 people in the previous decade, this loss of population seemed to signal a turn for the worse in Key West's fortunes.

Not all Cubans left for the south, however; other Key West Cubans packed their bags and headed north, drawn by news of work at the new cigar towns of central Florida. This northward exodus first began in 1886, in the immediate aftermath of the great Key West fire. While the city was still in ruins, a committee of citizens from Tampa arrived in Key West and tried to convince several cigar manufacturers, including Vincente Martinez Ybor, to relocate to virgin territory in Tampa. Ybor ultimately agreed, since he was tempted not only by the financial inducements offered by the Tampa committee, but also by the possibility of leaving behind the growing labor troubles of Key West. Indeed, by the 1880s, Key West cigar rollers had become notorious for their frequent strikes, much to the displeasure of local cigar factory owners. Key West's labor radicalism was fueled and strengthened by the growing influence of anarchism, which was spawned in the cigar factories of Havana, but had little difficulty in crossing the Florida Straits to Key West. Interestingly enough, the spread of anarchism was greatly facilitated by labor conditions within the cigar factories; the *lectores* frequently read Spanish language newspapers to their fellow workers, and the reading material of choice was often the Cuban revolutionary newspaper *El Productor*. By 1889, Cuban anarchists had become so powerful in Key West that they organized the island's cigar rollers into a general strike, bringing the cigar-dependent city of Key West to its knees.

In order to combat the growing radicalism of Key West's Cubans, local owners began to import outside laborers, especially those of Spanish descent. Needless to say, given the already-existing antagonism between Cubans and Spaniards, this was just asking for trouble. When a certain Mr. Seidenberg announced in 1894 that he would substitute Spaniards for Cubans at his factory, Key West Cubans threatened to kill any Spaniards so unwise as to seek employment at Seidenberg's establishment. Key West Cubans had two reasons to be concerned about the arrival of a large number of Spanish cigar rollers: not only might Spaniards cost Cubans their jobs, they might also infiltrate the Cuban revolutionary cells that were active in Key West, and thus uncover the clandestine plans of the Cuban independence movement.

Whatever the exact motive of the Key West Cubans, the incident soon erupted into a long and complicated legal battle between the Cuban cigar rollers of Key West and the factory owners, which eventually rose through the American legal system all the way to the Supreme Court. Finally, after months of bitter courtroom battles, the Cubans walked away with a partial victory. The U.S. government agreed to invoke the alien contract labor laws and deported the Spanish cigar rollers whom Seidenberg had brought to Key West from Havana.

The Key West Cubans may have won the battle, but they ultimately discovered that they had lost the war. Stung by his defeat in the courts and fed up with the uncompromising radicalism of Key West's Cuban workers, Seidenberg followed in Ybor's footsteps and set up shop in Tampa. Nor was he alone; at least four other major cigar manufacturers also transplanted themselves to Tampa Bay at around the same time, attracted by Tampa's railroad connection to the north and its less unionized labor market. As a result, Key West's cigar production began to drop steadily, while Tampa's production began to rise. By 1900, the cigar-making company town of Ybor City boasted over seventy cigar factories, providing daily employment for as many as thirty thousand cigar rollers, and as a result, Ybor City had earned the reputation as the cigar-making capital of the world.

Cigar-making did not die off entirely in Key West—indeed, many discriminating smokers still professed to prefer a cigar rolled in Key West's tropical climate—but competition from Tampa slowly smothered the once-mighty cigar industry of Key West. By 1909, Key West cigar-making was in such a sorry shape that Henry Flagler, who enjoyed the taste of a well-rolled Key West cigar, volunteered $50,000 of his own money to induce a large cigar manufacturer to relocate from Tampa back to Key West. No one took Flagler up on his offer, however, and Key West cigar-making continued its slide into oblivion.

By 1910, the city of Key West was in dire straits. The industries which had once supported the island city, making it the largest town in Florida for half a century, were failed or failing. As a result, Key West's population remained virtually static between 1900 and 1910, and during the same period of time, Key West went from being the state's second-largest city (behind Jacksonville) to the third-largest, due to the steady development of the lumber port of Pensacola. Within another ten years, Tampa's headlong urban expansion would push the stagnating Key West into fourth place, and the phenomenal growth of Miami would soon knock Key West even farther down the list. Once at the vanguard of Florida's cities, and one of the richest towns per capita in America, Key West was now in imminent danger of economic collapse and political irrelevance.

This fact was not lost on visitors to Key West at around the turn of the century, who took note of the atmosphere of gloom and decay which was already beginning to descend on the old island city. Charles Richard Dodge, for one, was quite unimpressed by the "dusty old town" of Key West, and noted in his account of his 1894 voyage along the Florida Keys that "there is very little of interest here to hold the tourist." John Gifford of *National Geographic Magazine,* who visited the island in 1906, departed with an equally negative impression of the old city of wreckers, declaring it a "dirty, unattractive city with a large proportion of Negroes and Cubans in a population of about 20,000." Key West was first and foremost an industrial town, all but devoid of high culture, fine architecture, and institutions of learning. Without its industries, there was nothing left.

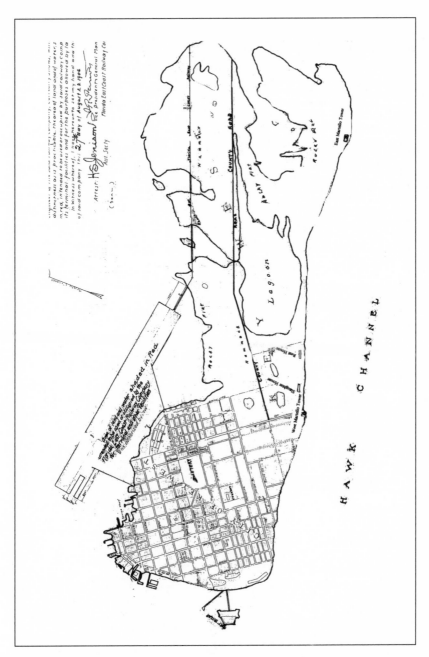

1906 Florida East Coast Railway Company map. Trumbo Island would soon be created (in the rectangular area at the bottom left) for the terminal of the Overseas Railway. (Florida State Library)

So what could save this dusty old industrial town, bypassed by the flow of time, from the inevitability of decline? To answer this question, the people of Key West fell back to the city's oldest and most cherished dream, which had haunted the city's ambitions ever since 1831. If the railroad came, the people of Key West reasoned, it would breathe new life into the tired old city and create new industries to replace those that had been lost over the past three decades. Back in 1831 the railroad had been the over-ambitious dream of an upstart village, the childhood conceit of a newly born settlement. By 1910, however, the idea was a matter of life and death; it was a lifeline thrown in the nick of time to a drowning town. The railroad was the city's only chance. So the people of Key West turned their eyes towards the mainland and prayed that Henry Flagler, the uncrowned king of Florida, would see fit to extend his rail line to Key West's shores. As the saying goes, be careful what you wish for.

5

A Perfect Wilderness

On the 3rd of March, 1896, at five o'clock in the afternoon, a gentleman by the name of John Sewell stepped off the steamship *Della* onto a dock alongside the Miami River and paused to survey his surroundings. Unlike the dusty old town of Key West, already overripe, already slouching into a gradual decline, the future city of Miami was still just an obscure frontier settlement in a neglected corner of America. Indeed, Sewell would later write that "I found Miami all woods," and he would likely have been hard-pressed to find a decent place to stay the night, if not for the fortuitous appearance of Captain Vail's "floating hotel," a steamship converted to living quarters that had just arrived from West Palm Beach. Although his background was humble—he was a former day laborer, a disillusioned schoolteacher, a bankrupted saw mill owner, and a failed student of medicine—this man Sewell was destined to become one of the founding fathers of Miami, and it may be worth our while to follow him around.

According to his memoirs, which provide historians with a fascinating account of the inaugural moments in Miami history, Sewell was not impressed by his first glimpse of the aspiring metropolis. Although several of the future streets had already been laid out by Julia Tuttle, most of the area which would later become downtown was still heavily forested, and outside of Fort Dallas and the Brickell compound, a few small tents and shacks were the only signs of human habitation which had yet appeared on the Miami River. This would soon change, Sewell knew—in fact, it was his job to change it. After failing at so many previous professions, Sewell had proven himself a gifted work crew foreman, and by March of 1896 his talents had become known to Henry Flagler. As it turned out, Flagler was in great need of a man like Sewell in the spring of 1896, since his railroad was already on its way to the Miami River, but the land had not yet been cleared; indeed, a previous work crew sent to the area had been defeated by the area's thick vegetation and rocky soil. For the next few months, it would be William Sewell's job to succeed where they had failed and transform this "perfect wilderness," to use Sewell's own phrase, into marketable real estate.

But first things first. After a short and pleasant visit with Mrs. Tuttle, whom he judged to be "a good business woman," Sewell set out to reconnoiter the area. To the north of Miami lay several small settlements, including the village of Buena Vista, which was inhabited at the time by the French Count, Jean d'Hedouville of treasure-map fame. Farther north, Sewell came across Lemon City, the uppermost community on Biscayne Bay and the terminal of the stagecoach line from Fort Worth, which the railroad was about to make forever obsolete. Lemon City also boasted a drugstore, a fairly large general store, and two honest-to-goodness medical doctors, which were still a rarity along the south Florida frontier. These small communities, however, were mere islands of cleared lands in an ocean of trees, connected only by rough trails that wound their tortuous way through the pines and hammock-land alongside Biscayne Bay.

Sewell then headed south. After crossing the Miami River by

The Peacock Inn in Coconut Grove, which became a fashionable place to stay for those drawn by the rustic delights of Biscayne Bay. (Florida State Archives)

means of a small hand-powered barge, since the river was not yet bridged as of early 1896, Sewell arrived at the Brickell compound, which he noted was "quite a trading post for the Indians"; indeed, it was common at the time to see dozens of Seminole canoes pulled up on the banks of the river near Brickell's store. A few miles farther south, Sewell came to the charming town of Coconut Grove, still the largest settlement on the Bay in 1896, where he enjoyed the hospitality of the Peacock Inn, which had "one of the finest reputations for a hotel that there was in Florida." Here, Sewell made the acquaintance of several of Coconut Grove's eccentric inhabitants, including the Commodore, Dick Carney, and Mr. and Mrs. Kirk Munroe; indeed, Kirk and his wife would later become two of Sewell's best friends. One wonders if Dick Carney attempted to play any practical jokes on Sewell; if he did, they were most likely lost on the matter-of-fact Sewell, whose autobiography is generally devoid of humor. While in the Grove, Sewell also formed a fast friendship with Dr. and Mr. Simmons, a frontier doctor and a retired lawyer/sea captain living together on a house near Biscayne Bay. At the time Sewell met the odd pair, the captain, who would later become Sewell's political confidant, was trying his hand at developing methods of preserving citrus fruits. We will return to Captain Simmons and his physician wife later.

In the meantime, Sewell headed inland, following a rough trail, and discovered a "great many homesteaders scattered through that section." Most of these backwoods pioneers, he found, were making a go at grapefruit farming, though he came across one couple still engaged in the almost extinct profession of making coontie starch. Sewell gradually worked his way back north through the pines of the rocky limestone ridge west of Biscayne Bay and eventually reached the Miami River, where he found that a few British families had set up "an English colony" of several adjoining homesteads on the river's bank. At this point, Sewell decided that he had seen enough of the surrounding country to satisfy his curiosity and

1897—Miami Avenue between Flagler Street and the river, showing John Sewell's shoe store. (Florida State Archives)

resolved to settle down to his appointed task, preparing Miami for the coming of the railroad. Sewell's survey of Biscayne Bay, incidentally, also convinced him of the wisdom of opening a shoe store at the mouth of the Miami River, since during his walkabout, Sewell discovered that the rock-impregnated Biscayne Bay soil made short work of the soles of shoes and boots. As a result, Sewell and his brother E. G., who had accompanied John to Biscayne Bay, decided to try their luck in the shoe business, and the Sewell brothers' shoe store would be a Miami fixture for years to come.

Before the Sewell shoe store (or any other store for that matter) could be built, however, the land had to be cleared, and quite a bit of land at that: the Flagler, Brickell and Tuttle land tracts covered a total of two square miles, one above the river and one below. Undaunted, Sewell tackled the task with gusto. At first, Sewell was forced to use the convict labor that Flagler had hired, but he soon switched to "Negro" workers, who had come to Biscayne Bay in anticipation of securing steady employment with Flagler's railway. Sewell did not disappoint them, as there was plenty of work to be done. Miami's soil, Sewell soon discovered, was quite thin, and barely covered a thick layer of limestone rock, which broke tools and made the removal of trees a back-breaking ordeal. Until the later invention of "rock plowing" with heavy machinery, in fact, Miami-area citrus farmers who wished to plant trees in the Bay's rock-bound soil were obliged to blow holes in the ground with dynamite charges, and Sewell ultimately was forced to use the same methods to clear the land near the mouth of the river. The worst land of all was the hardwood hammock at the edge of the Bay, which was so thick with trees, brush, and vines that Sewell discovered "a man could not walk through it." Unfortunately for Sewell, he had little choice but to tackle this difficult land first, since his top priority was to clear scenic bayfront land needed for the construction of Flagler's Royal Palm Hotel.

Sewell's ultimate goal was to create a blank slate in the Florida wilderness upon which Flagler's landscapers and architects would erect a wonderland paradise for the enjoyment of wealthy tourists; the idea, in other words, was to destroy Florida so it could be created anew. To this end, Sewell fought with nature all along the Bay, determined to clear the area of its native vegetation. This proved to be no easy task, however, because nature retaliated against Sewell and his men. Ironwood trees, so-called because of the resiliency of their wood, proved to be so hard that they could shatter the edge of an ax, and Sewell later reported that "I frequently had as high as a dozen axes broken in a day from cutting this 'brand' of trees." Much worse, however, was what Sewell called the "poison tree," which was so toxic that even its fumes could incapacitate strong men and would cause its victims to suffer "untold agony . . . some of them their faces would swell so that one could not see their eyes." Sewell dealt with this noxious plant, which recent historians have identified as the manchineel tree, by hacking it down and burning it where it lay. Luckily for Sewell, he had men under his employ who were "as tough as an alligator," and who could withstand the noxious fumes of the burning poison-tree.

Nature fought back against Sewell in other ways as well. In 1901, Sewell was overseeing the construction of a bridge across the Miami River at Avenue D when one of the solid stone bridge piers Sewell had built caved in unexpectedly. Upon investigation, Sewell discovered that the weight of the pier had broken the layer of limestone rock upon which it had rested and had opened up one of the underwater veins of water that flowed through the limestone ridge separating the Everglades from Biscayne Bay. So much water boiled up from the underground river, in fact, that when Sewell borrowed a boat to examine the fountain of water erupting from below, his vessel was "thrown off" several times by the force of the upswell. Upon reflection, Sewell wisely chose to abandon the pier, and adjusted his blueprint of the bridge to better fit the dictates of nature. As we shall see, this sort of wisdom was generally lacking in those who developed the south Florida frontier.

After disposing of the pine woods, palmetto scrub, and hardwood hammocks which covered the future downtown Miami, Sewell was next assigned the duty of paving the streets. This might have been a difficult task, but Sewell soon made a fortuitous discovery: the local limestone rock, if pulverized, could be made into an excellent concrete. There was, however, a drawback. The limestone concrete, as it turned out, was a natural brilliant white, and as a result, many early Miami citizens complained that they could not walk on Sewell's streets on a sunny day for fear of going blind. Some Miami pioneers actually began to wear colored spectacles, much like the inhabitants of the storybook city of Oz, to combat what one settler called the "glaring whiteness of the streets." At night, however, the streets were lovely, since the moonlight on the alabaster streets created the illusion that they were dusted with snow.

At the end of a hard day's work of demolishing and paving over Miami's perfect wilderness, Sewell would look forward to an evening of rest, which begs the question: where do the men who build cities sleep in the days before the city yet exists? Sewell's black workers slept under tarps, in tents, in shacks, on boats, or out in the open, but Sewell himself had higher standards. After a few nights in Captain Vail's floating hostelry, Sewell and his brother were put up by the railroad company in a not-yet-completed Miami hotel. The furniture was crude—Sewell later remembered that the hotel provided nothing more than two cots for the two brothers, plus one water bucket, one tin wash basin, one tin "slop bucket," and a kerosene lamp—but as John Sewell was the hotel's most distinguished boarder, he did receive "more towels than the others, some with real handwork on them and fancy designs."

Perhaps the management provided Sewell the dainty towels in order to distract him from one of the hotel's greatest flaws: although it was a two-story structure, it had not yet been equipped with a regular staircase and Sewell was forced to enter and leave his room by means of a ladder. As for food, the unfinished hotel offered "the best the country afforded, but at that time the country did not afford much . . . bread, bacon and grits were the bill of fare usually, and poorly cooked." Sewell later recalled that you could ask the hotel's cook for any type of meat, be it steak, pork chops, or mutton, and the cook would happily agree to the requests, but in the end everyone received different cuts of the same dish: sea turtle, which had not yet been driven from the waters of Biscayne Bay.

If Sewell had looked out of one of his hotel room's two windows in late March and early April of 1896, and one imagines that he did from time to time, he could have watched as the Biscayne Bay wilderness begrudgingly gave way to a steady stream of settlers. Bit by bit, the native vegetation disappeared and was replaced by crude, unpainted wooden structures, mostly built out of shipwreck timber, though the supply of the latter was no doubt strained by the rapid pace of the city's growth. At first, many of these settlers arrived by sea, as had Sewell and his brother, hoping to stake their claim before the mad rush began. As is typical of frontier towns everywhere, nearly all of these first settlers were men, and young men at that, hoping to make their fortune and reputation in a newly minted corner of America. To a great extent they succeeded, and many of them would become filthy rich over the next few decades, though as we shall see in later chapters, more than a few of these fortunes proved to be fleeting.

This steady flow of young male settlers into Biscayne Bay continued for about two months after Sewell's arrival, until the appearance of the first passenger train on the just-completed railroad. After that, things happened very quickly; as Sewell put it, "it seemed that the flood gates were opened and people came from everywhere." Within another month, Miami's population had already reached the one-thousand mark, and the city produced the first issue of its first newspaper, which was given the rather grandiose title of the *Miami Metropolis*. Like many Florida newspapers of the time, it was initially bankrolled by Flagler and served for several years as an organ of the Flagler interest. By the summer, the population at the mouth of the Miami River had swollen to as many as three thousand souls, most of whom were living in tents and shacks, though a

The arrival of the first passenger train in Miami. (Florida State Archives)

lucky few were able to find lodging in the boarding houses, cottages, and small hotels which the Tuttles and the Brickells were hastily erecting along the river banks.

On July 28, 1896, the powers-that-be along the Miami River judged that the population of the town had reached critical mass and Miami was officially incorporated as a city. Interestingly enough, because of the speed at which the town was founded, Miami never went through the intermediate steps of village or township, which means that the city of Miami was never anything other than a city; like the Greek goddess Athena, who emerged fully grown from the head of her father Zeus, Miami was already a full-blown city when she sprang onto the stage of American history.

The incorporation of Miami was unusual in other ways as well. Throughout American history, as settlers of European origin spread throughout the continent, they replaced native Indian names with names of their own devising. Along Biscayne Bay, however, just the opposite occurred. In 1896, settlers decided to drop the old name of "Fort Dallas," which had appeared on maps of the area for decades, and named the town "Miami" instead, which signified "sweet water" in the Indian tongue, or so they thought. In actuality, the name "Miami" is a Tequesta Indian term meaning "big water," a title that does not apply well to the relatively short and narrow Miami River, but which suits the nearby Lake Okeechobee quite well indeed; the early pioneers of Miami, it seems, mistook one Indian name for another. In any case, the town was almost not named Miami at all, since the railway employees in the city at the time campaigned heavily to name the newly founded city "Flagler," in honor of their boss. According to one historian, these men would likely have succeeded if Flagler had not "gently urged" his employees to opt for the Indian name instead. Most likely Flagler thought that the name of "Miami" would hold more appeal with the tourists he intended to attract to the Royal Palm Hotel.

During this period, Sewell became a political power to be reckoned with in Miami, partly because of his high office in the Flagler organization, but also because of his paternalistic influence over the hundred-odd black laborers in his work crew, whom he referred to somewhat condescendingly as "my black artillery." Before the railroad came, in fact, Sewell was the virtual dictator of the developing town—he later claimed that "at that time I was very near law in Miami"—and in the absence of an elected government, people with problems generally brought them before Sewell for adjudication. Sewell also took it upon himself to cast a watchful eye over Miami's pool halls and cold drink stands, which sprang up within a week of Sewell's arrival and which tended to attract baser specimens of humanity. At one point, in fact, Sewell rounded up the whole lot of them and forced them to attend the sermon of a traveling Episcopal preacher, in hopes of improving their supposedly degenerate moral character.

Sewell's authority did not end with the coming of elected government to Miami; indeed, it only grew stronger. During the 1896 elections held immediately after the incorporation of the city, in fact, Sewell set himself up as an unofficial party boss and tried to secure the election of men favorable to the Flagler interest. In order to ensure that his candidates were elected, Sewell relied upon his "black artillery," who were temporarily registered to vote, to tip the balance of the elections. Largely because of Sewell's influence, John B. Reilly, the chief clerk and paymaster of the work crew constructing Flagler's Royal Palm Hotel, became the first mayor of Miami. The third mayor of Miami, incidentally, was Sewell himself, who held office between 1903 and 1907. In the meantime, Sewell deployed his "black artillery" once again during the county referendum of 1899, when he used their voting power to ensure that Biscayne Bay would reclaim the status of the capital of Dade County, which it had lost to Juno ten years earlier. Once the election was won, the declining town of Juno, which had been bypassed by Flagler's rail line, obligingly shipped all of their government documents and equipment to Miami. As part of the package, Miami received their small wooden jail, which was shipped whole from Juno to Miami in 1899 with a single prisoner still incarcerated therein.

Our Mr. Sewell had quickly become a big man in a small town. When he walked the gleaming streets of Miami, which he himself had constructed, one imagines that he felt as if he were touring his own private kingdom—or perhaps his own private duchy, since no one who lived in Florida at that time ever forgot that Flagler was the real king. Whatever title he merited, it was incontestable that Sewell's subjects were many, and their numbers were growing by the day. On his tours, Sewell met J. E. Lummus, a long-time Florida businessman, who was looking to open a general store in downtown Miami. He met T. L. Townley, a transplant from Oklahoma, who intended to go into the drug business. He met J. W. Johnson, a grocer who was known as "Johnson on the Y" since also owned a store at the railroad "Y" at West Palm Beach. And he met Isidor Cohen, who arrived "with a big box of men's furnishing and opened up a little house south of Mr. Johnson's store."

Now that we have reached Mr. Cohen, let us depart from Sewell for a while and let him continue on his own his triumphant march through Miami history—no doubt he is tired of us looking over his shoulder in any case. Isidor Cohen, after all, has his own point of view about early Miami history, one that is quite different in many respects from that of Mr. Sewell. The time has come to let Mr. Cohen to tell his side of the story.

Like Sewell, Cohen arrived in Miami before the coming of the railroad by means of a small steamboat. The vessel stopped first at Lemon City, where Cohen was informed that Miami had no docking facilities and that it would be impossible for him to unload his merchandise at Miami. Disappointed but undeterred, Cohen arranged for storage of his merchandise in Lemon City and continued on his own to the mouth of the Miami River. Here he received a second disappointment—Mrs. Tuttle refused to sell him a plot of land on the north side of the river for his store, advising him instead to wait until the land was cleared and streets were laid out. Upon receiving this information, Cohen informed Mrs. Tuttle that he was too poor to wait that long and that he must find land for his store immediately. Julia Tuttle was not moved, however, and told Cohen that he could best alleviate his poverty by taking a job clearing the land of Miami, whereupon Mr. Cohen, who was Jewish, "tried to impress this naïve lady that the last labor of this character that my race had performed was in the land of Egypt, and that it would be a violation of my religious convictions to resume that condition of servitude." It would be interesting to know how Julia Tuttle responded to this remarkable and mendacious declaration, but Cohen's history of Miami does not say.

Following his unsuccessful interview with Mrs. Tuttle, Cohen's misadventures continued. Unable to secure a business location on the north side of the river, Cohen scoped out the relatively undeveloped south side and eventually secured business space on a tiny property which he sublet from the owner of a small sawmill. Before he could open the store, however, he had to retrieve his merchandise from storage in Lemon City, and to this end, he hired a sailboat from Captains Cuttrell and Gorry. Cohen and his hired captains arrived in Lemon City on the tenth of February, but to Cohen's dismay, while he haggled with the Lemon City dock owner over storage charges for Cohen's left-behind merchandise, the captains "retired to a neighboring tent for refreshments." By the time Cohen had completed his negotiations, the two captains had become so refreshed that they were "incapacitated for the performance of the services for which they had been hired," so Cohen attempted to load the vessel and sail back to Miami by himself. He was halfway done with transferring the cargo when the two inebriated captains stumbled back to the docks and saw Cohen attempting to leave without them. After what Cohen later described as "a noisy and incoherent conference," the captains attempted to take charge of loading the small sailboat, but they succeeded only in capsizing the vessel, spilling themselves, Cohen's cargo, and Cohen himself into the drink. Only the assistance of a "gang of Nassau Negroes" allowed Cohen to retrieve his lost merchandise from the bottom of Biscayne Bay. Isidor Cohen's career as a Miami merchant was off to an inauspicious start.

His problems soon became even worse. In his desperation at Lemon City, Cohen had promised a dollar to each man who assisted in the salvage of his submerged cargo, and he told the black men who had assisted him to report to his store in Miami the next day for their reward. On the following afternoon, however, Cohen was shocked to find "a gang of more Negroes than I had ever seen before at one time" at the doorway of his store, all claiming to be his rescuers and all demanding a dollar from poor Mr. Cohen. This could have bankrupted Cohen on the spot, but after some quick thinking, Cohen announced that he would honor his promise to all of them, but with store credit: he would grant each of them a one-dollar discount on the purchase of three dollars worth of merchandise. As a result, Cohen went to bed that night a wealthier man and managed to earn the goodwill of the local black population to boot. As Cohen wrote in his memoirs, "this proved a wonderful business start," and Cohen's fortunes in Miami were on the upswing from that time forward.

After languishing on the south side of the river for a little over a month, Cohen finally managed to secure himself a storefront on the northern "Tuttle" side of the river, which was the bustling part of the town at the time due to the lack of bridges; while on the south side of the river, in fact, Cohen had to provide a rowboat to transport his customers across the Miami. Once on the north side, however, Cohen began to do "good business," despite "keen competition" and relatively high rates of rent.

Cohen was far from the only Miami pioneer to be annoyed by the lack of bridges in the early days of Miami history, but none suffered more than William Brickell, who owned much of the neglected real estate south of the Miami River. Since the Brickell trading post was once the commercial and transportation center of Biscayne Bay, William Brickell found it hard to swallow the new reality that Flagler's railway had brought to Biscayne Bay, and he complained loudly that the development of Miami was occurring at his expense. In protest, Brickell vowed never to cross north of the Miami River again. If Miami legend is to be believed, he was true to his word, and never did.

Unlike the Brickell family, however, Cohen was generally quite happy with the course of events in Miami. True, the young city of Miami could become quite unpleasant in the summer, when mosquitoes and "a vicious breed of horse-flies" joined with heat and humidity to torment the new settlers along the Miami River. According to Cohen, mosquito netting and insect powder were staple articles of trade in early Miami, and many settlers burnt rags at night in an attempt to ward off the maddening pests. Still, Cohen noted that "in spite of the climatic and other discomforts, this is a wonderful town." What is more, Cohen had big hopes for the young city. "We are almost up to the population of West Palm Beach," Cohen wrote at the end of July 1896, "[and] we expect to beat Key West in population in a short time." It would not be long before Cohen's hopeful speculations came to fruition.

Although both Sewell's and Cohen's memoirs, penned long after the events they describe, examine the early events in Miami history through a rose-colored lens of nostalgia, it is clear from the writings of both men that early Miami history was characterized by high levels of violence—which is, of course, not unusual in a newly founded frontier town. Some of this violence was of the man vs. nature variety; one early settler, for instance, was attacked and seriously wounded by a "monster alligator" while night-swimming in the Miami River. Furious, the settler secured himself a rifle and rowboat and vowed to hunt down and kill the offending reptile. Several nights later, the determined settler managed to make good on his threat.

Most early Miami violence, however, involved conflicts between men. Indeed, the early inhabitants of Miami seem to have been willing to fight over nearly anything. Cohen recalled in his memoirs one "exciting incident" in which two well-known pioneers, members of Maimi's "aristocracy of the first train," once engaged in a heated argument in the Miami post office on the subject of Darwin's theory of evolution. Cohen's marvelous depiction of the ensuing struggle is worth recounting verbatim:

> When the controversy reached the boiling point, they embraced affectionately, fell to the floor and without breaking their strangle-hold rolled out of the lobby into the street. In trying to pull them apart, the spectators discovered that the defender of the negative side of the issue had imbedded his teeth in the ear of the affirmative and stubbornly refused to let go. This exhibition of brutality elicited the unanimous decision of the crowd of bystanders that there is something to the Darwinian theory of evolution after all.

Other early Miami violence was inspired by feuds between prominent Biscayne Bay families. A few years after the incorporation of Miami, for instance, a certain Mr. Gardiner, who edited a short-lived Miami newspaper called the *Sunny Land,* was shot and killed by the sixteen-year-old son of a prominent "pioneer merchant." The gun-toting lad apparently attacked Mr. Gardiner in response to a series of columns in Gardiner's newspaper which had "vilified his widowed mother." On the Miami frontier, revenge could be swift, and bloody.

Still other early Miami violence was the fruit of criminal activity. Like most newly settled cities on the American frontier, Miami tended to attract a fair share of whores, pimps, brigands, and desperados, and these dubious characters tended to gather themselves in North Miami, which had become a den of iniquity by the first decade of the twentieth century. According to the Miami historian Helen Muir, "sailors who docked in Miami said that Hell's Kitchen [a legendary red light district of New York City] could not compare with North Miami." In North Miami, saloons never closed, "roulette wheels ran in the middle of Miami avenue, and opium dens flourished." Worse yet, North Miami became a favorite hideout of south Florida's most hardened criminals, including the infamous Rice Gang, which would commit daring crimes and then lie low in the Everglades until the heat was off. During the height of North Miami's infamous career as Biscayne Bay's red-light district, "three reported killings a night were about average" in North Miami, and the more reserved citizens of Miami proper were aghast at the sordid goings-on just to the north of their beloved city.

Ironically, the founding fathers (and mothers) of Miami were themselves partially to blame for North Miami's moral turpitude. For years, the sale of alcohol within Miami city limits was forbidden by decree of Julia Tuttle, who managed to outlaw liquor by the simple expedient of including a no-alcohol clause into her property leases, which she enforced with vigilance. Flagler agreed to do the same on his own property, with the understanding that guests at his Royal Palm Hotel were exempt from this restriction during the tourist season. As a result, all of the bars, brothels, and gambling

The Royal Palm Hotel on the Miami River. (Florida State Archives)

houses which invariably sprang up in Biscayne Bay after the coming of the railroad became concentrated in one place, immediately north of the Miami city border, out of the reach of Flagler and Tuttle's lawyers. The situation did not improve until 1908, when lawman extraordinaire Dan Hardie was elected sheriff of the city of Miami, and even after several successful campaigns against North Miami vice and the Rice Gang, the area remained a notorious red-light district for years.

The hoodlums and villains of North Miami were troublesome, but in terms of overall violence, the disorders of North Miami were mere annoyances compared with the reign of terror that descended upon Miami in the spring and summer of 1898. In the aftermath of the sinking of the *Maine,* the town of Miami was overwhelmed with a sort of mindless panic, and the citizens of the town convinced themselves that they were in danger of imminent Spanish attack, despite the fact that their small city, with no industry to speak of and no deep-water port, was of negligible strategic importance. The military irrelevance of their city, however, did not prevent the citizens of Miami from organizing a militia, called the "Miami Minute Men" to protect the city against the grossly overestimated Spanish threat. In the end, the only shot of any consequence that this group fired was by accident. While drilling with the Minute Men in the hot sun, W. M. Featherly of the *Miami Metropolis* fainted, and John Sewell threw down his gun to catch Featherly as he fell. Sewell's gun went off, and the other Miami Minute Men immediately assumed that they were under attack from hostile Spanish forces—after all, a shot had been fired, and a man was down! The confusion was eventually straightened out, but not before Miami had reached a fever pitch of hysteria.

Terrified by the specter of Spanish invasion, the overexcited government of Miami forbade Commodore Munroe and his fellow yachtsmen to guide any ships into Miami's harbor lest they turn out to be Spanish gunboats in disguise—though Munroe, who thought this order was moronic, flatly refused to obey it. The Miami leadership also managed to convince the military to send a few obsolete old cannons to the city for shore defense, and the army obligingly shipped the ancient guns south to Miami, only to rush them back up the rail line again when a false rumor began to spread that a Spanish fleet was headed for the north Florida town of Apalachicola. Even if these guns had been deployed on Biscayne Bay, their influence on the war would likely have been utterly negligible, since these weapons, like the Civil War monitors mobilized at the same time to defend Northern harbors, were too antiquated to be of any military value. Munroe later wrote in his memoirs that "since they [the guns] were not needed on one hand, and useless on the other, the whole thing was little short of silly."

In the end, ironically, the citizens of Miami suffered far more at the hands of their own army than from that of the Spanish. Soon after Apalachicola snatched away Miami's guns for itself, the U.S. military announced that it was sending a garrison of seven thousand troops to Miami to protect it from Spanish attack. Citizens of Miami breathed a sigh of relief, assuming that they were now safe. Once the soldiers arrived, however, Miami realized their mistake. As it turned out, the troops sent by the army were a disorderly band of Texans, Louisianans, Mississippians, and Alabamans, many of whom were recently released convicts. Commodore Munroe later characterized the Miami garrison as "scum," an "infernal nuisance," and "completely out of control." While Teddy Roosevelt and his Rough Riders performed inconsequential acts of heroism in front of appreciative reporters in Cuba, the seven thousand soldiers stationed on Biscayne Bay ran riot on the gleaming white streets of Miami. Area merchants found themselves engaged in "frequent marathons," as Isidor Cohen put it, chasing after American servicemen in the act of absconding with stolen merchandise. Other soldiers took potshots at the coconuts atop Commodore Munroe's palm trees, much to the Commodore's chagrin. Munroe's palms fought back, however, and on one occasion the Commodore was gratified to see a soldier knocked unconscious after being struck in the head by several falling coconuts. The Commodore later pronounced the incident "an act of God."

Unfortunately for Miami, the soldiers did not limit themselves to petty theft and vandalism, and soon blood began to spill upon Miami's streets. According Helen Muir, during the military occupation of Miami, "men wore pistols as a matter of course, and there was hardly a night that someone wasn't murdered." Miami area doctors did brisk business during this period patching up knife and gunshot wounds, and after a typical night of violence, the path in front of Dr. Jackson's house in downtown Miami, "often looked in the morning as if animals had been butchered there." At least one soldier performed an act of violence, not against another person, but against himself, and was found dead in the old stone soldier's barracks at Fort Dallas, slain by a self-inflicted gunshot wound. This event so unnerved poor Mrs. Julia Tuttle, who still lived on the Fort Dallas grounds, that the army had to place a guard on her home.

When they weren't slaughtering themselves or each other, the rowdy militiamen of the Miami garrison amused themselves by terrorizing Biscayne Bay blacks. One soldier shot and killed a black man who had "happened to brush by a lady while making his exit from a dry-goods store." Another soldier, with no apparent justification, "chased a black man down the street and when he caught him twisted his neck until he broke it." Later on, after a rumor began to spread through Miami that a soldier had been killed by a black man, a mob of soldiers invaded the crude shacks of the "colored settlement" of the town and forced its panicked inhabitants to flee for their lives. With the possible exception of Miami-area women, who had lived for several months under the constant threat of rape, no group in Miami was happier to see the soldiers' backsides than the city's black population.

With the removal of the soldiers in late summer of 1898, the atmosphere of the town calmed down somewhat, at least until the outbreak of yellow fever the following year. The first case was discovered in Coconut Grove by Dr. Simmons, and the illness spread quickly from there. In order to contain the disease, the army set up a quarantine zone around the city, and yellow flags were tacked on the doors of any infected household. During the period of the "Black Vomit," as the disease was then called, the population of Miami remained virtually static, and nearly no business was conducted in the city, due as much to the panic engendered by the disease as to the disease itself. By 1900, however, the disease had played itself out, and the city was back to normal; indeed, the tourist season of 1900, by all accounts, was quite a success.

Even after the departure of the yellow fever and the return of prosperity, the newly born city continued to be plagued by violence, due in large part to the development of two distinct political factions in Miami. On one side stood the partisans of Flagler and the railroad, many of whom were employees of the Florida East Coast Railway. Gentlemen of this political persuasion, such as John Sewell, believed that Miami's best interests lay with Flagler, his railway, and his hotel empire. Other Miami residents, such as Isidor Cohen, strongly disagreed. Political outsiders like Cohen noticed early on that partisans of the railroad were calling all the shots in Miami—he wrote in his diary during June of 1896 that "the railroad crowd is certainly taking control of politics in this neck of the woods"—and they increasingly opposed the railroad's domination over Miami's civic affairs. By December of 1896, in fact, Cohen had become "convinced that a public utility monopoly possessing political power [such as Flagler's railroad] is a menace to the locality in which it operates," and he resolved to "do all in my power to support the courageous citizens in their efforts to destroy the growing political influence this ambitious corporation is wielding through its ubiquitous partisans in this promising town." Miami pioneers who shared Cohen's beliefs became known as the "Antis," and although they failed to elect any like-minded candidates onto the Miami City Council in the town's first election (due in large part to the electoral intervention of Sewell's "black artillery"), their influence increased over time.

Clashes between the two factions were often violent; indeed, Cohen noted in his memoirs that discussions of the FEC Railway and the political destiny of Miami "often culminate in fist fights with an occasional display of knives." One of the town's foremost political pugilists was none other than John Sewell, who later confessed that, during the early days of Miami politics, he was provoked into "several pretty lively fist and other kinds of fights" due to the "slanders" that the opposition was spreading about him. Unfortunately for Sewell, his display of fisticuffs came to the attention of the Miami papers, in which Sewell was portrayed in a highly unfavorable light.

In the aftermath of one such article, Sewell received some timely advice from Captain Simmons, his friend in Coconut Grove. John Sewell had come to trust the Captain's plain-spoken wisdom; as Sewell put it in his history of Miami, "the Captain did not mince words and used quite a lot of profanity, but his words were always to the point." On this occasion, the Captain explained to Sewell that "you are a damned fool getting into fights about what your opponents say about you in politics. The more they lie about you the more it will help you, when the people find out they were lies."

Sewell took Captain Simmons' advice, and from that time forward he used more restraint in political contests. Sewell's new-found forbearance was exceptional, however, and Miami politics continued to be tumultuous into the next decade.

Although they disagreed on many matters, the single most contested issue between the railroad partisans and the "Antis" during this period was the issue of the bayfront "park." The controversy started when a railroad crew began to string up barbed wire along the Miami bayfront, which technically belonged to Flagler as part of his negotiations with Mrs. Tuttle and the Brickells, but which the people in the town had long used as if it was their own; indeed, one of the Miami pioneers named "Judge" Worley had constructed a dock there for the use of the people of Miami. Before the forbidding-looking fence was even a day old, Worley signaled his defiance of the railroad company by cutting a hole in it. The railroad company repaired the fence, only to have Worley clip the wire again the next night. And so it went, for several days. Eventually the railway company, in an attempt to stop the nightly fence-snipping, hired the colorfully named "Peanut Johnson" to guard the fence at night, but he proved ineffective, most likely because Peanut was himself sympathetic to Worley's actions. In the end, the FEC turned to the courts for relief, and their lawyers had "Judge" Worley cited for contempt. The frustrated Worley responded by moving himself and his family several miles north of Miami to the town of Buena Vista.

The dispute over the bayshore land did not end there, however, largely because Worley, even in Buena Vista exile, did not let the matter drop. Instead, Worley, who was a defense lawyer by trade, raised a public outcry over the fact that Flagler was "bottling up the town," and contended that the bayfront land was supposed to belong to all of the town's people. In support of this claim, Worley pointed to an early map of Miami, drafted in the aftermath of the Brickell/Tuttle/Flagler real estate agreement; in this map, the bayfront area was clearly labeled with the word "park." Eventually, Worley made such a nuisance of himself to Flagler and his partisans that the FEC brought suit against him a second time, and Worley the defense lawyer suddenly found himself in front of the judge's bench, not as an attorney, but as a defendant.

Why was the matter so important? The answer, simply put, was that control over the bayfront was crucial to Flagler's domination over Miami's trade. Flagler probably assumed that his FEC rail line would carry most, if not all, of the young town's passenger and freight traffic, excepting of course the odd Northern tourist who arrived at the Royal Palm Hotel at the helm of his own private yacht. Imagine Flagler's disappointment, then, when schooners and other small cargo ships continued to make Miami a port of call. Really, Flagler had only himself to blame; if he had lowered the FEC's rail prices, he might have been able to reduce the schooner traffic, or else drive the schooners out of business altogether. Rather than cut into his own bottom line, however, Flagler sought to exclude schooners from Miami's harbor entirely, and the easiest means of doing that was by fencing in the bayfront, which would effectively prevent small ships from landing or receiving cargo in the city of Miami.

Flagler and the FEC hoped that putting Worley on trial would settle the matter in their favor once and for all, since they had the law on their side; indeed, the only evidence that Worley could bring against them was the single ambiguous word "park" written on an old zoning map. Furthermore, Flagler had the support of the town council, which consisted of railway supporters to the man—during the trial, in fact, they passed a resolution rejecting "any dedication implied by the word park on the recorded plat of Miami." They even were able to produce J. S. Frederick, the railway engineer who had actually written the word "park" on the town map in the first place, who testified that he had no idea what had come over him when he wrote the word on the map of early Miami.

In the end, however, none of this mattered. Flagler had not counted on Worley's oratory, popular appeal, and showmanship (he wore a large amethyst ring which he claimed had belonged to the

Pope), and following months of legal wrangling, the charismatic Worley was able to convince the state supreme court that the land marked "park" on the early map of Miami belonged to the city's people. The railroad faction had been handed its first defeat, and schooners continued to conduct a vigorous trade in the city of Miami.

Despite his setback, Flagler apparently did not bear the city of Miami any ill will, and he soon began to bankroll a massive dredging scheme, designed to make the port of Miami accessible to vessels with deep drafts. Flagler hired the first dredges in 1897 out of his own pocket, but soon used his Standard Oil connections to obtain large-scale federal grants, and as a result, Miami's harbor was eventually deepened to a uniform eighteen feet. In 1905, the new sea channel was all but complete, and the mayor at the time, who was none other than the esteemed John Sewell, proclaimed the projected date of project completion a public holiday and gathered up a group of dignitaries and spectators to witness the first mingling of waters from the Atlantic Ocean and Biscayne Bay. Unfortunately for Sewell, the dredge removing the final few feet of earth broke

Some of the schooners that so frustrated Henry Flagler are shown here, tied up in the harbor at the mouth of the Miami River. (Florida State Archives)

down before the work was complete. With characteristic determination, Sewell removed his coat and tie, grabbed a shovel, and dug through the last few feet of earth himself. Thus opened "Government Cut," the main shipping channel into Miami's harbor even today. In the meantime, Flagler added a navy to the forces of his Florida empire, creating the "Peninsular and Occidental Steamship Company" in order to take full financial advantage of Miami's excellent new port.

The merchants of Miami were delighted by the increased volume of trade brought by the deepened harbor, but the "improvement" of Miami's harbor did not please everyone; indeed, the sailboat enthusiasts of Coconut Grove regarded the harbor project as an atrocity. In the process of deepening the bay, the dredges dumped most of the displaced rocks and sand into the shallows, and as a result, areas of the bay that had once been navigable became inaccessible to sailboats. In addition, the engineers building the deepwater cuts placed lines of large wooden poles on the sides of the channel, and while these poles made navigation easier for steamships, they proved quite hazardous to sailboat traffic. Worse yet, these poles had a tendency to rot down to the water line, which created underwater obstacles of sharp broken wood as perilous as the concealed spikes in a tiger trap. The Commodore complained, but nothing was done, and the days of carefree sailboating on Biscayne Bay came to an inglorious end.

Most Miamians paid little attention to the Commodore's grievances, however. The golden age of yachting might be a thing of the past, and Miami's days as a "perfect wilderness" were rapidly fading away, but new amusements had risen to take their place. Flagler's Royal Palm Hotel sported a lively social scene, especially in late February, when the "Washington's Birthday Ball" attracted a glittering array of Northern socialites. The Royal Palm also offered more prosaic pleasures, including billiards and casino gambling. If a tourist tired of the hotel's delights, he or she could patronize one of Miami's two moving-picture theatres, the Alcazar and the Kinedrome, which featured silent film shorts as well as an unappealing-sounding medley of what one contemporary observer described as "vaudeville artists, old tinpan piano, and the screeching gramophone." For a more rustic experience, a tourist might take the steamboat *Sally* to the head of the Miami River, where he or she could peer out over the trackless Everglades from the Musa Isle observation platform, or pay to watch "Alligator Joe," a three-hundred-pound giant of a man, risk his life wrestling twelve-foot gators. Clearly, the town of Miami was already beginning to evolve into the brash, tourist-minded vacation mecca we know today.

Miami still had a long way to go, of course. The town boasted only 7,111 people in 1909, and wilderness still lapped up against its edges; indeed, the peace of Miami's undeveloped south side was still occasionally shattered by the shrieking call of the Florida panther, much to the dismay of Miami's worried residents. The town itself was so small that, in the words of Miami historian Thelma Peters, "any good walker could have hoofed it around Miami's perimeter in an hour."

Still, the pioneer shopkeeper Isidor Cohen had it right: Miami was destined for great things. Between 1900 and 1910, in fact, the city's population more than doubled, and by 1913, the city could boast of nearly eleven thousand inhabitants, which put it in fifth place amongst Florida's cities, and only one ranking behind the declining town of Key West. Furthermore, during the winter tourist months, Miami's population swelled to almost ten times that number: by 1910, the city had the capacity to house one hundred thousand winter guests in comfort. Miami's inhabitants, it seemed, had every reason to be optimistic about their city's future.

Despite these signs of progress, however, there was a troubling shadow on Miami's tropical sun. When Flagler had first come to Miami, he had proclaimed that he had no intention of extending his line further south. Within half a decade, however, Flagler's FEC

Railway had begun to creep toward the tip of the Florida Peninsula, into the Redland agricultural area near present-day Homestead. What would happen, Miami's inhabitants began to ask themselves, if Flagler were to extend his rail line to Key West? What would it mean for Miami? Would their ambitious young town be enriched, or ruined? There was no way of knowing. Worse yet, there was no way of stopping the project, should Flagler decide to build it. The citizens of Miami might fret and fuss, speculate and debate, but in the end, the decision to build a railway to Key West belonged to Flagler, Florida's uncrowned king, and to Flagler alone.

6

Eighth Wonder

In June of 1896, only one month before the ambitious settlement at the mouth of the Miami declared itself a city, a curious article by Key West Customs Inspector Jefferson Browne appeared in the newly founded *National Geographic Magazine.* To the amazement of his readers, who probably knew Key West only as a remote and exotic cigar town if they were aware of it at all, Browne boldly asserted that "Key West will within a short time be connected with the mainland by a railroad." One imagines that this grandiose proclamation evoked guffaws of laughter from many *National Geographic* readers of the day. Why, Browne might as well have predicted the construction of a railway to Madagascar, or to the moon!

To Jefferson Browne's credit, however, he supported his outrageous prediction with a fairly exhaustive list of the possible advantages that this hypothetical rail line would bring both Key West specifically and America as a whole. Key West's harbor, Browne noted, was marvelously deep, and was perfectly located near the main shipping channels: "Ships putting into Key West for stores and repairs," he claimed, "need go out of their course but 10 miles, an advantage possessed by no other port in the United States." In addition, Browne made elaborate claims about the fertility of the soil in the Keys near Key West, arguing that "the most delicate fruits and vegetables" grow "luxuriantly" upon the Keys, and he predicted that, with regular transportation facilities, "the Florida Keys would supply the country with fresh vegetables all winter." Furthermore, Browne lavished praise on Key West's idyllic climate, claiming that "sooner or later the thousands of tourists who are restlessly seeking a milder and more equable winter climate than the mainland affords will find in Key West their ideal health resort." Given these evident advantages, Browne judged, the construction of a railroad to Key West in the near future was well-nigh inevitable, and Key West was soon "destined to become the Newport of the south."

But wouldn't the construction of a railway to Key West be prohibitively expensive? Not so, according to Browne, and to prove his point, he took his readers on a tour across the twenty-nine major islands of the Florida Keys. The first thirty-mile leg of the journey, between Key West and Bahia Honda, "presents no difficult problems of engineering and would be comparatively inexpensive." Several water gaps would have to be crossed during this portion of the route, Browne admitted, but these could be mastered through a combination of solid fill and short trestle bridges. After Bahia Honda, the railroad would be obliged to cross over eight miles of open water before arriving at Knight's Key, but Browne claimed to know of a shallow route across the channel which would make the construction of such a bridge practical. Past Knight's Key, the railway's path would become relatively easier, since much of the remaining distance was dry land, and what water existed was either narrow (such as the cut between Plantation Key and Key Largo) or quite shallow (such as the broad flats between lower and upper

Matecumbe islands). Building this railroad would be a difficult job, certainly, but one quite within the realm of human capabilities.

What is more, Browne assured his readers that a railroad on the Keys would be practical as well as possible, and he claimed that conditions there would make construction of the iron road simplicity itself. "By fortunate provision of nature," he wrote, the island of Big Pine Key was abundantly supplied with timber suitable for use as railroad ties. Furthermore, Browne predicted that much of the roadbed could be laid upon raised embankments, which could be easily constructed from the loose rock "found in immense quantities on all the Keys." In addition, Browne argued that iron bridge trestles could be driven directly into the coral rock native to the Keys, which was soft enough to be easily penetrated, yet hardy enough to withstand hurricanes, as proven by the longevity of the lighthouses built by the federal government atop the Florida Reef over the last forty years. A well-constructed railroad, Browne believed, could easily withstand the legendary wind and tides brought by south Florida's dreaded hurricanes.

As subsequent history would prove, most of Browne's predictions in his 1896 article were either exaggerated or just plain wrong. For one thing, the construction of the Key West railway proved to be vastly expensive; by the time it was completed, the so-called "overseas" rail line would be perhaps the single most costly project ever bankrolled by a single person in the history of America. Despite Browne's optimistic predictions about the easy availability of nearby resources, much of the construction materials would have to be imported, at enormous cost, from as far away as Europe. Furthermore, the engineers charged with building the project would find it a nearly impossible endeavor, requiring an unprecedented mobilization of men, manpower, and human ingenuity. In addition, Browne grossly overestimated the fertility of the Keys soil, and the hoard of vacationers that Browne believed would descend upon Key West once the railway was completed never materialized—at least not during his own lifetime.

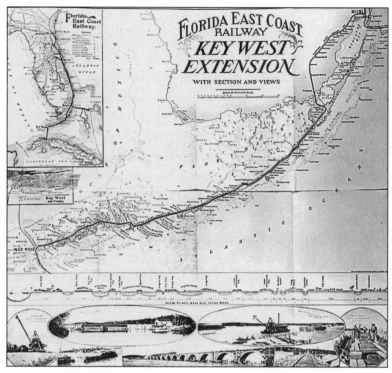

This map of the "Key West Extension" of Flagler's FEC railway clearly demonstrates some of the geographical difficulties that any railroad through the Keys would have to overcome. (Florida State Archives)

Browne was right about one thing, however. At the conclusion of his article, the Key West customs inspector ventured to guess that the Miami-to–Key West railway would be constructed by none other than Henry Morrison Flagler, "whose financial genius" had already "opened up to the tourist and health-seeker 300 miles of the beautiful east coast of the state." Browne concluded, "The building of a railroad to Key West would be a fitting consummation of Mr. Flagler's remarkable career," and he expressed his fond hope that Flagler would take on the project, thereby ensuring that "his name would be handed down to posterity linked to one of the grandest achievements of modern times." Within ten years, Browne's hopeful prediction became reality. Henry Flagler would spend a vast fortune to link Miami with Key West, and the island city's railroad dreams, first articulated in 1831, would finally be realized.

⑥ ⑥ ⑥

Why did Flagler choose to commit his heart, his soul, and (most importantly) his wallet to the construction of the Overseas Railway? Certainly not because of Browne's toadying flattery, though Jefferson Browne would later play an important role in the construction of the railroad. After he was elected to the Florida Senate, where he eventually rose to the rank of president, Browne became a key Flagler ally, and helped Flagler get the necessary political support for his railway. Still, Browne was just a pawn in Flagler's game, a mere means to an end. Although Flagler's actual motives for constructing the Overseas Railway can never be precisely known—indeed, Flagler may not have fully understood his motives himself—available evidence suggests that Flagler's decision was influenced by a number of considerations.

One motivating factor was almost certainly sheer spite. Although Flagler eventually gave in to Miami's desire for seaborne trade, and even financed the early stages of dredging himself, he must have harbored a grudge against the infant city. Sending his line past Miami was one way of punishing the young metropolis, which Flagler had originally envisioned as a mere "fishing village" thrown up for the enjoyment of the Royal Palm's guests, for its upstart presumption. Indeed, Flagler had already meted out somewhat similar treatment to the town of Juno, which he had bypassed with his railroad and thus condemned to obscurity.

Flagler was probably also motivated by his ongoing rivalry with Henry Plant, another Florida land baron, who was creating his own railway and hotel empire down the west coast of Florida, and who had his own ambitions to build a rail line to Miami and beyond. Plant, the reader may recall, was the Florida railway baron who had dispatched Ingraham's Everglades expedition in 1892 to investigate the possibility of a railway route from the west coast of Florida to the Miami River. Although Plant ultimately abandoned this idea, and surrendered the future town of Miami to Flagler's network, he competed heavily with Flagler in other fields.

The Flagler-Plant rivalry probably came to its head in 1891, after Plant opened a hotel in Tampa, called (not surprisingly) the Tampa Bay. Today, this massive Victorian structure has become the centerpiece structure of the University of Tampa, but at the time the Tampa Bay Hotel outshone Flagler's recently built Ponce de Leon Hotel in St. Augustine. Jefferson Browne, in fact, later claimed that a jealous Flagler had first mentioned the possibility of an overseas railway to him during the 1891 grand opening festivities at Plant's Tampa Bay Hotel. Flagler, Browne claims, was quite worried that Plant would "outdo" him, and the construction of a railway to Key West offered Flagler the tantalizing prospect of pulling ahead of his west-coast rival once and for all.

Flagler's competition with Henry Plant escalated to new heights during the Spanish-American War. At the start of that conflict, Plant managed to convince the U.S. government to use Tampa, which he had equipped with both a railway connection and deep-water port facilities, as the primary staging point for the invasion of Cuba, and during the war his newly built Tampa Bay Hotel hosted a large number of military officers and newspaper correspondents. Tampa and Plant profited greatly from the war, both in the short run (from the increased rail traffic and military business) and in the long run (as the newsmen brought the young city of Tampa to the attention of the nation). Key West flourished during the war as well and became the single most important American naval base during the campaign against Cuba. Since Miami lacked a deep-water port, however, the war bypassed Miami, with the notable exception of the seven thousand–odd garrison force which, as we have seen, proved to be far more dangerous to Miami's fair citizens than the much-feared Spanish. In any case, Flagler was disappointed that his FEC rail line was left in the cold during the war, and his decision to build a line to Key West was motivated, at least in part, by a desire to make sure that his railway, and not Plant's, received the lion's share of wartime attention and wartime profits in the future.

Still, Flagler was a responsible businessman, and personal vindictiveness probably played only a small role in convincing him to stretch his line to Key West. A far more important consideration, certainly, was the anticipated construction of a Central American canal. During the 1891 meeting between Browne and Flagler at the Tampa Bay Hotel, in fact, Flagler was already talking about the opportunities such a canal would provide for Key West, which was by far the closest U.S. port to the proposed canal site. In his 1896 *National Geographic* article, Browne expanded further upon Flagler's notion, and added the proposed canal to his list of justifications for building a railway to Key West. Once a Central American canal had been constructed, Browne claimed, "Key West would be a port of call for supplies and repairs for no small part of the shipping world," and he predicted that upon the canal's completion, "Key West will become the most important city in the South." Flagler himself told an interviewer in 1912 that the passage of the Panama Bill in Congress in November of 1903, which committed American resources to the construction of a canal through the Panama Isthmus, contributed greatly to his decision to build the Overseas Railway.

Indeed, the geographic realities of Florida and the Caribbean seem to support Flagler and Browne's shared belief that the completion of the Panama Canal would lead to an explosion of prosperity in Key West. A vessel traveling through the canal en route to the United States would reach land at Key West several days before it would reach any other port in America; indeed, it would have to steam northwards for another 850 miles before it could dock in New Orleans or Pensacola, which at the time were two of the most important American ports on the Gulf of Mexico. Key West's only close competitor was Henry Plant's Tampa, and even Tampa was no real competition, since our hypothetical vessel would have to sail another 250 miles past Key West before coming in sight of the gleaming minarets of Plant's Tampa Bay Hotel. American geography, then, seemed to dictate that the building of the Panama Canal would funnel an enormous volume of trade in the direction of the small city of Key West.

If that was not enough, the liberation of Cuba in 1898 provided Flagler with yet another compelling reason to stretch his railway to Key West. A mere ninety miles separated Key West from Havana, Flagler knew, and he envisioned that his Overseas Railway might eventually command Cuba's valuable traffic in pineapples, sugar, and oranges. Indeed, by the turn of the century, Flagler already had a vested interest in the economic well-being of Cuba: he owned $250,000 in stock in Sir William Van Horn's Cuba Railway Company, plus another $75,000 in Cuba Company bonds, and the two magnates were so closely allied that FEC railway agents actually sold tickets for Van Horn's Cuba railroad. Flagler may have even intended to trade entire trains between his FEC railway and Van Horn's Cuba line; Van Horn's other railway company, located in Canada, was already transporting twenty-six-car freight trains across 112 miles of water in the Great Lakes, so there was every reason to believe that trains could be carried whole across the mere ninety-mile gap separating Havana from Key West, once Key West was finally graced with a railway connection to the mainland. Flagler also enjoyed close connections to Cuba by way of his East Coast Steamship Company, which conducted a lively trade throughout the Caribbean by the turn of the twentieth century; indeed, one of Flagler's own vessels, the *Miami,* was enlisted to return Theodore Roosevelt and his Rough Riders back to New York City after the conclusion of the Spanish-American War. Like most of his contemporaries, Flagler assumed that the end of the Spanish era of Cuban history would open the island to rapid economic development, and Flagler felt that the construction of the Overseas Railway would give the FEC an unmatched opportunity to tap into Cuba's enormous economic potential.

Perhaps the most compelling reason of all for Flagler's decision to extend his line to old Cayo Hueso, however, was his desire to leave a permanent legacy for himself stitched into the American landscape. By the turn of the century, Flagler was seventy years old, and although he was still in relatively good health for a man his age, Flagler was becoming increasingly aware of his own mortality. Within a few years of the turn of the century, Flagler began to become hard of hearing, and by 1909 Flagler had lost his eyesight to such a degree that he complained to a cousin that "it is difficult for me to do more than sign the letters I dictate." Flagler's way of coming to terms with the inevitability of death was to keep himself busy, and the Overseas Railway project, which required Flagler's constant attention, allowed him limitless opportunities to do exactly that. Furthermore, the completion of the project offered Flagler the prospect of a certain form of immortality; future generations of Americans, he believed, would look in awe at his unprecedented Overseas Railway, and Flagler hoped it would become, in one historian's words, "his enduring monument."

Whatever Flagler's motivations, he was not the sort of man to jump into a project half-cocked, nor was he willing to entrust his fortune and his legacy to Browne's easy assurances that the route along the spine of the Keys would pose few problems for a determined builder. Before committing himself to the endeavor, he sent the young engineer William Krome through the Everglades to investigate alternate possibilities, such as the prospect of running a line west from Miami to Cape Sable and then across the shallow waters of Florida Bay to the lower Keys. Krome left in 1902, and if the records of his expedition are to be believed, he barely returned; Krome later reported to his supervisor that this portion of the Everglades was "a most God-forsaken region," and his men nearly starved to death before escaping from the sucking mud marshlands east of Cape Sable. Even if the Everglades had been less treacherous, however, the difficulties posed by this railway route would still have proven insurmountable due to the vast stretches of Florida Bay that would have to be bridged before reaching the Keys proper—and what is more, a railroad built along this path would not bypass the sizable water gaps separating the islands of the lower Keys. Clearly, then, the railroad would have to follow Browne's proposed route, or none at all.

Once the route was decided, however, Flagler still hesitated, and dispatched his FEC engineers for several more years of surveying and feasibility studies. Finally, in 1905, Flagler made his fateful decision. He summoned his general manager, Joseph R. Parrot, and asked him point-blank, can a railway be built to Key West? Yes, Parrot answered. "Very well," responded Flagler, "go ahead." Those four simple words mark the beginning of one of the most remarkable construction projects ever to be attempted on the North American continent.

Work on the Overseas Railway began in earnest in April of 1905, in the marshy lands south of Homestead, at what was then the end of the line of the FEC railway. Right from the beginning, the project was faced with a thorny problem of engineering—how could a railway bed be built through a wetland too damp to support either draft animals or motorized equipment? The engineers soon solved this dilemma by the ingenious expedient of employing floating steam dredges with shallow drafts, which dug trenches in front of themselves so that they could float forward and then deposited the Everglades muck in the area between their respective channels, thus raising it up for use as a railway bed. These canals are still easily visible along U.S. 1 south of Miami, which more or less follows the exact path taken by Flagler's railroad. By using four dredges at a time—two digging southward from Homestead and two northward from Jewfish Creek—Flagler's engineers ensured that this portion of the rail bed was completed relatively quickly, and by 1906 the railroad was approaching Key Largo, the first in the chain of the Florida Keys.

So far, so good. But as the railroad extended toward the Keys, difficulties began to multiply. One chronic problem was the atrocious living conditions on the Florida Keys, which greatly hampered

Two excavators piling fill in the middle as they built the eighteen-mile connection between Homestead and Jewfish Creek. If the water level was too shallow to float the barges, workers pumped water from one side to the other. (Museums at Crane Point Hammock)

the FEC's quest for a reliable workforce. South Florida was brutally hot, and contemporary visitors to Flagler's railroad project reported being eaten alive by clouds of mosquitoes, which contemporaries described as "almost unbearable," and which tended to drive away a sizable proportion of the workers recruited for the project. Furthermore, supplying these tormented workers with basic necessities proved to be immensely difficult, since nearly all supplies, including fresh water, had to be brought in by railroad or barge.

At first, most of the workers on the Overseas were either American blacks or "Negroes" from the Bahamas, but the discomforts of life in the camp soon forced the defection of these locally hired laborers, who found it relatively easy to return home if conditions became intolerable. As a result, the FEC increasingly recruited workers from distant New York City, which at the time was filled with both out-of-work laborers and impoverished recent immigrants from Europe. The FEC promised honest work, good wages, plentiful food, and free accommodations in the "sunny South."

Plenty of contemporary evidence, however, suggests that the majority of these imported workers were extremely displeased by working conditions on Flagler's Overseas Railway. Men hired to do skilled labor were often employed in mere grunt-work, perhaps in part because language barriers prevented Italian, Greek, and German workers from communicating their skills effectively to their foremen. Some men complained that they were charged $2.50 per week, the equivalent of two days' pay, for their supposedly "free" accommodations, which generally amounted to little more than a wooden plank under a tent. Others complained about the food, which they regarded as "scarce and hardly fit to eat." Worst of all, workers who were outraged by their treatment had little recourse but to grin and bear it, since the railroad refused to return laborers to New York unless they paid a full fare, and this was far beyond the financial means of most workers on the Overseas line—especially since the FEC deducted as much as $16 in "transportation fees," or about half of a month's wages, from a worker's first paycheck. Many who refused to work on the railroad eventually wandered to Miami, where they made such a nuisance of themselves that the FEC was forced to find them some employment.

The FEC's labor problems became yet more dire in the spring of 1906, when railway officials found that they had a full-scale exodus on their hands. As it turned out, quite a few of the workers hired during the previous fall had signed on in large part to escape the ravages of the Northern winter, and now that the spring had come, they were anxious to return to the North. In desperation, the FEC offered improved compensation for workers: it raised wages by a quarter per day for the summer months, and began to promise that workers would be given free board in "comfortably screened quarters." These efforts seem to have worked since by July of 1906 the FEC had managed to attract large numbers of Italian laborers to its south Florida work camps. Still, although the FEC's problems had been resolved for the time being, securing enough workers continued to be an ongoing problem until the very end of the project.

Despite the chronic labor shortages, the Overseas pressed onwards, and by fall of 1906 Flagler's engineers were nearly at Key Largo. Just before reaching this largest of the Florida Keys, however, Flagler's work crews made a dismaying discovery: a large lake, which FEC surveyors had somehow missed entirely, lay directly along the projected path of the railway. The FEC immediately dispatched engineers to analyze this unexpected problem, but their report only gave the FEC further cause for concern. There was no good route around the lake, the engineers concluded, and no bridge could be build across it, since the peatlike bottom of the lake could not support a bridge trestle. In the end, Flagler's engineers had no choice but to create an embankment straight through the lake composed of ton upon ton of "marl," a quick-drying, cementlike substance found in abundance on the seafloor near the Keys. Building this embankment proved to be both expensive and time-consuming; indeed, crossing "Lake Surprise," as it came to be called, proved to be a fifteen-month headache for the FEC.

Anxious not to fall behind schedule while overcoming this unexpected obstacle, the FEC's engineers leapfrogged forward and established a number of work camps in keys farther down the line. Unfortunately, these advance camps suffered greatly for their lack of a railroad connection, which meant that all supplies had to be hauled to the camps by way of barges and steamboats. This proved easier said than done since the shoal water around the Keys made navigation nearly impossible. Even shallow-draft riverboats, imported from the notoriously shallow Mississippi, found themselves continuously running aground. Following one such incident, a frustrated paddleboat captain employed by the FEC complained bitterly that the Florida Keys contained "not quite enough water for swimming and too damned much for farming."

While the FEC went to heroic lengths to get some supplies to their workmen on the Keys, they also employed strong measures to keep other supplies out of the camps, especially alcohol, which Flagler expressly prohibited from the work camps of the Overseas.

Unfortunately for the FEC, however, keeping liquor away from the railroad workers proved all but impossible. Some laborers were respectable recent immigrants from Europe, anxious to work hard for a fair wage. Far more, however, were skid-row types whom journalist Ralph D. Paine described as "good-for-nothings" and "dregs of sodden and broken humanity," who arrived in Florida with already well-established drinking problems. Furthermore, despite some improvements, conditions in the camps were still miserable, especially during the summer mosquito season, and more than a few laborers welcomed the opportunity to drink themselves into a stupor.

To the delight of the Overseas workers, and to the dismay of their supervisors, a market soon developed to satisfy their demand. During the early years of the 1900s, the Keys became the haunt of "booze boats," which, in the words of a 1908 observer, "skulked among the key channels as old-time buccaneers did in these same waters." Fearful of drunken disruptions, and loyal to Flagler's teetotaler sentiments, the FEC made a concerted effort to drive these latter-day pirates out of the hooch business. Those caught carrying out this illicit trade might find themselves tarred and feathered, or even worse—the same observer quoted above claimed that bootleggers "took chances of being peppered with rifle fire or of diving overboard just ahead of a stick of dynamite" whenever they approached FEC camps. Despite the exertions of FEC officials, however, Flagler's personal campaign against alcohol enjoyed only partial success; as one historian of the Overseas Railway recently quipped, "the workers probably drank less than they wanted . . . [but] more than their supervisors wished."

In part due to the predations of the booze boats, which exerted a quite negative impact on worker efficiency, the FEC railroad project moved with painful slowness in the winter and spring of 1906. Finally, in frustration, FEC officials made a fateful decision: despite the possible danger, they would continue construction through the 1906 hurricane season. Even in the best of times, with the railroad running at full capacity, this would have been a risky choice. Given the conditions on the ground in 1906, however, the FEC's decision was sheer folly. Although the workers at Lake Surprise could be railed swiftly out of harm's way if danger threatened, the workers further out on the lower Keys were in far more peril, since they could not be evacuated from their camps except by water, and communication between these camps and the mainland was poor in any case. Furthermore, many workers in the lower Keys did not live in camps at all, but rather in large houseboats, which consisted of flimsy two-story barnlike structures mounted on wooden barges. Although housing workers in these "quarterboats" made a lot of logistical sense—after all, they could be floated from work site to work site—they were exceptionally vulnerable to inclement weather.

The FEC's decision to work through late summer and fall, then, was just asking for trouble, and trouble soon made an appearance. In mid-October of 1906, a hurricane swirled up in the windward islands of the Caribbean, skirted the northern edge of Cuba, and then began to follow a northeasterly course directly towards the Florida Keys. A few of the FEC's foremen gained some forewarning of the trouble in store for them by means of homemade barometers, which consisted of little more than a glass column of water and a few floating pieces of seaweed: by the evening of October 16, the weeds in these homemade barometers began to bob upwards, and uneasiness began to spread on the camps and quarterboats of the FEC. Still, despite the warning, no effective preparations were made, in large part because few residents of the camps and quarterboats had any understanding of the power of a Florida hurricane.

On the morning of October 17, however, the hurricane's power became dismayingly clear. Over the course of the previous night, rain and savage gales had battered the moored houseboats, and by early morning the winds were blowing at hurricane strength. After hours of punishment, the mooring chain finally gave way on quarterboat #4, though few on the storm-tossed boat noticed at first;

one survivor latter claimed that the massive chain's breaking was "felt no more than if a thread had been popped." Once released from its mooring, the vessel and its 145 helpless inhabitants drifted out into the Gulf Stream in the direction of the Bahamas, though the boat foundered long before reaching that distant destination. Although one account of the 1906 storm claims that quarterboat #4 eventually dashed up on the Florida Reef, most eyewitnesses asserted that the houseboat was splintered to pieces, not by the reefs, but by the incredible violence of the fifty- to sixty-foot waves that broke repeatedly upon the boat and its horrified passengers.

As might be expected, the casualty rate on quarterboat #4 was quite high. Some of the workers were so overcome by fear of drowning that they raided the quarterboat's first-aid kits for laudanum, an opium-based painkiller, and committed suicide with fatal overdoses before they were sucked under the heaving seas. Other laborers who sought shelter under the decks were killed when the quarterboat's shallow hold caved in upon them, trapping them inside. Indeed, this was the fate of Bert A. Parlin, an FEC engineer and the ranking man on the vessel, who rushed below decks in an attempt to evacuate the men inside, only to be killed instantly by a flying beam when the roof of the hold collapsed. Other men were "cruelly beaten to death by timbers hurled against them" by the raging winds of the hurricane. Still other laborers suffered less dramatic deaths, and simply disappeared under the swirling water as the quarterboat disintegrated beneath their feet.

Given the ferocity of the storm, the fact that so many died comes as no surprise; what is perhaps more surprising is that so many managed to survive. Some saved themselves by huddling on the side of the barge which faced the wind, where they were less vulnerable to wind-blown debris torn from the fragmenting houseboat; when the ship finally went under, these determined souls grabbed onto anything that floated, including tables, chairs, steamer trunks, and the splintered timbers of the quarterboat. Other potential storm victims saved themselves by more creative means. One FEC worker found himself aboard a cement barge—a top-heavy piece of equipment that almost immediately began to founder in the wind-blown waters—and saved his life by unfastening a cypress-wood water tank bolted to the deck of the barge for use as a sort of one-man life boat. Two other workers, both Irish, saved themselves in a feat of daring; they were ready to go down with the rest of the labor-ers on quarterboat #4 when "a barge [mostly likely a small construc-tion barge] whirled past her in a fog of spray." The two Irishmen made the snap decision to jump aboard, which must have been no easy task given the rolling seas and howling winds. After the two sons of Erin reached the barge, "a gray sea rose and swallowed them," and their comrades aboard quarterboat #4 assumed they had fallen prey to the storm. Nearly a week later, however, the two com-patriots, "crazed and almost dead for want of food and water," were rescued by a passing ship.

These two fortunate Irishmen were not alone; indeed, quite a few other FEC workers were scooped alive from the sea in the after-math of the 1906 hurricane. The crew of the passing Italian steam-er *Jenny*, in fact, pulled no less than forty-nine FEC workers from the still-stormy waters in the afternoon after the hurricane at con-siderable risk to their own safety; tragically, the crew of the *Jenny* later reported that they heard voices of still more storm victims in the waters but were unable to locate their owners in the gathering darkness. Twenty-six more were rescued by the British steamship the *Alton*, which then deposited the men in Savannah before con-tinuing its voyage back to Europe. Still others ended up in Mobile, Galveston, New York, London, Liverpool, and even the distant Argentinean city of Buenos Aires. Since the houseboat was not equipped with any life jackets, and most of the workers were unable to swim, the survival of so many men after hours or days of floating in the open sea seems little short of miraculous.

Still, despite these stories of survival, the 1906 hurricane cost the FEC dearly. In the end, the railroad put the death toll at about 125 men, but this may reflect wishful thinking and poor record-keeping more than objective reality; some historians, in fact, believe that the casualty figure for FEC workers was as high as two hundred, which represents a loss of over five percent of the total work force of the Overseas. Quarterboat #4 alone lost about a hundred of its 145-odd residents. In addition, the FEC lost several steamships, barge-mounted machines, and other pieces of heavy equipment during the storm, and quite a bit of already completed work, such as the raised railway embankments on the upper Keys, was ruined and had to be rebuilt entirely. Still, Flagler was not discouraged. When apprised of the hurricane's damage by his subalterns in the FEC, and asked what do next, he made this response: "Go ahead." Henry Flagler was not about to let a little wind and rain spoil his chance at immortality.

Despite Flagler's order to proceed, however, the railway project stood idle for most of the next year, as Flagler's engineers surveyed the storm damage and argued about what steps could be taken to prevent such damage in the future. In the meantime, Flagler's FEC found itself in legal hot water over the issue of its labor policies. By the early 1900s, the New York press had taken up the cause of the treatment of the Overseas Railway workers, in large part because of the local interest angle; many of the workers were recruited from the New York area, so provocative headlines like "Brooklyn Lads Lured South into Chain Gang" were a surefire way to sell newspapers. The same newspapers published graphic (though often fraudulent) exposés about the horrors of the FEC camps. "They have Shanghaied us to a little island in the ocean about 90 miles from Florida," one correspondent claimed. "We are surrounded by rattlesnakes and dangerous animals. For God's sake," the author pleaded, "send us some money and food." Eventually, on the basis of such evidence, the New York federal grand jury decided to charge the FEC and a New York labor agent named Francesco Sabbia with peonage practices, in violation of an 1866 federal slave-kidnapping law.

Francesco Sabbia, incidentally, was by all accounts a particularly shady character, and his story demonstrates the lengths to which the FEC was willing to go to in order to make Flagler's Overseas Railway ambitions a reality. Sabbia was employed by Flagler and the FEC to persuade as many people as possible to come to Florida for employment in the project, and the unprincipled Sabbia, who proved expert at telling people what they wanted to hear, did not disappoint. Some people were promised cushy jobs as foremen and interpreters. Others were promised specialized employment as plumbers or blacksmiths. Needless to say, however, the bridge-building and railroad-grading labor gangs of the FEC had little use for plumbers, and Sabbia's promises proved valueless once the hapless laborers were deposited in Miami. To add insult to injury, Sabbia received a "finders fee" of $3.00 for each person he lured to Florida, and for the most part this sum was paid, not by the FEC, but by the misled worker himself, who found that two dollars of Sabbia's three-dollar bonus had been deducted from his first paycheck. The peonage charges leveled against the FEC, in fact, were inspired primarily by the horror stories which Sabbia's deceived victims brought with them back to New York after escaping from the FEC's clutches.

In the end, however, the entire sorry episode proved to be much ado about nothing. Once the charges were brought before a judge, he dismissed them outright on the grounds that the government had failed to prove that the FEC laborers had actually been enslaved, which was a necessary element of the crime under the 1866 slave-kidnapping statute. Still, despite his sudden and complete courtroom victory, Flagler was greatly unsettled by the whole affair, which he later wrote had "an air of mystery about [it] that we do not understand." Flagler suspected the entire thing was an elaborate attempt to besmear his reputation, and he blamed then-President Theodore Roosevelt for the whole mess. Flagler, in fact, held a long-standing grudge against Roosevelt dating back to 1898, when he helped Roosevelt get elected governor of New York, only to find Roosevelt repaying him for his support by passing laws levying taxes on public corporations (like Standard Oil), an action which Flagler considered a betrayal of trust and a personal attack. Flagler's private letters reveal the depth of his hatred for the former Rough Rider: "I have no command of the English language that enables me to express my feelings regarding Mr. Roosevelt," Flagler wrote. "He is shit."

In the meantime, while the peonage case was still ongoing, Flagler's workmen began to pick up the pace once again. The sixteen miles of track washed out during the 1906 hurricane were rebuilt, and the FEC planted work camps as far south as Knight's Key, about halfway to Key West. While some workers built railroad grades on the keys themselves, others were employed to bridge the gaps between them, which was done with a combination of trestle bridges and solid fill embankments—long, artificial islands built out of coral rock blasted from the Florida Keys.

The use of solid fill to bridge gaps saved the FEC money, but it did stir up a good deal of controversy. Long-time Florida residents like Commodore Munroe complained that solid railroad embankments closed many natural inlets, and thus caused the dramatic decline of many local fish populations, which depended on such inlets for food and shelter. Furthermore, Munroe claimed the construction of the "sea-going railroad" made the Keys much more dangerous for sailing vessels, since Flagler's solid fill embankments closed up many of the channels and small bays which had long been used for emergency shelter by Miami yachtsmen. Other critics charged that Flagler's miles of solid fill would stop up the natural flow of the tides and thus alter the course of the Gulf Stream. Years later, in 1927, it appeared that these critics were right; Europe suffered a winter of unprecedented cold, and many Europeans blamed Flagler's Overseas extension, which they claimed had disrupted the warm water currents which normally ameliorated northern Europe's weather. A U.S. government investigation, however, turned up no evidence to support this claim, and Europe's weather returned to normal the following winter.

Despite the complaints, Flagler's workers picked up the pace dramatically by the end of 1907. Construction was completed on Key Largo and continued over onto Plantation Key, which was separated from Key Largo by an easily bridged tidal inlet. At the end of Plantation Key lay two smaller islands known as the "Umbrella Keys," and to cut costs, Flagler's engineers linked the two islands with solid fill, creating what is today called Windley Key in the process. Since the next few keys were either solid land, or easily linked with fill, they presented no major problems to Flagler's workers: only one major bridge had to be built in this section of the track, across Indian Key Channel. And so it went, mile by mile, day by day, until Flagler's workers reached the end of Long Key, about one hundred miles out from Miami.

Here, Flagler's engineers were put to their first major test. Between Long Key and Conch Key, the next in the chain, lay about 2.68 miles of open water, a formidable obstacle to Flagler's railroad ambitions. To traverse it, Flagler ordered the construction of what came to be called the "Long Key Viaduct," a bridge made up of 180 concrete arches, each spanning a distance of about fifty feet. A project of this magnitude required the importation of a huge volume of needed building materials, and Flagler's managers were obliged to charter every freight steamer available on the Atlantic coast to haul cargo. In all, the construction of the Long Key viaduct consumed 200,000 tons of coal (as steam engine fuel), 286,000 barrels of cement, 177,000 cubic yards of crushed rock, 106,000 cubic yards of sand, plus 5,700 tons of steel supporting rods and 2,600,000 board feet of railroad timbers. Building a bridge on this scale would have been difficult even on dry land, but to build it at sea posed still further challenges: nearly all work had to be done by boat-mounted machinery, and Flagler employed an entire corps of hard-hat divers, many of them Greek sponge-divers, to build the arch foundations. Work on this engineering marvel was finally completed in January of 1908, and Flagler was so delighted with the result that he revised the official seal of the FEC railway to include an image of a passenger train chugging its way across the stately arches of the Long Key viaduct.

An FEC train crossing the Long Key viaduct. (Florida State Archives)

Observers who visited the newly built bridge were awestruck. Ralph D. Paine, for instance, wrote that the viaduct had "the aspect of a Roman aqueduct built of solid stone, and its colossal strength and dignity of outline are framed in a setting altogether lovely. Seen from the shore of Long Key," he continued, "its arches march across the water, away, away, until they seem to run sheer into the horizon with nothing to mar their splendid isolation." Railway passengers, unfortunately, could not appreciate the beauty of the arches, since a passenger's vantage-point from atop the viaduct obscured the arches below from view. Still, the bridge afforded them other pleasures. Paine speculated that "a passenger on a train crossing the Long Key viaduct may be lucky enough to see a school of flying fish skitter past and a porpoise or two hurtling in chase of them." And indeed, some years later, just as Paine had predicted, the first voyagers across the Long Key viaduct were enchanted by the experience; one wrote that "passengers in the railway trains may sit in the windows of Pullman cars in serenity and have an opportunity of seeing how the Atlantic Ocean looks in a gale." Flagler had created a bridge with no real match in the world, which allowed human beings to join the world of seagulls and pelicans, gliding effortlessly thirty feet above the open sea.

The Long Key viaduct was a marvel, one of several that Flagler would construct before reaching his final destination at Key West. In 1908, however, Flagler's project suffered an unexpected setback that threw the entire enterprise into sudden doubt. Since Key West was already a crowded town, Flagler planned to build his Key West terminus on built-up land, using mud dredged from the seafloor, which was nominally the property of the U.S. Navy. The Navy, however, objected to Flagler's plans on the grounds that they might need the same mud for their own projects. Flagler suspected that "shit" Roosevelt had thwarted him yet again, and he lobbied hard to get the Navy to change its mind.

In the meantime, however, Flagler seriously considered terminating his railroad at Knight's Key, about halfway to Key West, where he planned to build a major deep-water docking facility. For a while, in fact, it looked like Flagler had abandoned his resolve to continue to Key West, a suspicion which seemed confirmed in 1909, when the FEC established regular rail connections between New York City and Knight's Key with continuing service by steamboat to Havana harbor. Flagler's Knight's Key terminus quickly became the center of a thriving little town, which soon sported a post office, a power plant, recreation facilities, and a great deal of company housing. This growing settlement eventually sprawled onto nearby Key Vaca, where it evolved into the modern-day town of Marathon, still the second largest city in the Florida Keys today.

Speculation that Flagler would stop at Knight's Key was further fueled by the geographic realities of Florida. If Flagler were to continue his line past Knight's Key, skeptics noted, he would have to contend with a full seven miles of open water, a distance so vast that the curvature of the earth prevented observers standing on the shore of Knight's Key from seeing the distant islet of Little Duck Key, the next in the chain. Ralph D. Paine wrote in his 1908 article that "even after seeing Long Key viaduct, the present observer cannot view this great expanse of sea below Knight's Key without a sense of wonder and incredulity at the thought that it is to be bridged . . . so far as can be seen," Paine concluded, "it is a matter of launching a railroad straight into the blank horizon of the Atlantic."

In the end, however, Flagler decided to continue his line into the "blank horizon" despite these obstacles. By 1908, Flagler had reached seventy-eight years of age, and having come so far already, he was resolutely determined to reach Key West before his death. In that same year, therefore, Flagler assigned his engineers with the task of determining the feasibility of crossing the Knight's Key–Bahia Honda Channel, and one year later, his workmen began the arduous task of bridging this massive water gap. It was an unprecedented undertaking—no bridge like it had ever been built before anywhere in the world—and it taxed the ingenuity of the FEC engineers to the utmost.

After considerable consultation, Flagler's engineers decided to

Tourist postcard showing the construction of the "Overseas Extension's" Seven-Mile Bridge. (Florida State Archives)

span the seven-mile water gap between Knight's Key and Little Duck Key using a variety of different architectural techniques. In the shallows, the FEC constructed a bridge of 210 arches quite similar to those of the Long Key viaduct. Elsewhere, in deeper waters, Flagler's engineers laid steel deck girders atop a chain of 546 concrete piers, some of which had to be planted as much as twenty-eight feet below the water line. In the deepest waters of all, at Moser Channel, Flagler's engineers built a section of the bridge on a pivot, which could be opened to allow the passage of tall ships between the Atlantic Ocean and Florida Bay. To assure that each of these sections of the bridge were placed properly, Flagler's engineers resorted to constructing wooden platforms at five-hundred-foot intervals, from which Flagler's surveyors determined the exact location of each of the railroad piers in the vast, featureless ocean.

By this time, Flagler's work crews had become skilled bridge builders, and despite the massive scale of the seven-mile bridge project, construction progressed at an astounding pace; indeed, some FEC officials came to believe that the entire project could be completed by no later than 1910. This optimistic forecast, however, was undone by the return of the hurricane. On October 10, 1909, a fast-moving, late-season hurricane spun its way across the island of Cuba and then bore down hard on the Florida Keys. At Key West, winds reached 94 miles per hour, and an incredible 6.13 inches of rain fell in a 135-minute time period; other locations in the Keys reported as much as ten inches of rain overall. Key West was also battered by hurricane-swollen tides, which tore buildings off their foundations, and destroyed over three hundred boats in Key West's harbor.

By midday on the 11th of October, the hurricane had finished its demolition of Key West, and it continued towards Miami along the exact line of the Florida Keys, almost as if the storm were a vast, thundering train and the Florida shore were its track. For Flagler and the FEC, the hurricane's route could not have been more unfortunate, since almost every mile of railroad track they had built so far was exposed to the storm's wrath. Although most of the bridges withstood the storm quite well, including both the Long Key viaduct and the already-completed portions of the Knight's Key Bridge, the solid fill embankments constructed by the FEC in the upper Keys suffered severe damage from the tidal surges of the hurricane, leaving the rail line inoperable for months. Worse yet, much of the FEC's floating equipment was destroyed during the storm and had to be replaced or salvaged from the bottom of the sea. In the end, it took millions of dollars and months of work to undo the damage which the 1909 hurricane had wrought in a single day. The only silver lining in this cloud, as far as the FEC was concerned, was the paucity of human casualties—this time around, the FEC had ample forewarning of the approach of the hurricane, and only fourteen railroad employees perished.

Sobered by the second storm, FEC engineers entirely rethought their building plan. The solid fill, they realized, had been washed out in part because it offered no outlets for the storm tides; as a result, the railway embankments gave way to the pressure exerted by the millions upon millions of gallons of seawater piled high by the winds of the hurricane. This phenomenon, called the "storm surge," packs a terrific punch. Indeed, the engineers inspecting the damage after the storm noted that six- to ten-ton rocks had been washed from the railroad embankments of the upper Keys and into Florida Bay by the sheer force of the surge. In order to diffuse the power of future storm surges, FEC engineers replaced much of the solid fill they had already built with bridges, thus creating release valves for the pressure of the storm-driven water. In addition, they began to adopt the practice of covering over solid fill embankments with a coating of marine marl, which dried to form a hard, smooth shell, and which stood up very well against the erosive forces of the storm surge. These were sensible steps, but as history would prove, they would not be sufficient to spare the Overseas Railway from disaster.

In any case, the hurricane forced the FEC to spend much of its resources to rebuild and redesign track that had already been laid, but in the meantime, the railway's engineers continued to forge forward as well, knowing full well that any delays might deprive the rapidly-aging Flagler of the chance to see his grand project completed. To that end, the FEC continued the line onto Little Duck, Ohio, and Missouri Keys even before the Knight's Key Bridge project was finished. Past Missouri Key, however, they were forced to confront the greatest engineering problem the Overseas Railway would face: the Bahia Honda Channel. "Bahia Honda" means "deep bay" in Spanish, and the description was apt. Although only a mile and a half wide, much of the Bahia Honda Channel exceeded twenty feet in depth, and in places the sea bottom lay thirty-five feet under the low-water mark. Ironically, bridging this deep-water channel required a very tall bridge, since all of the railroad bridges of the Overseas were designed to be higher than the highest possible storm surge crests, and the maximum height of a storm surge wave depended largely upon the depth of the water—which at Bahia Honda was very deep indeed.

During the construction of the Bahia Honda Bridge, Flagler's engineers ran into problems they faced nowhere else during the construction of the Overseas. Due to the great depth of the water, which made the construction of underwater railroad pilings both difficult and expensive, the FEC engineers decided to build relatively few foundation piers. The piers they did build, however, were quite massive, and were able to support cagelike steel trusses as long as 247 feet. Building these enormous piers was no easy task, though, and one pier in particular caused the FEC no end of trouble. Flagler's engineers decided to plant one pier at the very center of the Bahia Honda Channel, where the water was at its deepest, but all attempts to locate a firm foundation on the ocean bottom failed; indeed, it seemed to Flagler's engineers that they had discovered a bottomless hole, capable of swallowing all works of man erected upon it. Eventually, an entire shipload of sand, gravel, and cement was dumped into the water in an attempt to create a firmer footing on the sea bottom.

While work on the Bahia Honda Bridge was still under way,

The Bahia Honda Bridge was one of the most problematic components of the
Overseas Railway. This postcard shows the bridge when it was finally complete.
(Florida State Archives)

Flagler's engineers penetrated still farther into the lower Keys. The
next major key past Bahia Honda was Big Pine Key, home of the
diminutive key deer. Jefferson Browne, it will be remembered, had
predicted that the trees of Big Pine Key would greatly assist the construction of the railroad, but as it turned out, these pines were more
of a hindrance than a help; the FEC building crews on the island
were constantly threatened by forest fires, which were ignited either
by errant sparks released by the island's resident charcoal-burners, or
by Conch hunters, who often used fire to flush the tiny key deer
from the island's thick underbrush. According to one historian of
the Overseas Railroad, FEC workers "were often forced to stop
work or literally flee for their lives when a wind-whipped wildfire
raged across the right of way."

As natural disasters go, however, wildfires cannot hold a candle
to hurricanes, and to remind the FEC of that fact, yet another hurricane made an unwelcome appearance in October of 1910. This
time around, the hurricane did not strike the Keys directly, but it

did stir up huge storm tides throughout the lower Keys, completely overwhelming the solid-fill embankments which FEC engineers
had just constructed to bridge the water gaps between Bahia Honda
and Key West. In some areas, tracks that had already been laid atop
the roadbed were washed six hundred feet away. Worst of all, the
same deep-water pier in the Bahia Honda Channel that had already
caused such trouble for Flagler's engineers was shifted during the
storm and had to be completely rebuilt.

Not all the news of the October 1910 hurricane was bad, however. To the delight of the FEC, not a single employee of Flagler was
killed. True, one FEC foreman was seriously injured, but he had
only himself to blame. At the hurricane's height, he climbed into a
tree and lashed himself fast, hoping to ride out the storm from atop
the tree, safe above the crest of the storm surge. Unfortunately, the
tree he picked for his salvation was a manchineel (a.k.a. William
Sewell's "poison tree") and for a whole agonizing night, the hapless
foreman could not escape from the thick toxic sap which oozed
from storm-broken tree. The foreman survived the experience, but
he spent the next few months convalescing in a mainland hospital.

The 1910 hurricane was a bruising setback, but there was nothing to be done but pick up the pieces yet again, since Flagler was
still utterly determined to see the project through before he died. In
order to ensure that the Overseas extension was completed during
his rapidly expiring lifetime, in fact, Flagler abandoned his long-
standing policy of funding the project entirely from his stock revenues and secured a loan of $10 million in bonds to hasten his proj-
ect along. Bolstered by this infusion of cash, his work crews once
again redoubled their efforts, and as 1910 verged into 1911, the
project approached completion. By degrees, the Bahia Honda
Channel was bridged, the railway embankments of the lower Keys
were completed, and the railway finally inched its way into Key
West. There, it linked up with a newly constructed railway terminus built upon 134 acres of man-made land which Flagler's engineers had built using mud and marl pumped up from under Key

West's harbor. The Navy had tried to object to the appropriation of this submerged fill, just as it had in 1908, but this time its complaints were drowned out in the crescendo of popular enthusiasm that the approach of Flagler's line had unleashed in Key West. In order to palliate the Navy, Flagler's engineers promised them that if the Key West naval base ever found itself in need of the mud and marl the FEC had borrowed, they would be happy to return it. Ironically, the built-up land created for Flagler's railway station is now U.S. Navy property; in the end, then, the Navy got its mud and marl back after all.

At long last, in January of 1912, Flagler's workmen put the finishing touches on the Knight's Key Bridge, and Key West was officially linked by rail to the continental United States. In order to celebrate this momentous event, Flagler himself set out for Key West in a train dubbed the "Extension Special" on January 22nd. He arrived in the island city amidst scenes of wild celebration; more than half of the population of the town came to await the appearance of Flagler's train, and when he emerged onto the observation

A view of the Overseas Extension's great seven-mile bridge, called the Knight's Key Bridge, with land just barely visible on the distant horizon. (Florida State Archives)

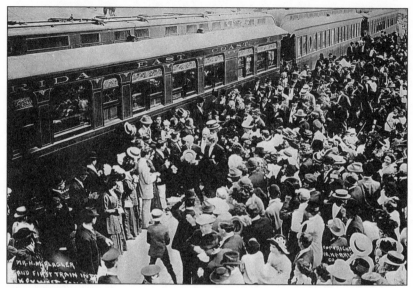

Flagler's triumphant arrival in Key West, January 22, 1912. Flagler is visible near the center-left of the photograph holding his hat in front of his chest. (Florida State Archives)

platform of his private sleeper car, he was greeted with effusions of praise. The Mayor of Key West read a laudatory speech, and while a military band played, a chorus of a thousand children sang patriotic songs for the aging tycoon's benefit. Overcome, Flagler told the crowd, "I thank God that from the summit I can look back over the twenty-five or twenty-six years since I became interested in Florida with intense satisfaction at the results which have followed." Privately, he confided to one FEC official that "I can hear the children, but I cannot see them." By 1912, the eighty-one-year-old Flagler was nearly blind.

Although Flagler's Overseas Railway achievement is little known today, it still deserves a prominent place in the annals of American history. The total cost of the railroad was astounding; according to FEC files, Flagler spent somewhere between $27 and $30 million on the Overseas, the equivalent of over a half-billion dollars in modern-day American currency. By way of comparison, the first transcontinental railroad, which linked Omaha to Sacramento, cost about $50 million to construct. Unlike the transcontinental railroad, however, which was funded by scores of investors, the Overseas Railway was bankrolled by just one man, who was able to pay for construction almost entirely out of his deep Standard Oil pockets. The fact that Flagler was unwilling to share the costs, and the risk, of the project with anyone else is especially surprising given the fact that the Overseas was not a certain money-maker. Indeed, Flagler's other rail lines in Florida barely broke even, and all predictions about the future profitability of the Overseas Railway were mere speculation. Rarely in American history has a single entrepreneur risked so much of his own fortune for such uncertain returns.

Still, any rational cost-benefit analysis of Flagler's achievement misses the essential point: how can a price be assigned to the quest for immortality? Perhaps more relevant than dollars and cents to this calculation is the number of workmen Flagler was willing to put at risk while constructing his legacy. All told, the storms, rip-tides, and construction accidents led to the deaths of hundreds of FEC workers, foremen, and engineers—and one of the construction chiefs hired by Flagler literally worked himself to death while direct-ing the project. Flagler's quest for eternal glory, then, came with a high price tag of human lives.

⑥ ⑥ ⑥

Ironically, given the fact that Flagler built the rail-road to secure his immortal legacy, he did not long survive the rail-way's completion. Less than one year after he "rode his own iron" to Key West, Flagler was badly injured in a fall down the grand stair-case of his palatial Palm Beach home, and he never recovered; after four months of gradual physical and mental degeneration, Flagler died in his bed on May 20, 1913. Three days later, he was buried in his beloved city of St. Augustine, where he and his second wife had honeymooned over thirty years before. Flagler's passing was head-line news throughout Florida, as well it should be; after nearly three decades of rule, Florida had lost its uncrowned king.

In the year before he died, however, Flagler must have been greatly gratified by the effusive praise that contemporaries lavished upon his Overseas Railway. During the construction of the line, some skeptics had dubbed it "Flagler's Folly," but now that it was complete, contemporaries jumped eagerly upon Flagler's bandwagon. Flagler's great achievement was widely touted in the press as the "Eighth Wonder of the World." One commentator in the *Manufacturer's Record* wrote that "it is within the realm of conservatism to say that at no previous period of the world's history, referring to construction or engineering undertakings, can a parallel case be cited." Even the construction of the transcontinental railroad and the mastering of the Alps, this commentator judged, "sink into insignificance when compared with this latest project in railroading." Editorialists for the *Tampa Tribune* declared January 22, 1912, the "greatest day" in Key West's history, and pronounced the Overseas Railway to be "one of the costliest railways ever constructed and one of the most unique and picturesque." Not to be outdone, the *Miami Herald* declared Flagler to be "one of the master builders of this country," and predicted that his unprecedented Overseas Railway would inaugurate "a new epoch" in the history of Key West.

Indeed, nearly all commentators agreed that the construction of Flagler's Overseas line would pump new life into the dusty old town of Key West. Jefferson Browne had predicted as much in 1896, and later observers expanded upon his claims. In his 1906 *National Geographic* article on the Florida Keys, John Gifford foresaw that the completion of the line would cause Key West to "develop into a metropolis of great importance," and he noted that "it is said by those who are well informed that this island of about 1,000 acres will have a population of over 100,000 in less than 10 years." A 1912 pamphlet published by the FEC to commemorate Flagler's achievement made still more elaborate claims about Key West's brilliant future. According to its anonymous author, the Overseas Railway would become the terminus of a "new artery of life which [would connect] the whole length of our coast line on the east of the United States," and the author anticipated that the flow of trade it produced would "make the island [of Key West] in a few years the queen of the southern seas."

As it turned out, however, these gentlemen were betting on the wrong horse. Despite the boastful predictions of Browne and the FEC, Flagler's railway utterly failed to revive Key West's fortunes. Quite the contrary, in fact—as we will see in later chapters, the Overseas Railway may have actually contributed to Key West's decline. In the meantime, the city of Miami at the other end of the Keys would experience unheard-of levels of growth, and would quickly surpass the city of Key West in both population and prosperity. Indeed, by the end of this period, Miami had become the true "queen of the southern seas," and seemed poised to become one of the largest cities in the United States. Once again, the upstart city of Miami had vastly exceeded Flagler's expectations.

7

American Frontier, American Riviera

On December 29 of 1911, the work crew operating a digger dredge in the swamps to the northwest of Miami pulled a decomposing body out of the muck of the Everglades. The police were summoned to investigate this gruesome discovery, and they soon determined that the body belonged to Desoto Tiger, a fur trapper, alligator hunter, and Seminole Indian who was well known in the Miami area. An investigation was immediately begun to examine the circumstances of Desoto Tiger's demise.

In a way, the death of Desoto Tiger serves as a perfect symbol for the decline in the fortunes of the Seminole Indians after the turn of the century. Before 1900, the Seminole Indian trade had been a crucial component of Miami's early prosperity, and the alligator hides, bird plumes, and otter skins purchased from Seminole trappers were a mainstay in the city's economy. As the nineteenth century gave way to the twentieth, however, the Seminoles entered a period of gradual decline, due in large part to the work of digger dredges just like the one that scooped Desoto Tiger's corpse from the Everglades.

There was nothing new about swampland drainage in Florida—observers such as James Covington had made note of it as early as the 1880s—but most early schemes had not penetrated the core territories of the Seminole Indians. By 1911, however, vast expanses of Everglades land south of Lake Okeechobee were being absorbed by settlers, developers, and speculators, and as a consequence the Seminoles were fast running out of productive hunting grounds. Worse yet, as the 1910s gave way to the 1920s, white hunters and trappers equipped with modern firearms, automobiles, and power-boats took advantage of the new routes opened by the dredging schemes into the previously impenetrable Everglades and made deep incursions into what was formerly an exclusive Seminole domain. In the process, they decimated wildlife populations and drove entire Everglades animal species to the edge of extinction. Since the Seminoles depended on these animals for their livelihood, these latest white invasions all but destroyed the basis of the Seminole economy.

Everglades drainage managed to accomplish what three bloody Seminole wars could not: it finally cost the Seminoles both their independence and their self-respect. As time went on, the Seminoles increasingly began to eschew the Miami Indian traders of old, who generally refused to sell alcohol, and began to frequent the rough taverns of North Miami, which were more than willing take alligator skins and otter pelts in exchange for booze. Other Seminoles gravitated to black sections of Miami where they eagerly consumed their favorite drink: a noxious concoction brewed out of red pepper, whiskey, and a dollop of cocaine. To pay for these beverages, Seminoles might carry clubs at one of Miami's golf courses; indeed, Miami boosters of the day proclaimed that Seminoles were "ideal golf caddies" due to their "marvelous eyesight," made keen by years of hunting in the Everglades. Still other Seminoles abandoned hunting altogether and joined one of the many Seminole "tourist camps" that sprang up in the vicinity of Miami after the turn of the century. These camps allowed the Seminoles to scratch out a miserable existence by selling cheap handmade knick-knacks and performing dances for the visiting motorists, but only at the cost of further injury to Seminole dignity. By the 1920s and 1930s, the remnant Seminoles had been reduced to the status of roadside curiosities in lands they had once counted as their own.

Desoto Tiger, however, was not killed by alcoholism, nor did he die from the boredom and frustration bred in the tourist camps. As the police quickly discovered, Desoto Tiger was the victim of foul play. According to another Seminole, Jimmy Gopher, Desoto and a white man named John Ashley had recently returned from an extended hunting and trapping expedition into the Everglades. Jimmy Gopher told the police that Desoto was still alive and well last time they met, but according to witnesses in Miami, John Ashley turned up several days later at a Miami trading post, alone, with $1,200 in pelts and hides. What is more, the police discovered, this same John Ashley had been arrested just the night before for "recklessly displaying firearms" in West Palm Beach. This was enough to convince Sheriff George B. Baker, who was handling the case, that John Ashley was almost certainly their man, and he immediately dispatched deputies to make an arrest. So begins the saga of John Ashley, who would blaze a path of terror across south and central Florida for much of the next decade.

As it turned out, arresting John Ashley was no easy feat. The first deputies who attempted the job were bushwhacked by John and his brother Bob, who sent the terrified lawmen scurrying away with orders to "tell Baker not to send any more chicken-hearted men with rifles or they are apt to get hurt." After that, Ashley left south Florida for three years for parts unknown; he certainly ventured to New Orleans, and the authorities suspect that he may have reached distant Seattle, where he supposedly worked in a

John Ashley, wearing an eye patch, bides his time in the Florida State Penitentiary, guarded by an unidentified prison official. (Fort Lauderdale Historical Society)

logging camp. John himself later claimed that he had gotten as far as Canada during this period, and boasted of robbing a Canadian bank, though this cannot be corroborated. In early 1914, however, John returned to his south Florida haunts, and claimed (through his attorney) that he was tired of running. Deputies brought him to the courthouse, and John Ashley was imprisoned pending his trial.

The trial, however, did not go quite as Ashley had planned. In all likelihood, Ashley only produced himself for judgment on the assumption that a jury in his home county would acquit him, either out of sympathy, or out of fear of retribution from other members of the large and violent Ashley clan. Unfortunately for Ashley, the West Palm Beach prosecutor seems to have been of the same opinion, and he foiled Ashley's scheme by petitioning with the judge for a change of venue to Miami. Even before closing arguments on this motion were completed, though, John Ashley made his escape, probably suspecting that a Miami jury would be less sympathetic to him than a jury of his peers. According to contemporary accounts,

Ashley exited his confinement by sprinting out of an unlocked door during mealtime and scaling a ten foot fence; Sheriff Baker, astounded by the ease of Ashley's escape over the fence, later claimed that Ashley "simply melted through it." This was John Ashley's first escape from prison, and it would not be his last.

Following his jailbreak, Ashley gathered together a motley band of kinfolk, ex–Rice Gang toughs, and Chicago gangsters that became known as the Ashley Gang. Under John's leadership, this rough crew staged a series of bank robberies and other daring heists in the backwoods towns north of the city of Miami. He and his men even attempted to rob an entire passenger train of the FEC, though the execution of their complicated plan failed after several of Ashley's henchmen bumbled their assignments.

No crime spree lasts forever, though, and John Ashley was eventually recaptured in Stuart, a town to the north of West Palm Beach, in the aftermath of an otherwise successful bank robbery. Details are unclear, but at some point during the escape, one of Ashley's lackeys accidentally shot him in the head, damaging his jaw and destroying his left eye. Ashley wore a glass eye for the rest of his life, but his partial loss of sight did not effect his legendary marksmanship; even after the injury, Ashley was reportedly able to shoot the heads off quail thirty yards away with his revolver, and witnesses swore that he could "shoot through the mouth" of a glass bottle placed on a stump thirty steps away "and knock the bottom out of the bottle without [the bullet] touching it anywhere else." Still, because of Ashley's serious injury, he was unable to flee into the sanctuary of the Everglades following the Stuart bank robbery, and Sheriff Baker's deputies finally managed to capture John Ashley for a second time.

Following his arrest, Ashley was taken to Miami for trial for the murder of Desoto Tiger, though the prosecution against him was eventually dropped since the state attorneys believed that they could marshal a better case against Ashley back in West Palm Beach on charges stemming from his Stuart bank robbery. In the meantime,

John's brother Bob tried to break Ashley out of prison, and managed to kill both a jailer and a sheriff's deputy before being gunned down himself. Enraged by Bob's killing spree, the crowds of Miami almost erupted into violence, and John Ashley just barely escaped being lynched in his jail cell by a mob of several thousand irate Miami townspeople; in the end, the mob only dispersed after the police paraded Bob Ashley's body through the assembled Miamians to satisfy their blood-lust. Even as late as the 1910s, revenge could still be swift and bloody in the city on Biscayne Bay.

Following his narrow escape from Miami mob justice, Ashley was brought before the bar in West Palm Beach, where he pled guilty for the Stuart bank robbery and was sentenced to seventeen and a half years in the state prison. By 1918, however, the crafty Ashley was free again. For two years, Ashley had played at being a model prisoner, and as a result, he managed to secure a spot in a prison roadwork crew, which offered more chances for escape. Ashley bided his time until the opportunity arose and then made his break for freedom with the assistance of Tom Maddox, another notorious Florida bank robber. For the second time in five years, John Ashley had escaped the clutches of the Florida penal system.

Ashley soon rejoined his old gang, and they resumed their villainous habits. This time around, however, they focused not on robbery but on rum running, a profession that became wildly profitable after January of 1919, when the Eighteenth Amendment to the Constitution made Prohibition the law of the land. During this period, Ashley and his gang set up a profitable empire of alcohol, maintaining moonshine stills in the woods of central Florida and sneaking booze across the Florida Straits from the British-owned Bahamas, where liquor was still readily available. In addition to hauling their own cargoes of booze, Ashley and his men had a lucrative sideline hijacking the cargoes of others. Indeed, during this period, the Ashley gang earned a reputation as ruthless liquor-pirates, and they became the terror of central Florida bootleggers, who feared the Ashley gang far more than the Prohibition enforcement police.

At about the same time, Ashley became romantically involved with Laura Upthegrove, a.k.a. the "Queen of the Everglades," who was nondescript in appearance, yet possessed of a fiery will. Laura served primarily as the gang's lookout; when the law approached one of the Ashley Gang's wooded hideouts, Laura would tear through the woods at night in a car with unlit headlights, following a secret trail known only to Ashley's followers, in order to warn her fellow gang members to seek safety in the sanctuary of the Everglades.

Laura's skill as a lookout no doubt shielded John from the law for several years, but in June of 1921, John was apprehended yet again, this time while unloading hooch in a garage just outside of the small town of Wauchula. For a while, Ashley managed to hide his identity behind the alias of "Davis," and was thus treated as just another penny-ante rum runner. Eventually, however, one of his fellow inmates ratted him out to the authorities, and Ashley was carted back to his prison outside West Palm Beach to serve out the remainder of his sentence.

In the meantime, while John languished in the clink, Laura Upthegrove kept the Ashley Gang alive by the sheer force of her personality. By the early 1920s, in fact, Ashley's gang was becoming a victim of its own success. Since so many bootleggers were relieved of their property or even their lives while passing through the Ashley gang's domain, bootleggers began to seek safer routes into southern Florida, far from the Ashley Gang's clutches. As a result, the pickings for liquor piracy grew increasingly slim and the gang was forced to return to its bank-robbing ways of old.

At around the same time, John Ashley somehow managed to free himself from jail for a third time; on this occasion, Ashley simply vanished from his prison cell. To this day, no one really knows how Ashley managed to escape, and Ashley himself later refused to explain how he accomplished his exit, most likely because he absconded with the assistance of confederates whose identity he wished to conceal. Once free, Ashley declared his intention to "embark on a real career of crime," and he vowed that he would never be taken alive by the authorities again. Ashley also issued a personal challenge to Sheriff Baker, who had become his personal nemesis, in the form of a single bullet, which he sent to the sheriff by way of a black man who had been forced against his will to assist in one of the Ashley gang's bank robberies. The meaning of the bullet could not be clearer: next time the two men met, either John Ashley or Sheriff Baker would not survive the encounter.

Soon after his third escape, Ashley and his gang pulled off their most daring escapade in their long career of crime. Since the Ashley gang had driven bootleggers out of their territory by the early 1920s, Ashley decided to attack the bootleggers at their source: the rum-running town of West End in the British Bahamas, which, thanks to Prohibition, was swimming with cash. Although details of the raid are unclear, it is known that Ashley and his gang stole $8,000 in cash and liquor from the various shops and warehouses of West End, and he just barely missed out on a much greater score; on the morning of the raid, an express boat had taken $250,000 from West End to the Bahamian capital of Nassau for safekeeping. Ashley also just barely missed an ambush set for him by Sheriff Baker, who had been tipped off to Ashley's plans by a local car salesman who had stumbled onto the gang's preparations on the eve of the raid. If the paranoid Ashley, who suspected that the law had caught wind of plans, hadn't chosen to enter the Atlantic unexpectedly via the dangerous and little-traveled St. Lucie Inlet, he would likely have been nabbed at sea by the sheriff's men.

Although thwarted in his attempt to seize Ashley on the high seas, Baker did not give up, and he resolved to pursue Ashley deep into the trackless expanses of the Everglades. After months of fruitless searches, Baker and his men finally learned the location of John Ashley in February of 1924; according to their sources, John Ashley and members of his family were holed up in a small moonshiner's camp located in a swamp about two miles south of the Ashley family homestead. Ashley's choice of a hideout was excellent, since the short bushes and palmetto scrub around the camp made it virtually impossible for anyone to sneak up undetected. The determined Baker, however, resolved to lay siege to the camp, and at three o'clock one February morning, he sent eight of his deputies, under cover of darkness, to surround Ashley's hideout. One imagines that their early morning crawl through the mud and thickets, towards the known location of a notorious murderer, was a terrifying experience for these Florida deputies. These men had all heard the story of the bullet and were all too aware that John Ashley was willing to die, or kill, rather than return to prison.

By daybreak all the sheriff's men were in position, ready to strike, but their plans were upset at the last moment by John Ashley's dog Shine, who sniffed out and charged several of the concealed lawmen. The deputies fired at the dog, and Ashley shot back. In the ensuing gunfight, one deputy was killed (almost certainly by John Ashley), Joe Ashley (John's father) was slain, and Laura Upthegrove, who had followed her lover to his swamp hideaway, was badly hurt by buckshot from a deputy's shotgun. John Ashley himself managed to escape unharmed, thanks in part to a secret escape route, but also thanks to the wounded Laura's agonized screams, which caused the disconcerted deputies to hold their fire. Still, Ashley did not go far, and despite a manhunt of over two hundred men, he remained at large for several months in the vicinity of the county prison where Laura was imprisoned, hoping for a chance to stage a jailbreak. In the end, though, the opportunity never arose, and Ashley eventually elected to flee to California until the heat had died down.

Even from his temporary exile in distant California, however, John Ashley cast a dark shadow over the city of Miami, since Ashley and his gang were the living embodiment of south Florida's deepest fears. The story of John Ashley, after all, was a story of Indians and desperados, bank robbers and lawmen, gunfights and blood feuds— it seems almost to have been plagiarized from the annals of the Wild West. Yet the Wild West is precisely what the Miami area was anxious not to become. The history of the Western frontier, the citizens of Miami well knew, was punctuated by sudden growth and equally sudden collapse, by boom towns transformed into ghost towns almost overnight, forgotten even by their former inhabitants. These lessons in history were of immediate relevance to Miami, since by the mid 1920s, the city on Biscayne Bay was showing all of the signs of a boom of legendary proportions.

Would Miami's prosperity withstand the test of time? Or, Miami's citizens worried, would their town become another Dodge City, swollen by ephemeral wealth and then abandoned by fickle fortune? Only time would tell; in the meantime, all the city of Miami could do was wait. At least the momentary absence of Ashley from his Florida haunts removed one nagging reminder that Miami was still basically a young, unproven outpost on America's southern-most frontier.

⑥ ⑥ ⑥

Frontier outpost it might have been, but the Miami area was growing, and what is more, it was growing in several directions at once. Anxious to make a buck from the region's unique geography and lovely climate, speculators and developers divided nearly every square mile of Miami and its hinterlands into marketable real estate, from the swamps of the Everglades to the sandbars beyond Biscayne Bay. In the process, they laid the foundation for what was almost certainly the most impressive real estate boom in American history.

To the north and west of Miami, for instance, a number of land developers began to carve out real estate plots in Everglades marshlands south of Lake Okeechobee. One early speculator named Richard Bolles made a small fortune by selling real estate subdivisions near the banks of Lake Okeechobee, land that for the most part was submerged under several feet of water, though Bolles, quite understandably, downplayed that fact in his sales pitches. One unhappy buyer later complained that "I have bought land by the acre, I have bought land by the foot; but, by God, I have never bought land by the gallon." Although successful in lining his pockets, Bolles ultimately contributed little to the development of the Everglades land.

Other developers, however, had a far more lasting impact on the map of south Florida. Take James A. Moore, for example. Moore arrived in south Florida in 1915 after trying, and failing, to make the city of Seattle a steel capital. To recover his fortunes, Moore purchased ninety-eight thousand acres of land southwest of Lake Okeechobee, and sold it to would-be farmers who were tempted by the reputed fertility of the Everglades soil. As it turned out, Moore's timing was perfect: almost immediately after he began selling land plots, the United States became involved in the First World War, and U.S. food prices skyrocketed. Moore also benefited from several years of low rainfall, which normally spells trouble for farmers, but which was a definite boon for settlers living on the banks of Lake Okeechobee, since the lake's declining water level opened up thousands more acres of rich, moist lake bottom for cultivation.

The dry spell, interestingly enough, had a second and unexpected consequence. As the waters receded, they uncovered hundreds of human skeletons on Kreamer and Ritta Islands along the southern shores of the lake; one settler later commented that skulls were so thick on the ground of these muddy islands that they resembled "pumpkins in the field." Although some have speculated that these remains might be ancient Indian water burials, the presence of these waterlogged skeletons on the bottom of the Okeechobee remains a mystery.

Despite these macabre reminders of the past, most indications seemed to suggest that Moore Haven, as it came to be called, was a town with a bright future. As a result of agricultural prosperity, the town of Moore Haven boasted several hundred residents by 1917 along with a school, a bank, and a regular newspaper. A year later, the town was connected to the FEC line by a rail spur, further stimulating its growth. Three years after that, the town of Moore Haven had become so prosperous that it petitioned successfully to become the county seat of the newly formed Glades County, a distinction which the town still enjoys today. Furthermore, though Moore Haven was certainly the largest town on the shores of the Okeechobee, it was by no means alone. Other towns rapidly followed, including South Bay, Belle Glade, Chosen, Pahokee, and Canal Point, a town that had the dubious distinction of being the dwelling place of Laura Upthegrove's immediate family. One of America's last frontiers, then, was finally giving way to human ambition.

At the same time that some developers were carving towns out of the Everglades swamplands, others had set their eyes on the marshy strip of land to the east of Miami that separates the waters of Biscayne Bay from the Atlantic Ocean. Early settlers of Miami made little use of this land, other than to walk its fine white-sand beaches in search of turtle eggs and shipwreck salvage. Homesteaders who might have considered carving out homesteads on the land across the Bay from Miami tended to think again once confronted with the peninsula's formidable vegetation. Although some coconut palms grew here, left over from the failed 1882 attempt to plant a coconut plantation along the shores of Biscayne Bay, much of the rest of the island consisted of mangrove-covered mudflats, and other locations were guarded by a spiky cactuslike plant with the intimidating name of Spanish bayonet. Not surprisingly, then, "Jolly Jack" Peacock's tiny naval rescue station long remained the only human structure on this remote peninsula.

At first, the coming of the railroad to Miami had little impact on this underdeveloped and overlooked strip of land. Although the territory became a favorite spot for hunting expeditions launched from Flagler's Royal Palm Hotel, the peninsula remained wild and served as a sort of private game reserve for Flagler's guests. Visitors reported in the 1890s that the island's vegetation was still so thick with palms and live oaks that they had to slash their way into the interior with machetes. Once they managed to penetrate the jungle, however, they marveled at its wildlife: the wooded peninsula was still well stocked with the now-endangered Florida crocodile, and at least one visitor was pleasantly startled by the sight of a "a big tawny, fierce looking" Florida panther, which made a "scream as of a woman in agony" before leaping away into the underbrush.

Although some visitors appreciated the wild, untouched beauty (and the excellent hunting opportunities) of this muddy peninsula, others were more attracted by its commercial prospects. One such developer was John Collins, one of the investors in the 1882 coconut planting fiasco, who found himself poor in coconuts but rich in undeveloped Florida real estate. Collins was already in his seventies by the 1910s, but he had the restless ambition of a much younger man, and he resolved to put the land which had fallen into his lap to some use. To that end, he established a large avocado plantation across the Bay from Miami, and planned the construction of a wooden bridge across the Bay to convey his produce to market. When his bridge scheme was opposed by two self-interested ship captains who had long run a ferry service across the Bay, John Collins drove his car to the docks and demanded passage for both himself and his automobile to the land he owned on the other side of Biscayne Bay, a request which both captains sheepishly admitted that they could not accommodate. The Miami City Council conceded the point to Collins and gave him a permit to build his bridge across the Bay.

Collins began construction of his bridge in mid-1912, about six months after Flagler's trains first rattled their way over the Knight's Key Bridge and into the new FEC terminal at Key West. At first glance, at least, Collins' bridge did not present nearly the same level of difficulty as Flagler's Overseas Railway; while Flagler had to contend with water at depths of up to thirty-five feet, the Biscayne Bay waters which Collins proposed to cross were quite shallow. In addition, whereas Flagler's bridge was constructed to withstand the ages, Collins contented himself with a bridge constructed of relatively inexpensive wood.

As it turned out, however, the choice of wood as a construction material caused Collins' costs to expand enormously. To keep the wood pilings of the bridge from disintegrating in the salt water, Collins was forced to plant the pilings in concrete cylinders, and the construction of these cylinders quickly drained the Collins family's considerable yet not inexhaustible resources. When the money finally ran out in November of 1912, Collin's bridge was still half a mile shy of the other side of Biscayne Bay. As one historian has quipped, John Collins had managed to build "the world's longest vehicular bridge leading nowhere."

Luckily for John Collins, he received assistance in his hour of need from an unlikely source: Carl Graham Fisher, a handsome young Indianapolis industrialist and entrepreneur. As the story goes, Carl Fisher and his young wife were tooling about on Biscayne Bay in their motorboat when they spied, against a backdrop of tropical jungle, an impeccably dressed older man standing pensively on the shore. Carl was immediately impressed by the old man's patrician countenance and later described him as looking like "a bantam rooster, cocky and unafraid." A conversation developed between this old rooster, who was none other than John Collins, and the much younger Carl Fisher. At some point following this exchange—the accounts differ as to when—Fisher resolved to use some of his vast fortune to help the old man finish construction of his bridge. In return, Fisher received partial control over the bridge and a strip of Collins' land eighteen hundred feet wide, reaching from Biscayne Bay to the Atlantic Ocean. Fisher soon augmented his land holdings with other purchases, until he became the dominant landowner on the peninsula.

This Carl Fisher, incidentally, was quite a character. Fisher was a self-made man from a humble family who left school after only five years and broke into the business world in the 1880s at the tender age of thirteen, selling newspapers, books, candy, and tobacco on railway cars. Fisher thrived in this environment, in part due to his unique business technique of flipping up the front of his apron to reveal a picture of a naked woman in order to pique a prospective

Carl Fisher, who constructed the Dixie Highway and built the town of Miami Beach from nothing, is shown here on one of his polo ponies. (Florida State Archives)

customer's interest.

Fisher's tactic of "flashing" customers was no childish whim, however, and he continued to employ it (with variations) throughout his life. When Fisher later started a business as an Indianapolis bicycle salesman, for example, he publicized his store by releasing thousands of balloons into the air, fifty of which bore a "lucky" number that entitled its finder to a free bicycle. Fisher also publicized his bicycle shop by hurling bicycles off of high buildings at a pre-appointed time, and awarding a free bike to whoever returned to his store with the fallen bicycle's frame. The fact that "Crazy Carl" was arrested by the police following each of these incidents only added to his growing fame and notoriety.

With his bike shop a success, Fisher then moved on to selling automobiles, and dropped one of those off a building too, to the dismay of the local police. Amazingly, Fisher's car not only survived the fall in one piece, it also sputtered to life when Fisher's brother turned the car's hand-crank, much to the delight of the appreciative crowds. Fisher then executed his biggest publicity stunt yet: he hitched one of his cars to a balloon and sailed over crowds of gawking spectators over Indianapolis. This incident made Carl both a local hero and a national celebrity, at least for a fleeting fifteen minutes.

In the meantime, Carl co-founded the "Prest-O-Lite" automobile headlight company, which experimented with ways of producing light using highly unstable carbide gas. For several years, the only thing this company managed to produce were well-publicized explosions, which left several dead and which flung hundred-plus–pound chunks of iron into the surrounding neighborhoods. The good citizens of Indianapolis were outraged, and Carl's carefully cultivated reputation suffered. By 1911, however, Prest-O-Lite had developed a marketable product and had begun to produce large profits for Carl and his business partners. Two years later, Fisher and his partners agreed to sell their shares of the company to the Union Carbide Company for about $9 million in stocks and cash, the equivalent of $160 million in modern American currency. For the first time in his busy life, Carl Fisher had indisputably joined the ranks of the American rich.

Like Flagler, Fisher was never content to sit idly upon a fortune, and he constantly plowed his profits into new endeavors. Even before the Prest-O-Lite gamble paid off, Fisher had co-founded the Indianapolis Motor Speedway Company, which hosted the first Indianapolis 500 race on May 30 of 1911. Fisher also became heavily involved in the effort to build the first paved automobile road across the country, which Fisher named the "Lincoln Highway" after his favorite U.S. president. After the Lincoln Highway began to enjoy some success, Fisher began to promote another paved road, dubbed the "Dixie Highway," which eventually stretched from Chicago to Miami, passing through Fisher's native Indianapolis in the process. Fisher's motives in constructing the Dixie Highway were somewhat self-serving: he hoped this highway would form a vital link between North and South, but he was not blind to the fact that a better north-south road connection would also bring thousands of visitors to his new real estate holdings in the Miami area. It was no coincidence that Fisher's Dixie Highway terminated at John Collins' wooden bridge across Biscayne Bay.

Indeed, by this time, Fisher had hatched big plans for the real estate he had acquired from John Collins. Despite the hostility of Fisher's new wife, Jane, who greatly disliked the mosquito-infested mangroves which her husband had acquired, Fisher (like Flagler before him) was possessed with a vision: he would transform the Florida wilderness into a man-made paradise. To do so, however, proved enormously expensive, since the land was wholly unsuitable for development. Although some land had already been cleared and planted with avocados or grapefruit, most of it was still choked by mangroves, palmetto scrub, Spanish bayonet, and pines. Worse yet, much of the land was at or below sea level and would have to be raised up considerably before any construction was possible.

Fisher was not deterred. To clear the land, he hired dozens of black workers, and after labor costs began to mount, he commissioned a custom-built plow equipped with three-cornered digging blades to shred the stubborn tropical vegetation. The same plow assisted Fisher with the destruction of the mangrove thickets as well; Fisher's men wrapped the mangroves with long steel chains, and attached the chains to the digging plow, which then snapped the stubborn mangroves with what Jane Fisher later described as "a sound like machine-gun fire."

In the meantime, anxious to create a seawall to protect his property from the tides, Fisher employed three large digger-dredges to scoop muck and marl from the bottom of Biscayne Bay and deposit it along his shoreline. This process created unnatural-looking shelves of new territory, quite light in color due to the marl, flat as a blackboard, and utterly devoid of vegetation. They were not, however, devoid of odor, since Fisher's dredges hauled up a great deal of sea life along with the mud and marl, and the rotting organic matter filled the air with the foul stench of decomposition. This already-unpleasant aroma was further worsened by the decaying corpse of a construction company mule, which sank into the not-yet-dry marl and died before it could be rescued.

Not surprisingly, the respectable citizens of nearby Miami gaped in horror at the stinking moonscape that Fisher was building on the other side of Biscayne Bay. What did Fisher possibly think he was accomplishing? Why was he building up new land on a muddy, mosquito-ridden sandbar when millions of Florida acres were still unsold, unpeopled, and uncultivated? "Crazy Carl," they told each other, had lost his wits.

But Fisher had a plan. After his dredged-up lands dried out, which took as much as six months, Fisher sent in hundreds of black workers to meticulously landscape his newly formed territory, gradually transforming it into a veritable garden of Eden, covered with a rich layer of grass and ornamented with carefully chosen tropical plants. In 1916, Fisher even hired two expert Japanese horticulturalists to maintain his grounds. In the meantime, the completion of John Collins' bridge brought more and more visitors to Fisher's man-made paradise, and the population of "Miami Beach," as the peninsula across the bay came to be called, began to increase steadily.

Still, since the population increase was not nearly as rapid as Fisher would have liked, Fisher began to rely on the same old "flashy" sales tactics that had served him well since he was thirteen years old. Hoping to attract the upper crust of American society, Fisher built a world-class polo field on his nearly unoccupied lands, and by 1919 his polo grounds had attracted both national and international interest. Then, when the country embraced the golf craze, Fisher laid out a championship-quality golf course on Miami Beach and offered a prize purse large enough to attract the very best American golfers. To further "flash" the attractions of Miami Beach, Fisher populated the town with a number of elephants that he acquired from the Florida-based Ringling Brothers Circus Company. One of these elephants, named Rosie, provided Fisher with his most priceless photo-op. In 1921, Fisher managed to persuade President-elect Warren G. Harding to play a game of golf

Rosie the elephant (here, being used as a golf tee) was of enormous assistance to Carl Fisher in his efforts to popularize Miami Beach. (Florida State Archives)

with him in Miami Beach, and Rosie was enlisted to serve as caddy; as a result most national newspapers, on the next day, featured photographs of Rosie the elephant carrying the future president's golf clubs. This was a public relations coup of the highest order, and almost overnight, Miami Beach became a household name.

Given her invaluable assistance in promoting Miami Beach, Rosie should probably be forgiven for the occasional headaches that she brought to Carl Fisher. On one occasion, Rosie smelled the odor of peanuts wafting out of a passing Miami Beach trolley car and stuck her trunk into the car to investigate. Unfortunately, the peanut-carrying passenger, who mistook Rosie's inquisitive trunk for a snake, screamed and leapt from the window of the trolley, breaking his leg in the process. He later sued Fisher for a tidy sum of money. On another occasion, Rosie was taken to Miami Beach's newly founded First National Bank, and as a publicity stunt, she was given a five-dollar bill and a passbook so that she could open her own elephantine bank account. Rosie, however, was so frightened by her new and unfamiliar surroundings that she responded with what one historian has described as "a long, loud defecation which drove customers helter-skelter from the bank." Miami residents later joked that Rosie's terror-induced bowel movement was "the biggest deposit that the Miami Beach First National ever had."

Despite Rosie's penchant for mischief, or perhaps because of it, Miami Beach experienced unheard-of growth as the 1910s gave way to the 1920s. Back in 1915, when Miami Beach was first incorporated, it could claim only thirty-five registered voters, and by 1920, it still had only 644 permanent inhabitants. Long-time residents later recalled that living in Miami Beach in 1920 was like "living in a big park, quite beautiful and more or less untended." In the first few years of the 1920s, however, the population of Miami Beach exploded. Hotel after hotel sprouted up on the Atlantic and bayfront shorelines; indeed, by 1925, Miami Beach boasted fifty-six hotels with four thousand available rooms, along with two hundred apartment buildings. Others came to Miami Beach, not as temporary visitors, but as permanent residents, and Carl Fisher finally began to find buyers for his Miami Beach land plots. Land sales, which had totaled only half a million dollars in 1920, rose to six million in 1923, and exceeded twenty-three million by the end of 1925. Fisher's Miami Beach gamble was finally paying off, and "the Beach" was rapidly earning a reputation as a new American Riviera.

In the meantime, at the other end of Miami, a real estate developer with even more ambitious plans was beginning to harvest his own millions from south Florida's subtropical soil. George Edgar Merrick was the son of a small-town New England minister named Solomon who had fled Massachusetts for the warmer climes of Florida following the ferocious blizzard of 1895. Although a man of God and an orange farmer, Solomon Merrick shared William English's old dream of founding a resort city on Biscayne Bay; Merrick later recalled that his father had fantasized about building "a place where castles in Spain are made real." For several years, the Merrick family's dream of building a "city beautiful" went nowhere, largely because they were unable to convince bankers that their grandiose plan would ever make any profits. Carl Fisher's stunning success on Miami Beach, however, caused the banks to change their minds, and in 1921, George Merrick broke ground on what he hoped would be a world-renowned model community.

Merrick's Coral Gables, as he called it, was designed to be a planned town, built in a consistent architectural style that Merrick called "Mediterranean." Merrick later explained that his structures were part Spanish and part Italian in inspiration, "a combination of what seemed best in each, with an added touch of gaiety to suit Florida mood." Whatever you termed Merrick's chosen style, it proved popular with home-buyers, and before long money was pouring into Merrick's coffers.

Not content to sit on his profits, Merrick immediately ladled the money right back out and used it to fund improvement after improvement within his model community. In early 1923, Merrick announced the upcoming construction of the Coral Gables business section, which was to line the newly built, 140-foot-wide

George Merrick's sales office in Le Jeune Plaza, Coral Gables. (Florida State Archives)

"Alhambra Plaza," and he began work on a garage and an electric plant, both built according to "the best Spanish design." Later in 1923, Merrick began the construction of an ambitious new Coral Gables city park, which was to include two waterfalls and a twenty-foot-tall diving rock complete with steps carved into the face. At about the same time, Merrick opened a nine-hole golf course, complete with a clubhouse. By the time the clubhouse was completed, however, Coral Gables had grown so much already that the structure was judged to be entirely inadequate for the needs of his model city, and Merrick plunked down an additional $60,000 to top it off with a second floor. Merrick's fondest hope was that Coral Gables would eventually become "Miami's master suburb," attracting the best and the brightest residents of Miami. By the end of 1923, he was fast approaching the realization of his dream; as we will see in the next chapter, Coral Gables would soon rise from the status of a mere housing development to become a nationally known real estate phenomenon.

Although the growing boom was most clearly visible in the outlying communities of Coral Gables and Miami Beach, metropolitan Miami benefited as well, and during the early 1920s the city registered quite impressive growth. The population of Miami, which had already topped 20,000 by 1920, shot up to an estimated 50,000 people in 1923, an increase of well over one hundred percent in only three years. If this surge of population growth continued, experts declared, Miami would reach 100,000 in 1925 and 250,000 by 1930, which would elevate Miami to the status of one of the nation's largest cities.

Other indicators also seemed to suggest that Miami was on the verge of greatness. Newspaper circulation increased by over one hundred percent between 1922 and 1923. Sales in Miami shops were up by nearly a third over the same year. Miami hotels reported a fifty percent increase in business. Inbound shipping freight increased by as much as seventy-five percent. Real estate and property tax revenue in Miami jumped up $4.9 million in a single year, which indicates robust growth rate of seven percent, and the pace of development was rapidly accelerating; real estate permits valued at $1.2 million were issued in July of 1923 alone.

There could be no doubt that Miami had entered into a period of dizzying, almost unprecedented expansion. Few in Miami disagreed with Warren H. Manning, a Miami-area architect, when he pronounced that Miami was destined to become the "big city of the South." Skeptics might have reminded Manning that exactly the same grandiose claims had been made about the now-struggling city of Key West only a single decade earlier, but there were precious few skeptics in Miami in the 1920s. With the possible exception of Commodore Munroe and his cronies in Coconut Grove, who continued to lament what they saw as the progressive mutilation of their beloved Biscayne Bay, nearly everyone in Miami had become mesmerized by the prospect of perpetual growth.

To ensure that this level of growth remained perpetual, the developers of Miami, Miami Beach, and Coral Gables all relied on innovative, high-profile publicity campaigns. Carl Fisher, for instance, did not rely solely upon the talents of Rosie the elephant; he also paid large sums for advertising, most notably for the construction of a lighted sign in downtown New York City that proclaimed in bold letters to cold-weary Northerners that "it's always June in Miami Beach." Not to be outdone, George Merrick managed to get William Jennings Bryan, the "Great Commoner" and a three-time Democratic Party candidate for president, to make his home in Miami and sell the aesthetic ideal of Coral Gables to prospective buyers. Bryan, who is today best known for championing the doctrine of creationism in the famous Scopes "Monkey" Trial of 1925, received $100,000 a year, and blocks of Coral Gables real estate, in return for the invaluable national publicity he brought to Merrick's "suburban utopia."

In addition to these more dramatic and visible publicity stunts, the towns of Miami, Miami Beach, and Coral Gables all made extensive use of print media to sell Florida to the American people.

Advertising the wonders of Florida was nothing new—in fact, the city of Miami had been running ads in Northern newspapers and magazines ever since 1916—but the scale of the Florida publicity campaigns reached dramatic heights during the early 1920s. Newspapers and weekly magazines in the North were bombarded by "news stories" written by Florida writers that contained no actual news, but were instead designed to introduce the dream of Florida into the national psyche.

The tack taken by these pseudo-journalists varied. Some announced that Florida was the land of the fountain of youth, a "pioneer" state endowed with unparalleled opportunities, where even an impoverished man could rapidly make his fortune. Other Florida boosters declared that Florida was a veritable Garden of Eden, a mecca for sportsmen, and the playground of the nation's most illustrious citizens. Nearly all Florida promoters agreed, however, that Florida was a land of unending prosperity, which would continue rather than fade with time. Many articles, in fact, loudly denied that Florida was experiencing a "boom" at all, and argued instead that the price of long-neglected Florida land was merely rising to its true value. A typical author of this genre assured his readers that "this is not a boom; Florida is just coming into its own."

According to one historian of the Florida real estate boom, these boom-time articles were characterized by a certain degree of conformity; Florida advertisers tended to rehash the same general arguments over and over again in a relentless effort to sell the state of Florida to the people of the North. This conformity resulted not from coincidence or from a lack of creativity, but from the operation of market forces combined with relentless peer pressure. One Florida reporter of the period complained that:

> If the editor becomes lax and forgets to shout [Florida's praises], he is reminded by the Secretary of the Chamber of Commerce. If he grows honest and declares that main street is a fright and that trash barrels should be kept in the alleys, he is instantly

damned as "anything but a booster." If he keeps it up, he faces a future barren of advertising and subscribers.

If a Florida newspaper was willing to be a team player, however, and "broadcast the virtues and splendors of its home town at the top of its voice" (as one commentator put it), then the rewards could be considerable. By 1925, for instance, the *Miami Herald* had become the thickest newspaper in the world, mainly on the basis of page after page of real estate advertisements; indeed, advertising in the *Herald* was in such demand that the editors had to turn away as many as fifteen pages of ads each day due to lack of space. Boom or no boom, Miami was certainly "coming into its own."

◎ ◎ ◎

By the mid-1920s, Biscayne Bay seemed to be on the very edge of greatness. Lured by the grandiose claims of the Florida publicity mill, Northerners were flocking into the state, and the Miami area was enjoying phenomenal growth. Only the long shadow of John Ashley still darkened the Miami area's otherwise unclouded skies. Imagine, then, the transports of joy which convulsed Miami in November of 1924: after a crime spree that spanned a decade, John Ashley's specter was finally and permanently exorcised from south Florida's sunny shores.

When last we saw John Ashley, the reader will recall, he had fled into a self-imposed California exile, hoping to lie low for a while following his father's death and his lover's capture at the hands of Sheriff Baker's men. As it turned out, however, Ashley could not bring himself to stay in California for very long. People who knew John Ashley well later said that, while he was out West, he had been "haunted by his father's moaning," and his inner demons eventually forced him to return to Florida in hopes of making Sheriff Baker pay for his father's death.

In the end, however, it was John Ashley, and not Baker, who

paid the final price. Tipped off that Ashley and his men were heading to Jacksonville, Baker set up an ambush at the Sebastian River Bridge, a little over 160 miles north of Miami. When Ashley and his men arrived at the bridge, they found it blocked with a chain, and before they could turn around their car to escape, six deputies armed with rifles emerged from concealed positions by the side of the road and approached the Ashley Gang's car from behind. What happened next is not entirely clear. Sheriff Baker later insisted that Ashley and his henchmen pulled out concealed weapons and opened fire, but some Florida residents sympathetic to the Ashley clan charged that Ashley and his men were handcuffed and then killed in cold blood.

Either scenario is plausible. Ashley, after all, had vowed never to be taken alive, and it would have been entirely in character for him to fight Baker's men to the bitter end. Sheriff Baker, in turn, had every reason to want John Ashley dead, since John Ashley had vowed to revenge his father's slaying, and no prison seemed capable of holding the elusive John Ashley. The truth of the matter will never be known.

Whatever the circumstances of Ashley's demise, his passing away on the night of November 1, 1924, seemed to bring Miami's era as a frontier outpost to a welcome close. For many, Ashley was the last in a long line of "dubious characters"—from Civil War deserters to the backwoods bandits of Prohibition—who had troubled the prosperity of south Florida for over half a century. Now that Ashley was gone, Miami residents assured themselves, the real boom could begin.

8

Castles in the Air

When T. H. Weigall, a young but ambitious English writer, stepped from his train onto the hot streets of New York City in August of 1925, a journey to distant Miami was the farthest thing from his mind. Weigall's avowed goal, rather, was to make a name for himself in the cosmopolitan city of New York, and he had come to America armed with letters of introduction from well-connected British acquaintances in order to accomplish exactly that purpose. As it turned out, however, Weigall's timing was terrible. New York City, he discovered to his dismay, was entirely barren of anyone of social consequence; most men with the means to do so had abandoned the sweltering summer streets of New York for the countryside and would not be back until after Labor Day. Since Weigall was suffering from what he called "financial stringencies of a very delicate nature," he simply could not afford to wait for their return.

So what would he do? Where would he go? While still mulling

over these questions, Weigall decided to squander some of his dwindling cash reserves on a ticket to the Ziegfeld Follies, an extremely popular New York stage show of the time. During that fateful performance, Weigall was struck by "a particularly attractive song . . . being sung by a particularly attractive lady, who was dressed for the occasion in black tights, a species of green waistcoat, and an immense black hat with a green feather in it." When writing later about his American experiences, Weigall acknowledged that this lady's costume "sounds completely revolting," but he assured his readers that "as a matter of fact, in practice it was rather the reverse."

Whatever the merits of her outfit, the lady in question loudly extolled the virtues of Florida, and immediately afterwards a back-lit scene dropped across the stage advertising "Biscayne Bay, Florida—The Eternal Summer Paradise, Where Work is No More." Soon after that, the lasso-toting cowboy comedian Will Rogers took the stage and "proceeded to tell an endless stream of semi-humorous stories dealing with the fortunes that were being made in Florida." Almost in spite of himself, Weigall was intrigued, and the idea of Florida began to grow in his mind.

Weigall had barely left the Follies that evening before being bombarded with yet more advertisements touting the attractions of Florida. "The first thing that caught my eye on the way home," Weigall remembered later, "was the great illuminated sky-sign at the corner of Fifth Avenue and Forty-Second Street, displaying an incredible tropical paradise with immense, brilliantly-lit castles towering among the stars." A few steps later, Weigall happened to notice a sign hanging in a realtor's window claiming to recount the "authenticated story" of a "young man who had made 500,000 dollars [in Florida] in four weeks by a judicious judgment of land values." This rags-to-riches story, Weigall discovered, was just one of hundreds which had deluged the newspapers and magazines of New York City.

Although not a particularly naïve fellow, Weigall came to the conclusion that "there must be *something* in all this; no matter how much the boom was a puffed-up affair, there must be *something*, at least, behind it all!" By the time he returned to his hotel room that night, Weigall had resolved to give Miami a try. He was pushed along in this direction by the precarious state of his finances: on the morning after the Ziegfeld Follies, Weigall had only ninety-three dollars left to his name, and the lure of easy money in Miami was irresistible.

His decision made, Weigall set out for the offices of the Clyde Steamship Company the next morning to book passage to Biscayne Bay, but found himself "blocked by a struggling mass of humanity," which apparently had come to the same collective decision about the attractions of Miami. By listening attentively to the rumors circulating through the vast crowd, Weigall learned that no berths were available on Clyde Steamships to Florida for at least a month, unless of course the prospective passenger was willing to bribe a Clyde official, an expense well beyond Weigall's meager means. Far from dissuading Weigall, however, the crowd at the steamship company only strengthened his resolve to go to Florida since the rowdy throng seemed to offer further evidence that "something pretty big" must be happening in the Sunshine State. Weigall then hurried over to the railway station, where his luck was better, and he was able purchase a ticket on an express train for the very next day. Although the train car he booked proved to be "extraordinarily uncomfortable," Weigall was carried onwards by dreams of Florida—it *was* the finest country in the world, the freest, the most wonderful, and the most profitable for its inhabitants! Completely won over by Miami's relentless self-promoting propaganda, Weigall could hardly wait to arrive.

After an interminable ride through forests, cities, and croplands, the train finally reached Jacksonville, Florida, where Weigall was stunned by the heat and the noise, but energized by the intangible yet omnipresent feeling of boom in the air. Once the train lurched back into motion, headed for still-distant Miami, Weigall noted that the Dixie Highway, which ran almost parallel to the FEC train line, was choked with an "endless procession of cars" carrying an "incredible assortment of humanity" in the direction of Biscayne Bay. From Weigall's point of view, it seemed like all of America, rich and poor, young and old, was pouring with the force of a biblical flood towards the promised land of Miami. At long last, after an agonizingly slow passage through the endless subdivisions north of the city, Weigall was thrilled to see the large buildings of Miami gradually emerging out of the thick tropical air, and following one final lurch, the FEC train shuddered to a stop in the Miami station.

No sooner had the train arrived, however, than it was set upon by a huge crowd of men who swarmed the train carriages like "a hive of angry bees," all carrying huge bundles of papers, all determined to sell Florida property to the newest gullible arrivals from the North. Having no money to spare on real estate, Weigell resisted the blandishments of the paper-waving throng and hired himself a taxi, which he directed to take him to a hotel. Within ten yards of the station, however, the taxi was stopped cold by the most awful traffic jam Weigall had ever seen, which "made the worst congestion of London or New York child's play by comparison." Weigall's driver tried to combat the gridlock with the liberal use of his horn, as did nearly every other car caught in the jam, which created a racket "better imagined than described."

After a harrowing journey, which included a fender-bender and the unwelcome appearance of a silk sock salesmen so insistent on selling his wares that Weigall had to eject him forcibly from the taxi, our intrepid Englishman finally reached his chosen hotel, only to be told that "it was out of the question to get any sort of room at all." A second hostelry did have a vacancy, but only at the exorbitant price of $7, which bought Weigall a single night's stay in a tiny and stiflingly hot room on the top floor of a second-rate hotel. The room cost Weigall well over a third of his remaining funds, but what did it matter? He had reached Miami, the city of opportunity, and surely it would not be long before he made his fortune.

A few hours later, invigorated by a much-needed bath, Weigall emerged onto Miami's sun-drenched streets to seek employment, and his first impression of Miami was that of "utter confusion." To Weigall's eye, accustomed as it was to the more sedate landscapes of Britain, Miami appeared to be a town composed entirely of construction sites, traffic jams, clouds of dust, and real-estate offices. Weigall eventually managed to find his way through the bedlam to the office of the *Miami Herald,* where he sought employment as a staff writer, only to meet with rejection. Nor could he find a job at any of the other three newspapers he visited that afternoon. Since Weigall had worked in newspapers all his life, and his qualifications for "any other sort of business were nebulous," this was a serious blow to his hopes for an easy fortune. Perhaps coming to Miami had not been such a good idea after all.

With nothing else to do, the dispirited Weigall set off in the direction of the distant lights of Miami Beach, which were by then winking invitingly across Biscayne Bay in the gathering darkness of the evening. After buying himself a curious American treat called a "hot dog," which was destined to become one of his favorite foods, Weigall dipped further into his dwindling funds to purchase himself a swim at a private bathing beach. As it turned out, the swim was just what Weigall needed; the warm and silky water calmed his nerves and restored his spirits. "Florida," he told himself while floating in the Atlantic Ocean, "was not such a bad place—it was rather wonderful!" Surely, he mused, he would make his fortune tomorrow.

Early the next morning, the refreshed Weigall set back out on his search for employment. Before mid-day, he had secured his first Miami job: selling lifetime memberships for the "International Yacht Club," which an entrepreneur by the name of Cyrus P. Morton was planning to build inside of a derelict hulk purchased from the United States government. Weigall, however, proved to be a poor salesman and was only able to dispose of one membership over the course of the next week, mainly because his "International Yacht Club" memberships were generally regarded by Miamians as nothing more than a scam. And indeed, they *were* just a scam: to Weigall's dismay, Cyrus P. Morton and his government surplus hulk disappeared one night from Miami, never to be seen again.

Following his disastrous career as a salesman, which left him with only six dollars in the world, Weigall decided that he was thoroughly sick of the "Magic City" of Miami. "At that time," he later wrote, "I loathed Miami, heartily and absolutely." In a fit of bitterness, he wrote a scathing letter about Florida to his friends back in Britain. Although he did not know it at the time, Weigall's diatribe would come back to haunt him later in his Miami career.

The letter might have brought Weigall the bitter joy of revenge, but it earned him no cash, and since he couldn't escape from this loathsome city without funds, Weigall resolved to tighten his belt and roll up his sleeves. In order to save money, he hired himself a "cot-bed" on an upper floor landing in a Miami Beach hotel for the sum of $7 per week; living in the landing meant that he was forced to "dress and undress in full view of a much-used passage," but by this time Weigall could hardly afford to be choosy. To earn the money needed to escape from Miami's clutches, Weigall secured himself a job the next day as a night shift stevedore, unloading cargo ships for the pitiful wage of 50 cents an hour. The job proved to be just awful—Weigall later learned that stevedoring in Miami was widely regarded as one of the worst jobs in America—and given the enormous weight of the cargo, the breakneck speed of the labor, and the baking heat of the subtropical night, it is remarkable that the bookish Weigall survived the ordeal.

After only one shift of stevedoring, Weigall resolved never to return, and on the next day, he secured himself a different blue-collar job, this time at a plant that manufactured cement blocks for the booming Miami house-building industry. The cement factory, however, proved no better than stevedoring, since the labor proved to be almost more than Weigall could bear. "To those who have never shoveled sand to the height of their shoulders, with long shovels, for five hours at a stretch, in the bottom of a shallow pit under a blazing tropical sun," Weigall later advised, "I do not recommend the experiment." Complain though he did, Weigall managed to withstand the rigors of the shift, and earned $5 for his efforts.

Unwilling face another dispiriting day of manual labor, Weigall resolved to take his hard-earned cash and "squander it on one last desperate effort to improve the situation." On the next day, therefore, Weigall slept in late and then made another job inquiry at the *Miami Herald.* To Weigall's disappointment, he was told once again that no positions were available. The manager at the *Herald,* however, did happen to mention that Coral Gables was looking for new staff writers—why not try his luck over there? Weigall was skeptical, but he had no other prospects, so he paid the 10-cent fare on the electric tram and headed into George Merrick's dream city.

Coral Gables, incidentally, had grown quite a bit since 1923. After the coming of the great Miami boom of 1925, sales in Coral Gables had skyrocketed, and almost overnight, the price of George Merrick's lots rose by as much as two extra zeroes: property that was selling in the hundreds before the boom was now valued in the tens of thousands. As his coffers bulged with cash, Merrick's dreams for Coral Gables became more and more ambitious. Merrick bought up hundreds of acres of outlying land, and decorated them with tree-lined boulevards, grand plazas, vast hotels, and at least one artificial mountain.

Although the scope of Merrick's projects became progressively more grandiose, Merrick did not compromise his aesthetic ideals, and he refused to approve any building that did not conform to his architectural vision of a "Mediterranean" community. According to Weigall, who later became an employee of Coral Gables and was thus in a position to know, Merrick believed that something worth doing was worth doing right the first time, and he "would allow nothing whatever to be done without lengthy committee meetings and interminable conferences." Coral Gables was just not a business to George Merrick, it was his life's work, his passion, and his masterpiece.

Merrick's consistent Mediterranean style of architecture probably did not please everyone, but it certainly impressed the young Weigall. Although Coral Gables was still just barely begun when he first entered the aspiring city, the work that had already been completed caught Weigall's fancy. "Everywhere," he wrote, "there was brilliantly-colored foliage and running water . . . houses stood back in their gardens, and even the offices, with their brightly-colored sun-blinds, gave an impression of being almost countrified. Everywhere there were dazzling colors—white walls, striped awnings, red roofs, brilliant greenery and the intense blue of the Florida sky." Weigall would eventually become somewhat disillusioned with the city of Coral Gables—he wrote in retrospect that Merrick's "insistence on conformation to type resulted in a tendency to weary and bewilder the eye"—but at first, Weigall found Coral Gables to be astonishingly wonderful.

Coral Gables was beautiful, but would it offer Weigall employment? The young Weigall no doubt approached the administration building with an anxious heart, but his fears were soon lifted by Mr. Yoder, the director of the Coral Gables news department, who immediately offered Weigall a position as a staff writer. From that moment onward, Weigall's experiences in Miami changed dramatically—"my poverty-stricken and hand-to-mouth existence of the previous few weeks ended for good and all . . . a boom is a much more pleasant thing," he soon discovered, "if you happen to be sharing in it." Weigall knew in his heart that the tide of his life had turned.

Weigall's change in fortunes, in fact, could not have been more complete. Several weeks before, Weigall had been lured down to Florida by the creative emanations of Miami's mighty publicity machine, which worked aggressively and ceaselessly to burn the idea of Florida into the national psyche. But now the tables had turned. His new job in the Coral Gables "news department," which was in actual fact concerned with propaganda rather than news, transformed Weigall into an organ of the same publicity machine that had lured him to Florida in the first place. Weigall had left the herd of sheep and had joined the ranks of the wolves.

The next few months were among the best in Weigall's life. He generally woke before six, energized himself with a dip in the

Atlantic, washed and dressed, broke his fast in downtown Miami, and eventually reached Coral Gables by eight o'clock. Once there, Weigall threw himself into his work, which he later declared to be "extraordinarily interesting, and never the same for five minutes at a time." After a normal working day in the office, Weigall rarely returned to his Miami Beach stairwell, but dined out instead with friends and co-workers, and then either went back to work until all hours of the morning, or else danced the night away. He got little sleep in the process—an average of only two or three hours per night—but as he later explained, "there was an electricity in the air which made sleep seem too futile a thing to bother about." During the boom, Miami was a city of frenetic action, not of rest.

Weigall's job, while at Coral Gables, was to write publicity for the city of Miami in general and for the Coral Gables housing development in particular, and Weigall soon proved quite adept at the trade. Whenever Merrick announced a new building plan, Weigall and his fellows wrote glowing copy and dispatched it through the news services to every newspaper in America on the same day. If anyone with the slightest fame, importance, or notoriety visited Miami, Weigall rushed to the scene for an interview, which was then quickly distributed throughout the country—assuming, of course, that the subject of the interview had favorable things to say about southern Florida.

What is more, Weigall's job in the Coral Gables news office only grew better with the passage of time. As he rose in the ranks of the Coral Gables organization, he was directed to write special interest news articles on aspects of Coral Gables life, an assignment that earned him a good income, near total artistic freedom, and a generous expense account. What is more, Weigall became a passionate believer in the dream of Coral Gables; he began to feel that he was "playing a part, no matter how insignificant a one, in carrying that gigantic enterprise to its conclusion." Weigall, then, had landed every writer's dream job: he had become a passionate and well-paid advocate of a cause he wholeheartedly supported. "I had no longer a care in the world," Weigall later recalled, "all my troubles were behind me." Biscayne Bay had finally lived up to the promises of the cabaret singer in the green waistcoat, and Weigall had at long last found his castle amongst the stars.

⑥ ⑥ ⑥

Although Weigall's account of the Great Miami Boom of 1925–1926 is exceptionally colorful, his experiences in Miami were by no means atypical. By all accounts, tens of thousands of people were flooding into Miami during the summer and fall of 1925, some to make money at real estate, some to enjoy the celebrated Miami climate, and some simply to see what all the fuss was about. Because of the influx, the population of Miami may have swollen to a quarter-million people by the summer of 1925, which represents a remarkable population increase of over two hundred thousand in a single year.

Like Weigall, many of these would-be residents had extreme difficulty in finding lodging, especially since they had to compete with the estimated 2.5 million temporary visitors who descended on Florida during the 1925–1926 tourist season. One reporter for the *New York Times* quipped that, during the Florida boom's height, the peninsula was "jammed with visitors from end to end and side to side," and the only topics considered worthy of discussion were real estate and "finding a place to sleep." Unable to find lodging, hundreds of hopeful new Miami residents slept in their cars, found space on Miami park benches, or else camped out on Miami-area porches, which enterprising residents rented out for as much as $25 a week. The situation across the Bay in Miami Beach was no better; Carl Fisher, in fact, was forced to house his legion of black hotel and construction workers in a small city of one hundred army tents. Considered alongside such miserable accommodations, Weigall's cot-bed in a staircase landing seems almost luxurious.

Why did so many people swarm into Florida in general, and Miami in particular, over such a short period of time? Historians who have studied the Florida boom point to a variety of causes. Changes in technology almost certainly played a significant role. Air conditioning, which helped to take the edge off of Florida's sweltering summers, was beginning to make an appearance in Miami homes and businesses. No less important was the new availability of mass-produced, budget-priced automobiles such as the Model T, which allowed even relatively poor families inexpensive access to the splendors of Florida. Wealthier travelers, who put more of a premium on speed and comfort, could voyage to Florida by means of the airplane; by 1926, in fact, nine Florida cities boasted airports, and commercial air flights to and from Florida were becoming an increasingly common occurrence.

Technology certainly fueled the boom, but other factors are needed to explain why the boom exploded so dramatically onto the Florida scene in the summer of 1925. Political decisions, such as the legislature's 1923 decision to eliminate the Florida sales tax, contributed to the boom as well. As far as Miami is concerned, random chance also played a significant role. On March 18, 1925, a disabled woman's electric hair cutter started a tremendous fire at the Flagler-built Breakers Hotel at Palm Beach. As a result, the resort town of Palm Beach was in disrepute during the 1925 tourist season, and quite a number of guests who might have visited Palm Beach opted to give the much-ballyhooed city of Miami a try instead.

The most important roots of the 1925 boom, however, are almost certainly psychological. According to the respected economist John Kenneth Galbraith, the Miami boom was just one manifestation of a much larger 1920s trend. During this period, Galbraith insisted, Americans displayed "an inordinate desire to get rich quickly with a minimum of physical effort," and Florida promoters capitalized on this sentiment by creating a "world of speculative make-believe," where great fortunes could be acquired effortlessly underneath swaying tropical palms. Although the boom was built mainly upon a foundation of hot air—namely, the bombastic utterances of the vast Florida publicity machine—it succeeded, for a while, since it was able to recruit a constantly growing number of new people with money in their pockets. What is more, the Miami boom did indeed make a few well-publicized people rich: those who earned a fortune in real estate and then wisely took their winnings off the table did in fact walk away far wealthier than when they arrived. As a result, many Americans came to believe that the Miami boom was more than just talk—as Weigall put it, "there must be *something*, at least, behind it all!"

Given the importance of good press to the Miami boom, the civic leaders of Miami were extremely sensitive to negative publicity and criticism, as Weigall himself learned to his dismay. Weigall, the reader might remember, had jotted off an angry letter to friends following his miserable failure as a club membership salesman, and unfortunately for Weigall, those friends had published his letter in a prominent London newspaper under Weigall's own name. When a copy of this Miami-bashing article made its way back to Florida, it precipitated a "tremendous row" between Weigall and his supervisor, who nearly fired Weigall on the spot. Weigall was only able to mollify his boss by claiming that, at the time of writing the letter, he had been under the influence of a sort of temporary insanity.

The Miami boom, then, functioned much like a pyramid scheme: so long as people were convinced that it was the real deal, and so long as an ever-increasing flow of new "prospects" rushed into Florida to push land prices ever higher, the boom generated vast sums of money for the people on top. If the base of the pyramid was not constantly renewed and expanded, however, the edifice of the boom would collapse like a house of cards. To prevent this from happening, real estate agents often resorted to half-truths or outright lies to attract the attention of prospective Northern customers. According to Galbraith, some real estate developers sold "seashore" property which, truth be told, lay a good fifteen miles inland. Other property was advertised as being "near Jacksonville," even though Jacksonville was actually sixty-five miles away. Still another developer advertised that his property was located near the "prosperous and fast-growing" city of Nettie, despite the fact that the city of Nettie did not in fact exist, except as a mere figment of the advertiser's imagination.

More respectable promoters of Florida real estate vigorously denied that anything like a pyramid scheme was going on in Florida: as one Florida booster insisted in a national economic journal in 1926, "the bubble will not burst for the very good reason that there is no bubble." In the meantime, however, the Miami bubble was being pumped ever larger by a new breed of professional pyramid-schemers who depended entirely on speculative transactions for their livelihood. Called the "binder boys" by their contemporaries, these gentlemen were nearly all outsiders to Florida who had ventured south expressly for the purpose of making vast fortunes in the real estate market. The trick to doing so, they soon discovered, was to purchase the rights to a property by paying a "binder" of ten percent or less of the property's value, and then find someone to buy the property for a higher rate, thus yielding the "binder boy" a substantial profit. The binder boy would then commit his gains to the purchase of a binder on a far larger property, and then resell it to a developer like George Merrick for greater profits still. As Weigall later noted, with more than a touch of envy, some binder boys were able to earn the fortune of a lifetime with only a single week's work.

Although definitive statistics are lacking, plenty of anecdotal evidence suggests that quite a few people managed to cash in magnificently during the Miami boom. According to Weigall, who knew them well, a "binder boy" might arrive in Florida with only $500, use it to purchase a binder on a property worth $10,000, and then sell it for $15,000, thus earning thousands in profits for a minimal initial investment. Such transactions were by no means exceptional during the Miami boom; Weigall, in fact, claimed that "this sort of operation was not only possible, but was actually for some months almost the normal way of doing business in Florida land."

Other stories about the boom suggest that even the minimal

starting capital of $500 was optional. One often-repeated legend of the period, in fact, held that an unnamed citizen "parlayed two quarts of synthetic gin into $75,000 in eight months." People with large amounts of starting capital could make more money still. According to Weigall, the great Carl Fisher purchased $8 million in property to the north of Miami Beach during the height of the boom, and then resold the property within two weeks for $11 million. "If this story is true," Weigall later noted, "as I have no reason to doubt, Mr. Fisher had made three million dollars in two weeks out of literally nothing at all!"

Although speculators and developers were the most visible beneficiaries of boom-time windfalls, long-standing Miami residents managed to reap fortunes as well. Those early pioneers who had purchased land for a few hundred dollars during the inaugural days of Miami found themselves able to sell it for hundreds of thousands

This Miami billboard advertises the sale of subdivision real estate lots during the Great Miami Boom. (Florida State Archives)

during the mid-1920s. A black man named John Givins, who had reportedly paid $250 for his land in Miami back at the turn of the century, managed to sell it for $175,000 in 1925. Although Givins' rate of profit was remarkable by any standard, other accounts of Miami-area land transactions seem to suggest that Givins could have held out for more. Another pioneer who had purchased his land for only $212 dollars in 1897 sold it for $250,000 in 1925. Still another plot of land, which had been purchased in 1914 for a modest $1,500, was sold for the princely sum $1.5 million in 1926, a profit of about one hundred thousand percent! As a result of these skyrocketing land values, old Miami land-holding dynasties, like the eccentric Brickell clan, found themselves rolling in cash.

Not all long-standing area residents were pleased about the dramatic increase in land prices around old Biscayne Bay, however. Commodore Munroe, for one, griped that the coming of the boom had spelled economic disaster for the residents of Coconut Grove, who had no intention of selling their beloved Biscayne Bay homes and thus were punished rather than rewarded by the rising value of their land. In his biography, Munroe noted of Coconut Grove residents that "the richer they grew the poorer they were," since the increased value of the land they inhabited forced long-time residents, most of whom were of quite modest means, to pay spiraling property taxes. Worse yet, Coconut Grove's residents were hounded day and night by speculators and real estate agents; one old resident, Mr. Gardner, complained that "I can't keep spec-ulators off the grounds, and no one is interested in any other sub-ject. It is in the air, like a fever, and there is no peace left."

In other parts of Miami, however, this real-estate "fever" was greeted with wholehearted enthusiasm, and lots offered for sale were snapped up within days, hours, or even minutes. According to boom legend, one Coral Gables subdivision was entirely sold out ten minutes after being put on the market. When the tiny, man-made islet of Fairisle in the lower bay went on the market in

September of 1925, $1.5 million of real estate was sold off within the span of four hours. Another housing development, Seminole Beach, was put on the market after a $300,000 initial investment, and was completely bought out in a few days for $7.6 million; not long after that, the first round of buyers resold the lots they had purchased for a total of $12 million. At about the same time, a four-hundred-acre property in Miami was put on the market at 8:30 A.M. and was totally sold out by 11:00 A.M. following a near riot, in which prospective customers literally threw $33.7 million in money and checks at the real estate salesmen. When the money was finally counted and the proper forms were filed, which took the better part of the next five days, the overworked sales staff discovered to their dismay that they had accepted more money than they had property to sell! In the end, a full $11 million would have to be returned to disappointed would-be purchasers of the Miami dream.

The numbers posted during the Great Miami Boom, in fact, are nothing less than remarkable. According to one estimate, Miami real estate sales in 1925 totaled as much as $1.75 billion dollars, the equivalent to over $18 billion in modern-day American currency. Sales and resales in Coral Gables alone accounted for $95 million of that sum. In order to administer this enormous volume of business, the Miami city government issued an astounding 7,500 real estate licenses over the course of a single year, and contemporaries estimated that the city of Miami, which had only fifty thousand residents in 1924, had three thousand active real-estate agents by the end of 1925. Thanks to the diligent efforts of these agents, Miami-area bank deposits rose from about $37 million to nearly $130 million from 1924 to 1925.

Although impressive, the statistics quoted above all represent transactions involving exchanges of pieces of paper, and a critic might point out that gains of this sort were mere ephemera, lacking in any real substance. In response to such a charge, a Miami booster would doubtless take the Doubting Thomas on a tour of Miami's numerous and busy construction sites. Between 1923 and 1925, the value of Miami building permits rose from $11 million to over $60 million, and only eight American cities—all of which were much larger than Miami—could boast of higher numbers. The number of miles of paved streets in the city rose by almost the same factor, from 32 to 420, over the course of that same period. During the high point of Miami-area construction, in July and August of 1925, no less than sixteen huge office buildings and major hotels were completed, and another fourteen large-scale projects were still under way. What is more, between January and December of 1925, a total of 481 hotels and apartment buildings were reportedly completed throughout the Miami area.

If these facts and statistics were not enough to convert the skeptic, the Miami booster would probably have taken the doubter down to Biscayne Bay and shown him the work being done on the "Venetian Islands," a small archipelago of man-made islets, each in the shape of a elongated oval, that Carl Fisher was constructing between the Miami mainland and his tropical utopia of Miami Beach. Carl Fisher, at least, was no mere paper-shuffler! Quite the opposite, in fact: Fisher was walking in the footsteps of the Creator, and at his word, dry land was raised up from the watery abyss. In the face of such breathtaking achievements, who could doubt that the prosperity of the Miami boom rested upon a foundation of solid, albeit man-made, ground?

Despite such sales pitches, there were still plenty of skeptics. The 1920s novelist Theodore Dreiser, for one, was quite unimpressed by boom-time Florida in general, and Miami in particular. In Florida, Dreiser complained in a December 1925 letter to a friend, realtors occupied "every third store" and dealt in promises of "clouds, rainbows & castles in the air & in Spain." In later letters, Dreiser expanded upon this theme, and heaped scathing comments upon the "swarm of realtors shouting about their subdivisions" that were thick upon the Miami landscape. There was beauty here, he admitted, though not yet to his taste: "In about 10 years," he predicted, "one might come back & find something—maybe." In the meantime, however, Dreiser was anxious to leave "this real-estate madhouse known as Florida," and eager to return to his home in "the chilly & unregenerate North."

By the end of 1926, Northern newspapers were beginning to turn against the Miami boom as well, in part because of a growing Yankee dismay at the vast sums of money being withdrawn from Northern banks for investment into Florida real estate boondoggles. Indeed, the Massachusetts Savings Bank League reported that a total of $20 million was withdrawn from its combined institutions alone for the purpose of Florida land speculation during the boom's height. To counter this capital drain, Northern newspaper editors cautioned their readers against the sinister designs of the Floridian "pirates of promotion," and predicted ominously that "the boom has reached such tremendous proportions that a terrific crash is inevitable."

Most participants in the Miami boom, however, paid little heed to such warnings. Indeed, conventional wisdom said that Miami was poised on the edge of greatness. Back in 1923, when the city population still totaled only about 50,000 inhabitants, people were already predicting that Miami would have 150,000 inhabitants by 1927 and 250,000 inhabitants by 1930, which (if realized) would have made the juvenile city one of the largest in the American South. Once the boom came, the people of Miami risked even bolder predictions. George Merrick foresaw that 100,000 people would soon live in his beloved Coral Gables alone, which would have earned Miami's "master suburb" a place of its own on the list of the nation's one hundred largest cities. Other Miami residents speculated that their city would soon become the hub of an enormous metropolitan area, over sixty miles long and several miles wide, which was destined to stretch from West Palm Beach to the Florida Keys, and which would rival New York City in both size and population. And why not? In Miami's boom-time atmosphere, where paupers could reap vast fortunes and land values could double overnight, anything seemed possible.

❧ ❧ ❧

In the end, of course, Miami failed to live up to these overblown expectations, and as 1925 gave way to 1926, the boom began to show the first signs of collapse. Land prices, which had been on a steady upward spiral through the first ten months of the year in 1925, finally began to level off in November, much to the dismay of the binder boys, who found that the perpetual inflation of real estate prices which had ensured their livelihood was a thing of the past. Soon after November, in fact, the binder boys began to leave Miami in droves, and Miami's permanent residents let out a collective sigh of relief; now that these parasites had left Biscayne Bay, it was widely believed, the city of Miami would settle into a period of slow but steady growth. But that didn't happen. Instead, Miami's real estate market entered into what boosters called a "lull," but which more objective observers recognized to be a recession. Investors who had purchased property in order to resell it at a profit were unable to find prospects, and were forced to dispose of the property for a loss. The boom was over, and the bust had begun.

The Miami bust, like the boom itself, defies simple explanation. The most obvious cause of the bust, as far as most observers were concerned, was the transportation crisis that paralyzed the flow of the city's cargo freight by November of 1925. Although commercial aircraft did make Miami a port of call in the 1920s, and automobiles were able to enter and leave the city via Fisher's Dixie Highway, these means of transportation mainly carried human passengers. Miami's freight traffic, on the other hand, was carried mainly by sea and by rail, and by November of 1925 both means of conveyance were proving increasingly inadequate. Although the arrival of Flagler's East Coast Railway had caused Miami's population to explode earlier in the century, this single-track line could not possibly handle the increased traffic of people, food, and building materials that accompanied the Miami Boom. As a result, by August of 1925, 820 rail cars were sitting on the terminals of Miami waiting to be unloaded, and another 1,300 were lined up on the tracks to the north of Miami.

In order to relieve this congestion, the FEC resolved on September 12 to "embargo" all non-necessary cargoes, such as building materials, in favor of needed staples, including both food and, more tellingly, newsprint—the Miami boom, after all, could not survive without constant and systematic publicity! By November, the FEC extended its embargo even to newsprint, and thereafter only food still flowed by rail into Miami. As it turned out, this embargo on non-foodstuffs was less than absolute, and some clever contractors found ways around the restrictions. According to one Miami legend, in fact, some particularly desperate building contractors packed their bricks on ice and shipped them to Miami as cargoes of "lettuce." Subterfuge of this sort, however, could not solve the underlying problem, and the railway embargo began to exact an increasingly heavy toll on Miami's boom-time prosperity.

Miami's railroad problems were aggravated by a similar and simultaneous collapse of the Miami shipping trade. Ever since 1905, Miami had boasted a deep-water channel into the Bay, and this avenue of trade was improved several times in the years before the boom. Still, Miami's unloading and warehouse facilities remained limited, and could not keep up with the unbridled growth that the boom brought to Miami.

By Christmas of 1925, in fact, Miami's harbor was choked with thirty-two ships that could not be unloaded due to lack of space and manpower, and another forty-odd ships were reportedly on the way. Some sea captains became so desperate to unload their wares that they anchored their boats next to the automobile causeway linking Miami to Miami Beach and unloaded cargo onto waiting trucks through holes cut in the hulls of the ships. Aware of Miami's difficulties, Carl Fisher offered to allow Miami officials to use Miami Beach's dock space for free until the congestion was relieved, but Fisher's assistance was not enough to solve the problem. Worse yet, in the midst of the crisis, the Miami-area stevedores went on strike for a 15-cents-an-hour wage increase, which further added to the backlog of ships. One imagines that Weigall, who had experienced first-hand the difficulties of their labor, felt some sympathy for the striking stevedores, though his memoirs on the boom are silent on this subject.

The Miami shipping industry was also hampered by the inadequacy of the Miami shipping channel, which proved in the end to be an even more serious problem than the lack of docking facilities. Since Biscayne Bay was serviced by only a single narrow shipping lane, the "government cut," even a minor mishap could block the channel for hours or even days. Weigall learned of this problem first hand one day in late 1925. On this occasion, Weigall had joined a delegation of prominent Coral Gables dignitaries to greet the arrival of the *Cuba,* the flagship of the Cuban Navy, which had sailed to Miami as part of a goodwill tour. Since the seas were too choppy to risk a rendezvous with the *Cuba,* Weigall and his fellows returned to port in their small motor launch, only to find the harbor entrance had been blocked by a "large-sized tramp steamer" that had managed to become "immovably jammed across the channel so as to make it quite impassible." The tramp steamer was eventually shifted through the united efforts of all other ships in the vicinity, but only after several hours of "yo, heave ho's" and what the somewhat prudish Weigall later described as "an incredible quantity of blasphemy."

On January 10, 1926, an even greater chorus of blasphemy filled Miami's harbor following the sinking of the *Prince Valdemar,* a two-hundred-and-forty-foot sailing vessel, at the mouth of the Miami sea channel. For nearly a month, the capsized ship brought all Miami-area shipping traffic to a standstill, and the FEC railway, which had serious congestion problems of its own, was unable to pick up the slack. The *Prince Valdemar* sinking all but paralyzed the Miami construction industry, which was heavily dependent on seaborne supplies; indeed, it was estimated that approximately forty-five million board feet of desperately needed lumber was stranded outside the harbor during January and early February of 1926. During this period, several construction companies nearly

An aerial view of the overturned Prince Valdemar, *which blocked the shipping channel into Miami for weeks and thus contributed to the collapse of the Miami Boom.* (Florida State Archives)

folded for lack of revenue, and more than a few major Miami-area projects were put on hold for the duration of the crisis. In particular, the construction of N. B. T. Roney's fabulous "Roney Plaza Hotel," one of the most ambitious projects of the period, was delayed for a full three months by the *Valdemar* sinking, and as a result, Roney was unable to make any profit on his Miami Beach hotel investment during the 1925–1926 tourist season. Roney later complained that this lost season proved even more disastrous to his finances than the bust of 1926.

Although the constriction of Miami's trade arteries was the most visible cause of the bust, other factors played a role as well. Increasingly bad press from Northern newspapers served to dampen Yankee enthusiasm for the boom. Word of mouth also dissuaded would-be visitors to Miami; many who visited Miami during the boom returned north with stories of overcrowded hotels and exorbitant prices, and their cautionary tales turned public opinion against the goings-on in Miami. In addition, the impending spring property tax deadline precipitated a panic sale of Miami real estate in March of 1926, as buyers who had purchased real estate only to resell it later suddenly found themselves faced with the prospect of paying hefty taxes on property they had no real interest in owning. In the end, so many Miami property owners proved unable or unwilling to pay taxes on their real estate that the city was forced to sell thousands of parcels of repossessed land at auction for a fraction of its former price, and this served to push down land values still further. By July of 1926, in fact, the city was finding it difficult to dispose of property that the general public had snatched up with wild abandon less than a year before.

The single most important root cause of the Miami bust, however, was psychological; just as the boom was fed by an over-abundance of enthusiasm, the bust was driven along by a progressive failure of nerve. As 1925 spilled into 1926, exhaustion with the frenetic pace of the boom had begun to set in, and the ever more grandiose claims of the Miami boosters began to sound increasingly hollow.

In his memoirs of the Miami boom, Weigall claimed that he felt his first stirrings of disillusionment during an interview with the esteemed Mr. Zeigen, a worldly and educated banker who was assisting in the founding of the University of Miami. According to Mr. Zeigen, the University of Miami was to be George Merrick's most ambitious project yet, and once completed, "Coral Gables was to become the Athens of the modern world, a center of learning and culture."

Mr. Zeigen's description of the proposed university beggared belief. At its center was to be a fifty-foot artificial hill topped by a hundred-foot tower, which Zeigen claimed would be visible from up to fifty miles away. This impressive spire, Zeigen claimed, would be surrounded by an enormous university endowed with "the finest libraries, the finest museums, the finest scientific equipment that ever existed." To take advantage of the gentle tropical breezes, each of the vast marble buildings of the university would be open to the air, but sliding plate-glass panels would shut them tight in case of wind or rain. As for the grounds surrounding the central buildings of the school, they were to be planted with "vast gardens" decorated with "shaded walks and marble fountains and canals wandering away into the woods." What is more, the faculty of this university was to be recruited from the upper crust of American and European scholarship, and Zeigen claimed to be in correspondence with professors, librarians, and administrators from across the world. "This is going to be," Zeigen concluded, "the greatest contribution to civilization that America has made for a hundred years."

At first, Weigall was entirely captivated by Zeigen's grand vision of the University of Miami, but soon after the close of the interview, skepticism began to creep into Weigall's thoughts. Drained by several months of sleep deprivation and overwork, Weigall was utterly exhausted, and he found it scarcely believable that such a gigantic undertaking could ever succeed. What is more, Weigall's British nationalism rebelled against the notion that this new University of Miami would "attain to even a remote particle of that almost holy eminence that belonged to such Universities as Oxford," and Weigall suspected that the upstart University of Miami, despite its vast endowments, "would always be a little crude, a little callow, a little young." For the first time, Weigall had lost faith in George Merrick's vision, and he was beginning to doubt the reality of the Miami dream.

After his disquieting interview with Mr. Zeigen, Weigall returned to his office in Coral Gables, where he typed his story and brooded through the rest of night. By the next morning, however, the shadows on his mind had dissipated, and he claimed that "I had become once again the [an] unshaken and enthusiastic believer." His faith restored, Weigall served out several more weeks as a willing cog in the Coral Gables publicity machine. In the meantime, though, doubts continued to gnaw under the surface of Weigall's mind. Finally, on one fateful morning in December of 1925, Weigall awoke in his cot-bed with a start, filled with the "absolute certainty that something had gone wrong."

Despite his apprehension, Weigall persisted in his normal daily routine, and eventually arrived at work, where he was "handed the usual mass of papers and sales contracts from which to make out the fanfare for the press." This specific ream of papers, Weigall discovered, announced the upcoming construction of a new Miami hotel, "The Towers," which would have been an accomplishment beyond the scale of anything yet attempted in Miami. The massive $9 million structure, Weigall read, was to have been built in the shape of a five-pointed star, and when completed, it would have boasted over eleven hundred rooms "all of a standard of luxury hitherto unknown." What is more, it would have featured a private waterway for yachts and steamships, a massive glass pavilion a quarter-mile long modeled after the Crystal Palace in London, and a built-in hospital wing with resident nurses, doctors, and surgeons. In earlier days, news of a project on such a scale would have caught Weigall's imagination. This time, however, Weigall was struck with the unreality of both this project in particular, and the Miami boom in general. As he later explained, "somehow the whole feeling of the place was different; something that was very faintly sinister seemed on that morning to have mingled with the air." Weigall continued to work dutifully for Coral Gables, but he increasingly felt himself to be a skeptical stranger in an unskeptical land.

The last straw, for Weigall, was the announcement of George Merrick's latest pet project, a "staggering" scheme that would have extended Coral Gables well into the Atlantic Ocean. Merrick's plan, apparently, was to blow up the entire Biscayne Bay seafront, dig out a deep-water harbor, and then use the residue from both projects to construct both an artificial mountain and a vast chain of islands stretching far out to sea. These islands, Weigall learned, would host a "whole series of hotels and casinos and palaces each one of which was to be the most magnificent of its kind ever built." What is more,

Merrick proposed to connect these man-made isles with "a great arc of illuminated viaducts five miles in length," thus making them accessible to automobile traffic. This new project was slated to cost "scores" of millions of dollars, and if realized, it would have made "everything else that had been done in Florida utterly insignificant."

Weigall helped his fellow "news" writers report on this latest Merrick undertaking, but his heart was not in it. "Even as I wrote," he later remembered, "it meant nothing to me . . . the pressure and the excitement which had kept me going during the last four months seemed suddenly to have gone, and I felt that we were all madmen." Weigall had finally come face to face with the truth about the Miami boom: that it was primarily built, not upon actual human accomplishments, but upon ever-expanding expectations—upon the rather naïve belief, not just in perpetual motion, but in perpetual acceleration. And now, Weigall realized, the entire affair was skittering towards collapse, since the grandiose claims of the Miami boosters were increasingly losing touch with reality. "There now came over me," he wrote, "the first feelings of real panic and the instinctive certainty of impending and unimaginable disaster. I felt that the whole thing had suddenly crossed the border-line of sanity, and that we were entering into a world where nothing meant anything any more." Whatever Miami's future might be, Weigall no longer wanted to be part of it.

Two days after his epiphany, Weigall decided to call it quits. He tendered his resignation that next morning to incredulous colleagues, who urged him to remain, and who regarded his decision to leave as "conclusive proof of sheer, stark insanity." Even the proprietor of a Miami coffee shop that Weigall had often frequented campaigned for him to stay in Miami, only to give up in frustration after a heated argument—"no use argufying wid an egg-head," the shop-owner eventually (and colloquially) concluded.

In the end, Weigall decided to leave Miami the same way that he had come, by train. As Weigall's Pullman car rattled northwards through the growing dark of a late December evening, he remembered that he could see no sign of life in the countryside around him—"Miami," he felt, "had disappeared utterly and absolutely, swallowed up in the night." The only lights he saw were the headlights of automobiles, headed (of course) southbound towards Miami, but eventually even they faded from view. After that, all that remained to Weigall of the Miami boom were the memories.

As 1925 gave way to 1926, departures like that of Weigall became increasingly common. True, many people still continued to stream into Miami; indeed, while passing through the Miami train station on the way north, Weigall crossed paths with the newest batch of "victims," whom he described as "fat, perspiring men," anxiously clutching their suitcases, blackened with "soot and two days' beards." In general, however, the tide had turned. Compared with the last year's tourist season, which had culminated in a summer's worth of boom-time excess, the tourist season of late 1925–early 1926 was quite modest. Since the boom depended on a constant flow of new prospects—or, as Weigall put it, "fresh grist for the mill"—the declining numbers of new visitors of Miami threatened to undermine the fragile edifice of the boom. The base was crumbling beneath the Miami pyramid, and the entire structure began to shudder.

Still, there is some reason to think that the Miami economy might have continued at a somewhat reduced level of prosperity after 1926 if outside factors hadn't disrupted the natural course of events. Real estate sales in 1926, after all, were marginally higher than in 1924. Admittedly, the numbers were down from 1925, but some in Miami rationalized that this was probably for the best—after all, 1925 was a freakish year, in which real estate had become a "gambling proposition," and most Miamians professed to be pleased that the realty market was now operating on a "saner basis."

Other signs also pointed to continued progress. Bank clearings, the boosters told their skeptics, were even higher in early 1926 than they had been in the first six months of 1925. Still more importantly, the construction industry continued to expand; although the total value of Miami-area construction for the first six months of 1926 was $1 million below the comparable numbers for 1925, the 1926 numbers were a full $3 million above 1924, which suggested long-term progress. For Miami boosters, such numbers were a sure sign that, despite the setbacks, Miami was still destined for a glorious and profitable future.

It is quite possible that the boosters were right, and that Miami was entering into a period of slower yet steadier growth. Alternatively, it may be true that Miami was on the verge of a fiscal catastrophe; indeed, that is the prevailing view amongst historians. Kenneth Ballinger, for instance, has argued that 1926 Miami businesses were "trembling on the edge of insolvency" due to the steady deflation of real estate values, and most historians who have considered the boom would probably endorse this view. Still, in the end, the point is moot. In September of 1926, the question of Miami's future was answered definitively by the coming of a ferocious tropical hurricane, which contemporaries described as the most horrific natural disaster ever to hit the United States and which all but wiped away five years of economic progress in Biscayne Bay. In the end, it took only a single day of hurricane winds to blow away half a decade of hot air.

9

Recurving Disturbance

On September 17, 1926, the perspiring citizens of Miami awoke to a stiflingly humid late-summer day, already hot in the early hours of the morning. Some Miami residents later claimed that, even as they arose from their beds, they were haunted by an inexplicable sense of foreboding. This feeling of unease was reinforced by the bizarre appearance of the sky; residents remembered that the overarching heavens had a luminous but sinister appearance and that the writhing mass of clouds which hung over Miami that day resembled nothing so much as "boiling gold" or "molten brass." As evening came, the natural pyrotechnics continued, and the sunset blazed with "outrageous colors . . . sprays of purple, orange, green, and gold flared and faded in the twilight."

These atmospheric phenomena were signs of dire times ahead, but few in Miami understood the warnings. For most Miamians, in fact, the 17th was a Friday like any other, and they reported dutifully to work despite the oppressiveness of the weather. If their city was in any real danger, most residents assumed, then the National Weather Service would surely raise the hurricane flags and give notice of the storm in the newspapers. But no such warnings appeared. The September 18th edition of the *Miami Herald*, for instance, which had been typeset late on the night of the 17th, admitted that a powerful hurricane was prowling about in the Atlantic ocean, but it assured Miami residents that the storm's path was "expected to shift due north or northeast as it nears the Florida coast," meaning that Miami would receive only a glancing blow from the hurricane. The *Miami Herald*, in fact, gambled that the worst of the storm would be over by midnight of that night and decided to refer to it in the past tense in the morning paper. "Little damage was done in the Miami harbor," the paper announced, as if the storm were already just a fading memory. Even as these words were written, however, the hurricane was angling to the west, on a path that would take it directly into the mouth of the Miami River.

Why were the residents of the Miami so complacent in the face of possible peril? Part of the answer lies in the psychology of the Miami boom itself. Although the boom was already sliding into stagnation, many Miami residents were still predisposed towards the same mindless, unthinking optimism which had characterized the height of the boom and which rendered the idea of impending disaster almost inconceivable. The fact that so many Miami residents were recent transplants to the Florida subtropics, and thus had little experience with hurricanes, almost certainly contributed to Miami's lack of preparedness as well. To make matters even worse, these greenhorn Northerners arrogantly assumed that they had already seen the worst that a hurricane had to offer. Less than two months earlier, Miami had been brushed by the edge of a late July hurricane, which had heaved up some impressive breakers, rattled a few Miami-area windows, and blown citrus fruit from the trees. As a result, most Miami citizens believed themselves to be grizzled hurricane veterans, entirely capable of withstanding the violence of a hurricane. The

"Magic City's" unjustified overconfidence would soon prove deadly.

There are many ways in which the severity of a hurricane can be measured. Meteorologists calculate the rainfall, barometric pressure, wind speed, and surge tides. Insurance adjusters tour the wreckage and tally up the property damage. Rescue workers count the injured, the missing, and the dead. Such statistics can tell us a great deal about the relative power of the storm. Numbers alone, however, reveal little about how people on the ground experienced the unbelievable fury of the hurricane.

Fortunately for historians, a number of people caught in the Great Miami Hurricane of 1926 survived to leave detailed eyewitness records of the fury of the storm. One such eyewitness was the Coral Gables construction manager L. F. Reardon, who watched the entire hurricane from his family home as it disintegrated around him during the height of the tempest. Another was Del Layton, who was destined to become a Florida supermarket tycoon later in life, but owned just a single grocery store when the hurricane struck in September 1926. The most vivid account of all, perhaps, was penned by the *Miami Tribune* reporter Al Reck, who became a main character in the story he sought only to chronicle, and who was obliged to perform acts of great heroism during the hurricane's height. We will return to the issues of wind speed and body count later in the chapter—and indeed, the 1926 storm posted some terrifying statistics—but first, these eyewitnesses must have their say.

If Leo Francis Reardon's later recollections are accurate, he spent most of September 17th barely aware of the coming of the hurricane. At four o'clock Friday afternoon, on the very eve of the storm, he left work at Coral Gables and played a carefree round of golf with a close friend from Boston. Reardon's lack of concern was due, in large part, to his serious underestimation of the danger posed by tropical hurricanes; as he noted somewhat dismissively in his memoirs, hurricanes "appear often down here this season of the year," and they rarely caused any trouble for Miami. Even late into the evening, Reardon remained blissfully untroubled by the approach of the storm, and eleven o'clock found him in his home discussing "the future of motion pictures in Miami" with friends from the North. By the time his friends left, however, the wind was beginning to rise, and Reardon realized for the first time that the storm might make a surprise appearance in Miami after all.

By this time, of course, it was far too late for any serious storm preparations, but Reardon did what he could, locking the windows and barring the double doors to the living room. At first, it seemed that these minimal preparations would be enough; other than a broken awning, which a shattered a window in Reardon's bedroom as it collapsed, Reardon's house suffered little damage in the early hours of the storm. By the small hours of the night, however, the wind had risen to a steady gale, and events took a more ominous turn. In a single moment, one powerful gust of wind tore every awning off the east side of the house, shattering several more windows in the process. Moments later, the power failed, and "we were left in the blackest dark I have ever seen." From that point onward, Reardon later wrote, he and his family were obliged "to do battle for our lives" against the terrific power of the hurricane.

After an unsuccessful attempt to pierce the darkness by striking a match, a task made hopeless by the gusting winds that were now ripping through the house, Reardon and his wife Deanie hurriedly dressed their children in the pitch-black night. But what to do next? Should they stay put in their damaged home, or brave the storm in an attempt to seek shelter elsewhere? As it turned out, the question was moot; when Reardon stepped out of his home, the bludgeoning winds of the hurricane hurled him several yards, and he was only able to get back to his front door by "grabbing the awning bars that were still fastened to the side of the house." Clearly, if Reardon could barely make headway against the storm by himself, there was no way that he could lead his wife and children out into the shrieking gales.

His decision made for him, Reardon hatched a new plan: he

and his family would wait out the storm in their automobile, which was located underneath the windward side of the house; Reardon's assumption was that "if the house came down it would fall towards the south and away from us." Getting to the garage, however, proved to be quite an ordeal. Reardon and his family first had to pass through the kitchen, but the winds were so strong that the kitchen door, once released from its latch, "shot back and was shattered against the electric range." In the end, Reardon and his family reached the garage only by crawling through the kitchen and laundry room on their hands and knees. Once there, Reardon piled his family into their sturdy roadster, and as an afterthought, he heaved an old mattress onto the sedan's roof. Perhaps, he thought, the mattress might soften the blow if the house were to crash down upon them.

Moments later, Reardon and his family became aware of an unearthly noise, a high wail "like the sound of an ambulance siren" which seemed to rise steadily with the increasing force of the wind. What could it be? "In my mind," Reardon wrote later, " I pictured a wall of water sweeping over the city . . . never have I heard a sound that froze one's young blood like that." Reardon was far from the only hurricane survivor to quail in terror at this horrifying wailing sound, which accompanied the worst winds of the 1926 Miami hurricane. Although the cause of this noise cannot be known with absolute certainty, it was most likely produced by vibration: the force of the wind in a class four or five hurricane is such that it causes any solid matter, including power lines, trees, and even house timbers, to quiver in place like a tuning fork. Taken together, these vibrating wails produce what hurricane historian Les Standiford has described colorfully as a "harmony of dread," and this baleful noise is usually described by survivors as one of the most terrifying aspects of the hurricane experience.

Whatever its cause, the nightmarish noise rose, dropped to nothing, and then rose again about ten minutes later. At almost the same moment, as if it had been waiting for the signal, a huge pine crashed to the ground only ten feet from the family car. Reardon and his family were nearly paralyzed with fear, "expecting every moment to be buried under tons of stucco and Cuban tile or swept away entirely." Not long after, however, the miraculous occurred; the sky began to lighten with the coming dawn, and the thundering winds died down to near total quiet. The Reardon family breathed a sigh of relief. "Thank God it was over," L. F. Reardon wrote later, "and we were alive!"

It had been an exhausting night, but Reardon decided there was no time to rest; in the aftermath of the storm, he judged, there would likely be a run on the food stores, and Reardon wanted to do his shopping before the grocery stores were swamped by the inevitable post-storm throngs. To that end, Reardon shifted the debris and wreckage from his driveway, tipped the mattress from atop his car, and set off in his roadster for town. "The scene of wreckage" in Coral Gables, he later remembered, "brought tears to my eyes . . . the beautiful foliage was laid low . . . [and] a few weather-beaten policemen were standing about the ruins of destroyed buildings." But Reardon had no time to mourn the ruin that the

A day after the end of the hurricane, many of Miami's streets remained under several feet of water. (Florida State Archives)

storm had visited upon the dream city of Coral Gables. His first concern was providing for his family, and after a search, Reardon finally found a single grocery store that was open despite the ravages of the hurricane.

Reardon did not record where he did his shopping in the early hours of September 18th, but it is possible that he patronized the establishment of young entrepreneur Del Layton, who was still only twenty years old in 1926. Layton had even less forewarning of the coming of the storm than Reardon since he was busy at work in his downtown Miami grocery all day on the 17th and didn't hear anything about the hurricane until he returned to the family home late in the evening. Even after his mother gave him news about the approaching weather, however, Layton didn't give the hurricane much thought. After all, he and his family had lived in Florida for thirteen years, and although he had heard tales of hurricanes told by long-time Miami residents, he had never personally experienced a hurricane's fury. As a result, Layton and his family retired at their normal bedtime of nine o'clock without having taken any precautions against the coming of the storm.

The hurricane did not let the Laytons sleep long, however. By midnight, heavy winds and soaking rain began to batter the house, and the roof began to leak. Soon after that, the storm flung a wooden board through one of the living room windows, and the Layton family began to have their first pangs of anxiety. These fears were intensified by the arrival of terrified neighbors who had fled their flimsier houses and were seeking refuge from the storm in the sturdy home of the Laytons. As Del Layton later admitted to an interviewer, the arrival of the neighbors, "rain soaked and near shock," caused "some of the fear . . . to rub off on us."

At around six o'clock, however, the winds suddenly quieted, and welcome rays of sunlight stole over the city of Miami. Relieved that they had survived the storm, the Layton family ventured into the streets to survey the damage. "Everything was wet," Del Layton later remembered, "and there were some trees and telephone lines down, but our neighborhood came through all right." But what about his grocery store in downtown Miami? Unable to restrain his curiosity, Layton left his family behind to begin cleaning up the mess, and set off for the Miami business district.

As he drove through the half-flooded streets, Layton noticed a lot of storm-blown debris, but little real destruction; billboards, flimsy wooden structures, and palm trees had taken the brunt of the damage, and most commercial buildings had survived virtually unscathed. There was, however, one notable exception; as he turned the corner on to Twentieth Avenue, he saw the ruins of a three-story furniture store that the raging storm had reduced to a "pile of match sticks." "For the first time," Layton later recalled, "I *knew* what a hurricane was." Layton's growing anxiety turned to elation, however, when he reached his downtown Miami storefront, which had gone "untouched" by the storm. Like Reardon, Del Layton imagined that he had emerged from the hurricane unscathed.

As for our third eyewitness, Al Reck, he was far better informed about the coming of the storm than either Layton or Reardon. It was, in fact, Reck's job to be informed; Reck was a reporter for the *Miami Tribune,* and the hurricane promised to be the big news of the day. As a result, Reck spent much of the 17th collecting what data he could about the storm's approach, but the information he ferreted out was contradictory. The local head of the Weather Bureau, Richard Grey, forecasted that the storm would veer to the north and Miami would suffer little more than forty-five-mile-per-hour winds. News dispatches from Jacksonville and Washington, however, predicted that the blow would be the "worst that south Florida had ever known." One thing was certain: the Bahamian island of Nassau, which had been struck by the tempest several hours earlier, had gone silent and was no longer communicating by radio with the outside world. Was Nassau's silence a portent of doom for Miami? Would the storm curve northward or would it plow directly into Biscayne Bay? Reck returned to his apartment that night still uncertain, his head swimming with questions. As it turned out, Reck did not have to wait long for his answers to arrive.

When Reck finally reached his apartment building late that evening, he discovered that the ground floor lobby was filled with tenants "gathered in frightened and wondering groups," all anxiously awaiting the coming of the storm. Reck decided to join them, and they listened together as the hurricane gales grew in intensity in the wee hours of the morning. At one o'clock, Reck later remembered, the wind was "howling and roaring like a hungry lion." By two o'clock, the "weather outside [was] as black as ink" and the wind began "humming like an elevated train." As if sensing the city's vulnerability, the hurricane chose that moment of deepest darkness to blow out the power, and Reck and his fellow tenants suddenly found themselves blind and trembling in the pre-dawn darkness.

For fifteen minutes, Reck and his fellow tenants waited anxiously in the pitch black, broken only by beams from a small number of flashlights with which a few clear-thinking tenants in Reck's building had thought to arm themselves before the coming of the hurricane. Then, with a horrible suddenness, the whine of the storm was interrupted by a "terrible crash." What had happened? An investigating expedition of several tenants ventured up the stairways to the third floor, "only to be met with a shower of brick and mortar." The roof, they realized, had been ripped clean off the building. Soon after, another terrific gust of wind made the apartment house shudder, and a terrible crash further jarred the frazzled nerves of the tenants; the now-unsupported walls of the third floor, Reck and his fellows realized, had crashed down upon the roof of the second. At almost the same time, the glass windows of the first floor shattered, and the lobby was filled with gusting winds and torrential rains. With the hurricane attacking the beleaguered tenants from both above and the sides, the situation appeared desperate.

Imagine the relief that flooded though the lobby, then, when

Damage–probably from the storm surge–in the Little River section of Miami. (Florida State Archives)

dawn finally broke and the winds finally subsided at six o'clock on the morning of the 18th. Reck emerged from the apartment lobby into a scene of devastation. "Looking around with fearful eyes," he later wrote, "all I could see were wrecked and ruined homes." Although many buildings were still standing, the storm-flooded streets of downtown Miami were "a mass of debris." Worse yet, the telephone lines were all down, which meant that Miami was now cut off from communication with the outside world. Since Reck was a journalist, and anxious to get word of Miami's disaster to the rest of America, the downed telephone lines represented a significant professional challenge.

With the phones out, Reck realized, there remained only one possible way to get word out of Miami—by radio. Before he could send a message, however, Reck had first to get to the radio station, which was easier said than done, since on the morning of the 18th "it was next to impossible to obtain any sort of transportation." The resourceful Reck, however, was able to cut a deal with the superintendent of a taxicab company, who agreed to transport him to the

Tropical Radio station in the nearby Miami suburb of Hialeah. Within minutes, Reck and the taxi driver were speeding northwards, "past scenes of ruin and desolation on every hand." Although the road was choked with fallen poles, trees, and telephone wires, the heavy taxi managed to smash through every obstacle along the way, and before long, Reck and his driver had reached the radio station—or what was left of it: the huge radio towers had been toppled by the storm and lay prostate on the ground. Reck realized, with a heavy heart, that no radio messages would be broadcast out of Miami for quite a while.

Reck did not have long to ponder his misfortune, however, since his journalistic attention was soon drawn to the human drama that was unfolding around him. Although one of the three radio station buildings had been smashed open by the falling radio towers, two others were still standing, and these solid steel-and-concrete structures were virtually the only buildings left intact by the hurricane in that area of Hialeah. As a result, the radio station buildings had become a magnet for those in the Hialeah district who had been displaced by the storm. "Tiny children were crying in the arms of their parents," Reck later recalled. "None of the refugees were dressed except in night clothes or clothing hastily donned. They were wet, injured, and miserable. One woman had her leg broken above the ankle. Another had a shoulder broken. One boy, about 12 years of age, was so badly cut in the leg by broken glass that we had to put a tourniquet around his leg." At least these poor unfortunates had one consolation—the terrible storm was over.

Or was it? Even as Reck helped to tend to the injured, the winds began to mount once again, though from the opposite direction. The storm, it seemed, had not ended at all, but had only been biding its time, as if to lull the people of Miami into a false sense of security. By 7:00 A.M., the hurricane had returned and was even more ferocious than before. As Reck later wrote, "the storm changed . . . [and] this time it was real."

⑥ ⑥ ⑥

In the aftermath of the Great Miami Hurricane of 1926, much was written about the deceptive calm in the center of the storm. Some survivors of the storm talked for years about the "second hurricane" which struck Miami shortly after the first, and one rather confused witness to the hurricane claimed that there had been three separate storms, each more destructive than the last. Still another commentator, believing that the hurricane had turned one hundred and eighty degrees in direction while passing over the center of the city, gave the storm the odd title of a "recurring disturbance."

In actuality, of course, the "lull" in the middle of the storm marked the passage of the hurricane's eye, which encompassed downtown Miami from roughly six to seven o'clock on the morning of the 18th. A few Miamians were aware that the lull was destined to be short-lived. The Miami Weather Bureau meteorologist Richard Grey, for instance, ran shouting through the streets of Miami during the lull, warning any who would listen to return to the relative safety of their homes. For the most part, however, the transplanted Northerners who made up the bulk of Miami's population were deaf to Grey's pleadings. Unaccustomed to Florida hurricanes, they assumed that the clearing skies and shining sun of the lull signaled the end of the storm. But the show was not yet over—Miami was merely enjoying a brief intermission, and the climax was still to come.

L. F. Reardon first realized that the storm was coming back while loading his car with groceries; in the course of only a few minutes, he noticed, the wind had risen from a moderate breeze to about 40 mph. Half-panicked, and fearing for the safety of his family, Reardon sped back home and made a frantic effort to lock windows, brace doors, and otherwise prepare his house for the return of the storm. By the time his rounds were completed, Reardon judged that the winds had reached 80 mph, and were still gaining strength. From his vantage point in the living room, Reardon watched with morbid amazement as the front door of his house, which was receiving the full force of the hurricane winds, bent and buckled under the pressure of the gale. As they mounted, the winds took on the sound of "hundreds of steamer whistles blowing at once." Then the gales grew stronger still, and Reardon heard once again the "terrifying siren-like moan" which had broken his nerve the previous night. Convinced that a tidal wave was about to wash over the battered city, Reardon and his family waited for the end.

At that dramatic moment, the large double doors of the living room flew open, "and the ripping, tearing hurricane found us." Reardon later estimated that the winds blasting through his living room must have topped 120 mph. Unwilling to give up ground to the storm, Reardon made an attempt to close the living room doors, and he actually managed to lock one of them into place despite the pressure of the wind. But the hurricane fought back. Before he could close the second door, the storm winds grabbed Reardon as if he were a child's doll and hurled him disdainfully into the air. Reardon landed painfully on his dining room buffet table, a full forty feet from the still-gaping living room doors.

As Reardon crawled back to where his family was hiding, he came to the conclusion that his house could not possibly last much longer in the storm, so gathering up his brood, he led them through the kitchen and down to the laundry room. Once there, Reardon and his wife placed their children in large slate washtubs, covered them with pillows, and stood guard over them against the ravages of the hurricane. Perhaps the washtubs would provide at least some protection, Reardon hoped, and might allow the children to escape the hurricane even if their parents did not—a possibility that seemed increasingly likely as the weather continued to worsen.

From their vantage point atop the washtubs, Reardon and his wife Deanie were able to appreciate the full power of the storm. They watched awestruck as the wind hurled heavy objects past their

Poor quality of construction meant that many Miami buildings suffered severe damage during the 1926 hurricane. (Florida State Archives)

home. "The air," Reardon wrote, "was streaked with garbage cans, automobile tops, doghouses, furniture, and parts of buildings." Rain fell in "white singing sheets," and the force of the wind inside the house was so intense that the glass on the kitchen door shattered with a sound "like the report of a gun." "Will this cursed storm never abate," Reardon asked himself, "or is it determined to decimate us and our beautiful city?"

Finally, after four more nightmarish hours, the storm began to subside. Reardon toured his house and found it all but destroyed. "What was a home," he lamented, was "now a scene of sickening desolation. Nothing was left. Those three words tell the story." Their house rendered uninhabitable by the storm, Reardon and his family gathered up the few dry clothes they could find, and set out for the shelter of the Everglades Hotel in downtown Miami.

The devastation they encountered along the way was almost beyond belief. Trees, poles, and telephone wires lay across every street. Roofs, torn from houses, had been deposited "whole and intact" several blocks from their original locations. Few people were to be seen, and those that they did spot were "either laughing hysterically or weeping." Whole sides of buildings had been shorn off by the storm, revealing "semi-naked men and women moving dazedly about the ruins of their homes." Most chillingly of all, "ambulances rushed in every direction," bearing the injured and the dead.

Finally, after circling the flooded downtown business district several times in an attempt to find a way past the water and debris, the Reardons reached the hotel. The ninth-floor room they were given was soggy, without running water, and without power, but the Reardon family didn't mind. After what they had seen and suffered, they were just thankful to be alive.

Unlike L. F. Reardon, who was caught by surprise by the "second storm," Del Layton had at least a few minutes to prepare himself for the return of the onslaught. When Layton arrived at his downtown Miami grocery, he found it untouched, but was surprised to see nearby shop owners frantically boarding up their storefronts. What was going on? "Don't you know anything?" the shopkeeper replied. "We're in the eye. We've got the backside of the hurricane to fight now." Although Layton did not quite understand the explanation, the shopkeeper's obvious anxiety convinced him that the danger was real, and he set out to make his shop as shipshape as possible.

Before he had finished, however, the hurricane returned. "The first thing I remember," Layton later recalled, "was the sound like a freight train coming down Twentieth Avenue." The storm came with such suddenness that the changing air pressure caused Layton's ears to ache, and before long, the glass windows of Layton's storefront popped as easily as soap bubbles, scattering broken glass throughout the store. Time to leave, Layton decided. The next time the gales moderated, Layton made a break for it and sprinted through the wind to the nearby house of Arthur DeCollins, from whom Layton rented the storefront. Layton found the old gentleman on his knees in prayer. "It's a little late for that," Layton told him.

Not long after Layton arrived, other neighbors began to arrive at the DeCollins' doorstep, abandoning their own poorly made houses for the sturdy, well-built DeCollins home. For the most part, these refugees huddled near the floor, but Layton was drawn to the window out of fascination for the unbelievable fury of the storm "I was standing there," he remembered later, "and the sight of the wind and rain wrecking things was strange and awesome. All of a sudden I saw the wind pick the roof off a nearby house and carry it away. It was done like you might pick up an ice cream cone and crush it."

Layton's awe at the spectacle quickly turned into dismay as he realized that the house in question contained a family with three small children. Someone, he decided, had to make sure they were safe! To that end, Layton joined with the other male refugees in the DeCollins house and ran through the gale and into the house next door. But the imperiled family was nowhere to be found; "There was nothing," Layton later recounted, "except the *whoosh* of the racing wind blowing over the open roof and sting of the rain beating down in the flooded room." Layton and his fellows were about to hightail back to the DeCollins house when they finally spotted the terrified family. All five of them, two adult women and three children, were "huddled under a small table in the kitchen—packed together like sardines under a table that wouldn't hide a good-sized man." Del Layton and his fellows shepherded them to safety, and the last hour of the hurricane passed without further adventures.

When the "second" storm was finally over, Layton returned to his store, or at least to the ruins of it. The windows were smashed in, the door was nowhere to be seen, and the store itself was gutted. "My heart sank down to my toes," Layton remembered, "to see all those fifty-cent cans of Maxwell House coffee floating down the street." Despite the scale of the disaster, Layton could think of nothing else to do than open for business as usual, so he gathered up the little merchandise that remained and placed it on the rain-soaked shelves or on the sidewalk in front of the ruined store. Within an hour, he was besieged with customers desperate to buy whatever foodstuffs they could find. "People would come up to me with a can with no label and ask me what it was," Layton told his interviewer, "[and] I'd look it over and render some sort of an opinion. Often as not, I'd just say that I didn't know, but that it was on sale!"

Layton's story of hurricane survival, thankfully, ends on a happy note. As Layton drove his way home that evening, it suddenly struck him that the family he had left behind during the calm might have perished during the second wave of the storm. But his fears proved groundless; his family was safe, and the family home was still intact. As we shall see, however, thousands of other Miami families were not so lucky.

In the meantime, back at the Tropical Radio station building in Hialeah, it must have seemed to Al Reck that he had stumbled upon the single most unlucky portion of the Miami metropolis. Since Hialeah was a rather poor district of Miami, the houses were of inferior quality and few were able to withstand the ravages of the storm. From the relative safety of his concrete enclosure, Reck watched with morbid fascination as the neighborhood of Hialeah was all but leveled by the fury of the hurricane. "Peering from the rain-clouded windows," he wrote, "I could see houses rolling along the ground like tin cans." At first, Reck observed the storm with the detached eye of a journalist. The force of circumstances, however, were about to oblige Reck to assume a new role, that of hero.

As Reck watched the storm, he became aware of the approach of a small human figure, crawling on its hands and knees in the direction of the radio station building. After an exhausting journey, the lone figure finally reached the station, and Reck realized it was a man of about sixty. The elderly gentleman pleaded for help. Nine people, he said, were trapped in a flimsy house only a block away, and one of them had a broken leg! Reck's taxi driver immediately offered his services. So did Reck.

The two brave volunteers ran out to the taxicab, which the driver managed to steer in the general direction of the threatened house, despite the battering wind and the sloppy muck of the rain-soaked landscape. After a short, weaving drive through the raging elements, they forced open the door to the battered house and quickly loaded the storm survivors into the taxi. At that cinematic moment, the foundations of the house finally gave way, and the structure, "in which the nine had been less than thirty seconds before, turned over and started rolling after the cab." It was almost as if the storm, thwarted at the moment of homicide, was making a desperate effort to strike out against its intended victims and their meddling rescuers. In the end, however, the taxi outran the rolling house, and the storm's death toll was reduced by nine.

Reck nearly paid a high price for his heroism. Soon after, as he was picking up a small child to carry him into the safety of the radio station building, the vengeful storm winds struck Reck with their full force. "The wind-driven rain stung like a thousand bees," Reck later claimed, "[and] it cut like a knife and tore my raincoat to ribbons." Just then, "a gust of extra heavy wind came swooping and bounding, picked my feet up and hurled me a good twenty feet and started me rolling." Luckily for Reck, he was able to grab onto a palmetto bush before he was swept too far from the station building, and he finally made it back to the station with the child after a torturous crawl on his hands and knees.

Reck's labors, however, were not yet over. As soon as he returned to the station, Reck learned that about thirty people were still caught out in the storm and had been "crouching in the palmettos for hours." Once again the taxi driver volunteered to help, and once again Reck screwed up his courage and followed. Their rescue efforts did not start well; almost as soon as they ventured back into the storm, a rogue gust caught the taxi driver and "hurled him high in the air." He recovered, however, and the two men eventually managed to find about thirty men, women, and children, all "blue and cold, in the palmettos, gripping the earth to save from getting hit by flying debris." One by one, Reck and the taxi driver herded these unfortunate souls to the refuge of the radio station.

At long last the storm subsided, and Reck finally had a chance to appraise the damage the hurricane had wrought on Hialeah. The Miami suburb, he decided, "was a picture of ruin . . . all around were buildings overturned or wrecked. Not a whole structure was standing." The Hialeah Racetrack, once a city landmark, was "ripped and torn." The nearby jai alai court was "shattered as if by a heavy bombardment." As Reck and the taxi driver made their way back to the flooded ruin of downtown Miami, he soaked in all these details with the trained efficiency of a news reporter. Despite all that had happened at the radio station, after all, Reck still had a job to do. Now that the storm was over, what Miami needed most were journalists, not heroes. It was imperative, Reck knew, that someone tell the rest of America as quickly as possible about the unprecedented catastrophe which had just befallen the "Magic City" of Miami.

MIAMI BEACH DURING THE HURRICANE WITH WATER WAIST DEEP AND WIND WHIPPING PALM TREES

Miami Beach flooded by the storm surge during the 1926 hurricane; this is one of very few extant pictures taken while the storm was still raging.(Florida State Archives)

As terrifying as these stories of hurricane survival might be, Reck, Layton, and Reardon at least had the luxury of facing the storm from the comparative safety of the mainland. The residents of Miami's offshore islands, however, suffered from even greater peril during the 1926 hurricane. At the height of the storm, the power of the wind and rain joined forces with the surging ocean, which was whipped up into crashing breakers by the fury of the hurricane. On the morning of the 18th, when the storm surge rose and overwhelmed Miami Beach, many witnesses must have wondered if the work of a decade would be undone in a day, and if Carl Fisher's man-made paradise would be swept clean by the angry tide.

In the desperate days following the Great Miami Hurricane, a number of survivors on Miami Beach penned stories of the storm, but few are as thrilling as the account given by Dr. George W. Woollard, the local head of the Coral Gables real estate office at Miami Beach. Woollard's office, before the storm, was luxurious to say the least; over $150,000 had been lavished on the interior decorations alone, including such fixtures as deer-hide chairs, antique lanterns, ornate hardwood desks, a Steinway grand piano, and two huge candelabra imported from a medieval Spanish cathedral. Woollard was reading an after-dinner newspaper amidst this extravagance on the night of the 17th when he received a telephone call from a Coral Gables colleague, warning him of the predicted storm. Woollard, however, was not worried; the July "flurry," as he put it, had done little more than dampen the rugs in his office, and he was confident that this storm would be no worse. Other than ordering his night watchmen to secure the doors and windows, Woollard did nothing to prepare for the approaching hurricane.

The Great Miami Hurricane proved to be far more than a "flurry." By ten o'clock, storm winds were getting "pretty high," and when Woollard went out to secure his huge Packard automobile against the storm, wind-blown sand "cut into [his] face like needles." Soon after, water began to flow under the doors of Woollard's building, and by midnight, this water had reached a foot in depth. At that point, Woollard decided he had better change from his day clothes into his bathing suit, and he even removed his watch and rings for safekeeping. As Woollard would soon discover, however, no place on Miami Beach was safe during the 1926 storm.

Not long after Woollard had donned his trunks, the lights went out, and Woollard was forced to light candles to illuminate the midnight dark of his private office. Then, "all of a sudden," Woollard heard an "awful crash." He opened the door to the outer office and saw that the front doors had given way, allowing huge waves to wash into the building, "carrying out furniture on their return." Horrified by the sight, Woollard rushed into the room in a futile attempt to close the doors against the storm, but he proved barely able to hold himself in an upright position against the power of the storm swells, even while clutching onto the outer office's walls. While Woollard strained against the riptide, "the remaining win-

An aerial view of storm damage in 1926 on Miami Beach. (Florida State Archives)

dows and doors crashed in at intervals until all were gone on the ocean side." Not knowing what to do, Woollard had decided to return to his private office when "a great wave came in from two directions, one from the ocean side and the other from Twenty-third Street, and a big bundle rolled up at my feet." The "bundle," as it turned out, was a policeman, who had been on duty outside the nearby Roney Plaza Hotel when he was picked up by a monstrous wave. This unnamed policeman would become Woollard's partner in survival for the rest of the ordeal.

After helping the hapless cop to his feet, Woollard led him into the office lounge, where the two rested for a while in armchairs near the only window still intact in the entire building. Soon enough, however, even that window shattered, and Woollard claimed that he could "feel the floor trembling" beneath his chair. At that point, the water "rose so high that the chairs we were sitting on were floating." Panicked, Woollard grabbed the policeman's arm and dragged him outside in search of more secure shelter.

For a brief moment after emerging from the building, Woollard and the policemen became stunned eyewitnesses to the full power of the storm—huge coconut palms and entire roofs of houses, Woollard later claimed, were sailing through the air. The two men had no time for sightseeing, however, and they searched frantically for shelter until they spied a building with a still-intact door. Success! Desperate for safety, the two rushed in and closed the heavy cypress door against the raging storm.

As it turned out, however, their place of refuge nearly became a deathtrap. At first, the level of the water was relatively low, but after a while it rose to waist height, so the two men decided to seat themselves on a wooden table. Not long after that, however, the water rose again, and pair was forced to stand atop the table and cling to an overhead chandelier in order to keep their heads above the water. Fearing for his life, Woollard tried to exit the room through the door, but he discovered that "sand and debris had piled up above the catch sash of the windows," thus entirely blocking their exit. Even if they did manage to escape, the two men feared they would be caught in the storm surge— "a raging torrent," Woollard remembered, "was racing by the windows carrying every thing in its wake." Escape, Woollard realized, had been cut off.

Just when it seemed that things could get no worse, they did. Woollard and the policeman watched in horror through sand-obstructed windows as the Roney Plaza Hotel's enormous swimming pool "split completely in two, releasing five hundred thousand gallons of water in one deluge." The effect, Woollard later wrote, was the same as "a dam bursting and carrying everything before it." The water in the room rose rapidly, until it was up to Woollard's chin, even though his head was already touching the ceiling. Desperate, Woollard resolved to attempt another escape as soon as the storm relented.

At about the same time, miraculously, dawn broke over Miami, and the storm appeared to subside. Woollard took advantage of the moment, and swam to a nearby closet, where he found a small window that had not been blocked by debris. Elated by his discovery, he returned to the policeman on the table, and the two men hatched a plan—Woollard would attempt to escape the building through the closet window and then rescue the policeman from the flooding room, while the policeman would come to Woollard's rescue if the storm tides swept him away. Woollard shook the policeman's hand, borrowed his pistol, and then set out to find a way out of this watery prison before it became a tomb.

After a short underwater swim, Woollard returned to the closet and, using the revolver, smashed open the window and the metal screen. He was free! Unfortunately for Woollard, however, the lull in the storm had passed, and he emerged from the flooded room only to face the full force of the resurgent winds of the hurricane. Woollard tried to hang on for dear life, but the wind "was now coming from the south at terrific force, making it difficult for me to retain my hold." At one point, the returning winds of the hurricane hurled Woollard across a courtyard and into a marble fountain, which he struck with a painful thud—after the storm Woollard discovered that six of his ribs had been broken. Despite the injury, Woollard eventually managed to make his way to the door of the room where the policeman was trapped, but found it blocked by an "exceptionally high" wall of sand. Luckily enough, however, Woollard happened upon a metal frying pan, which he used to dig the sand away from the cypress door. Moments later, the policeman was free, and the two men finally managed to find a safe shelter from the storm atop a mantle in the nearby courtyard.

After the wind and water had finally subsided, Woollard was shocked at the desolation it had brought. The beautiful furnishings of the Coral Gables office had been entirely washed away; even the Steinway grand piano, which had once been the property of the Emperor of Austria, had been carried off and smashed to pieces. The entire office complex was covered with sand, which in places reached six feet in height. What is more, the building itself had been all but demolished. "Floors of solid concrete and tile," Woollard later lamented, "had collapsed entirely, and some of them were carried as far as fifty feet away." Worst of all, "the huge front entrance arch of solid concrete standing forty feet high had fallen completely into the street." It would be awhile, it seemed, before Woollard would be able to sell any real estate on Miami Beach.

As for himself, Woollard was left destitute by the 1926 hurricane. His Packard was wrecked by the storm—it was later found half a block away, turned upside down, and completely buried in sand. Woollard also lost several thousand dollars in cash to the storm, plus jewelry worth $14,000, including the watch and rings he had removed, supposedly for safekeeping, at the start of the tempest. "Everything I had was literally swept away," Woollard complained, "leaving me with nothing in the world but a bathing suit." In one sense, however, Woollard was a lucky man; unlike many other Miami Beach residents, he at least managed to escape with his life.

Woollard was lucky in another sense as well;

although threatened by death at several points during the storm, he always had solid ground under his feet, and never had to worry about being swept to sea. Other hurricane survivors on the islands of Biscayne Bay, however, were deprived of even that small comfort. The Miami resident Gus Mitchell, for example, was caught by the hurricane while on Belle Isle, one of Fisher's artificial "Venetian Isles" built in the midst of Biscayne Bay. While traversing the island with a friend at the start of the storm, they were overtaken by surging waist-high water, and since it was pitch black, the two men feared to move, lest they accidentally step off the island and find themselves swept out into the open waters of Biscayne Bay. In the inky dark, without any landmarks to guide them, and without any way of knowing how close they might be to the edge of the island's seawall, the two men struggled for hours to hold their own against the force of the wind and the tide, which eventually rose to the level of their necks.

Finally, after battling the wind and current for what seemed like an eternity, the duo came upon a house, which (as they soon discovered) was already sheltering two women and a man against the storm. Their relief, however, proved to be short lived—ten minutes after they arrived, the house succumbed to storm surge and collapsed around them. Desperate to save their lives, the five refugees tied themselves together with bed sheets and "struggled out into the teeth of the awful wind that was by now crashing high waves over the island." According to Reardon's account of the Great Miami Hurricane, this storm-battered quintet "fought the elements for more than two hours, not knowing what direction they were proceeding or how soon they would be swallowed in the furious waters of the Bay." At long last, the storm began to subside, and in the first glimmerings of dawn, and the five survivors managed to locate a stronger Belle Isle home, where they found shelter for the remainder of the first part of the hurricane.

These five people were lucky to have survived the storm; after the passage of the hurricane, the first visitors to Belle Isle described a scene of absolute devastation. Belle Isle, however, was far from alone in its misery.

In the early afternoon of the 18th, survivors all over Biscayne Bay emerged from their storm shelters into a world that was drastically different than the one they had inhabited only twelve hours before. The flooded streets were strewn with debris and wind-blown wreckage, and many civic landmarks were damaged or missing entirely. Nearly every tree in the city had been toppled or stripped of foliage, and those that remained upright were bent in the direction of the "second storm's" winds. Dozens of ships, including several barges and large yachts, had been washed into downtown Miami during the storm surge and now lay hundreds of yards from the waters of Biscayne Bay amidst millions of rotting fish. Hundreds of people were dead, and thousands were missing. The power was out, the city water had failed, and with refrigeration fading and so

Miami automobiles driving past boats deposited far inland by the '26 storm.
(Florida State Archives)

much food now buried underneath ruined buildings, the specter of famine was rising over the city of Miami. In the words of one historian, "the miracle city that had been the center and pride of the Great Boom now lay flooded, battered, denuded of most of its vegetation, blacked out, eerily silent and cut off from the world."

In the bleak aftermath of the 1926 hurricane, rumors spread like wildfire. Miami Beach had been washed away completely, some claimed, and the dead were decomposing in "piles of thousands." As many as a thousand people were supposedly dead in the nearby development of Hollywood. Ft. Lauderdale had been utterly flattened by the storm, and hundreds lay dead under the rubble. Not a home was left standing in Coral Gables. The Everglades town of Moore Haven had been washed from the map by the storm-swollen waters of Lake Okeechobee. Typhoid had broken out in hurricane-smashed Miami. Or was it smallpox? And did you hear?—another storm was coming!

For the most part, these rumors were just that—rumors. But the rumor mill did have one fact right. Something terrible had happened in Moore Haven.

One of the first news reporters on the scene in Moore Haven was John W. Falconnier, a correspondent for the *St. Petersburg Times*. Moore Haven's destruction had already been surveyed from the air, Falconnier knew, and the observers had brought back reports of unimaginable desolation. But in journalism, there is no substitute for being there in person, and Falconnier wanted to see it for himself.

Just getting to Moore Haven, however, proved to be a harrowing ordeal. Falconnier was able to take the train from St. Petersburg to Palmdale, about fifteen miles west northwest of Moore Haven, but the train could go no farther due to damage to the track. Undeterred, Falconnier and his party set out on foot for Moore Haven, following the railroad grade underneath the scorching heat of the midday Florida sun. At first, the railway showed signs of only minor damage, but as they approached Lake Okeechobee, the damage to the railway bed bore increasingly clear testimony to the scale of the disaster that had overwhelmed the town of Moore Haven. In several places, the crossties had been washed out entirely, and Falconnier's party was forced to balance themselves upon "the swaying rails like a tight wire walker" over stretches of open water or "slimy black muck." Farther along, Falconnier discovered, the railroad track had been flipped on its back by the force of the storm, or else was missing entirely, forcing Falconnier and his party to press forward through floodwaters that might rise as high as a man's waist. And what water! It was, Falconnier reported, "polluted by the bodies of dead animals, the stench of which filled the air . . . dead snakes, rattlers four and five feet long, moccasins equally as large and a great number of non-poisonous snakes." Although Falconnier and his comrades were suffering badly from thirst, water of this sort offered few temptations.

About two-thirds of the way to Moore Haven, Falconnier's party happened across what was left of a Lake Okeechobee fisherman's settlement. A few houses still stood, but without roofs, and pieces of furniture were scattered haphazardly across the raised roadway, which rose mere inches above the level of the floodwater on either side. In the middle of the road lay the body of a ten-foot alligator, apparently killed during the hurricane. "When the storm is bad enough to kill alligators," Falconnier asked himself rhetorically, "what chance has a human being?" There were, however, a few live human beings about, most of whom had fled from Moore Haven during the hurricane and were waiting for the National Guard to give them leave to return to salvage what they could from their waterlogged city. After risking a drink of what they hoped was uncontaminated water from a half-filled water barrel, Falconnier and his fellows left these destitute refugees behind, and continued onwards toward Moore Haven, now only four miles away.

As they approached, Falconnier and his crew were heartened by the sight of rooftops and a water tower rising in the distance; something of the town, at least, had survived. Once they reached Moore Haven itself, however, this optimism gave way to dismay. Horrible water, befouled by animal corpses, was still several feet deep throughout the streets of the town. Although a few houses had survived intact, most structures had been reduced to piles of broken planks, and the stench from dead bodies still buried beneath the debris was almost indescribable. The town of Moore Haven, Falconnier realized, had been all but obliterated. "Moore Haven was," he wrote. "Whether it will ever be again remains to be seen."

What had happened? Survivors and rescue workers gradually pieced together the horrifying story of the Moore Haven catastrophe. In the months before the coming of the Great Miami Hurricane, heavy rains had swollen Lake Okeechobee nearly to the point of overflowing: over ten inches had fallen in both July and August, and nearly fourteen inches of rain had been recorded between the first and fifteenth of September. As a result, the lake's water level had risen to the dangerous height of eighteen feet, and the earthen dikes built on the southern bank were already straining to contain it. Even before the hurricane arrived, then, the overfull Okeechobee had become a disaster waiting to happen.

When the hurricane winds began to trouble the waters of the Okeechobee on the 17th of September, they produced a phenomenon that can best be described as a freshwater storm surge. The northeasterly winds of the "first storm" pushed the water almost completely away from the northeastern part of the lake, temporarily transforming lake bottom into mudflats and causing a perceptible upward slant in the surface of the lake towards the southwestern shore. Observers at Canal Point, on the northern edge of Okeechobee, reported that the lake floor, which was normally under as much as twelve feet of water, "lay dry for a considerable distance offshore." In the meantime, on the other side of the lake, sloshing waters piled up to a height of twenty-six feet along Okeechobee's southwest rim, directly above the imperiled town of Moore Haven.

In the early hours of September 18th, the citizens of Moore

Haven realized their peril, and the town's fire whistle summoned all able-bodied men to duty stacking sandbags. The defenders of the dike, however, were fighting an impossible battle, and by daylight the dike had begun to rupture, releasing what one witness described as "a six-foot wall of water." Panicked, the inhabitants of Moore Haven fled for their lives. Some reached their cars and motored away before the oncoming flood could overtake them. Others ran to their homes, but houses proved to be of little protection during the Moore Haven disaster. Battered by hurricane winds, and deluged with overflowing lake water, the houses of Moore Haven drifted from their foundation, smashed against each other, and broke into pieces.

In the aftermath of the storm, nearly every survivor had a nightmarish story to tell. One family's home was flooded to a depth of fourteen feet during the storm, filling the building all the way to the attic, and the family was eventually forced to chop a hole through the roof to escape the rising water. Another family was riding out the storm on top of their one-story house when it smashed into a two-story home; most of the family reportedly saved themselves by clambering into the two-story home through an upper-story window, but two family members died before they could scramble through the window as their house fell to pieces beneath them. Still another Moore Haven clan managed to keep their home on its foundations by opening their doors to the flood, allowing the storm waters to pass through the home rather than sweep the home away. As it turned out, however, this tactic entailed risks of its own. During the flood, a water moccasin invaded the home, apparently looking for shelter from the storm. Unwilling to share his family's refuge with a poisonous snake, however, the owner of the flooded house killed it with a broom handle.

Although Moore Haven's homes offered only dubious protection, they did at least provide their residents with handholds and footholds against the roaring floods. For those carried away by the freshwater surge, however, the Great Miami Hurricane proved to be a waking nightmare, and few survived to tell their stories. One who did was Mrs. Howell, a Moore Haven resident and mother of four. While her husband worked to shore up the dike, Mrs. Howell tied inflated inner tubes around each of her four young children to keep them safe from a possible flood and then bound all four tubes to herself using a pair of silk stockings. Whatever happened to her family, Mrs. Howell resolved, at least they would stay together.

When the floodwaters came, Mrs. Howell and her brood were swept out of their home and found themselves bobbing southwestward into the Everglades, propelled by the wind and tide through the howling storm. After an hour and a half, the currents changed, and the Howells were carried back towards the direction of Moore Haven. Relief turned to dismay, however, when they were swept into a storm-swollen drainage canal, and then dragged "through and over a barbed wire fence." The inner tube supporting Mrs. Howell's six-year-old son George was punctured, and since he was unable to swim, the child quickly drowned.

Stunned by the sight of watching her own son die before her eyes, Mrs. Howell refused to cut his body lose from her own, even though her own life was now endangered by the weight of her son's corpse. Soon after, Mrs. Howell's baby girl Eleanor drowned while still in her tube, since Mrs. Howell wasn't able to keep the little one's head above the wind-whipped waves. For two long hours, Mrs. Howell struggled to keep all four children with her, but her strength finally began to fail, and she decided at last to cut the two dead babes loose rather than risk the lives of her surviving children. Even then, however, she proved too weak to keep her oldest boy, Oliver, from being torn away from her by the unpredictable current, and Mrs. Howell watched despairingly as Oliver floated out of sight.

Finally, at four o'clock in the afternoon, Mrs. Howell and her one remaining child drifted near the house of the Steers family, where mother and daughter were finally rescued. The Steers tried to comfort the exhausted pair, but one imagines that the anguished Mrs. Howell was all but inconsolable after this night of tragedy. Thankfully, the coming of the next evening brought some small measure of relief to the decimated Howell clan—Oliver, who had been snatched away from his mother by the flood tide, had managed to ride out the storm on a raised ridge of land and eventually waded back to the ruined town after the waters began to recede.

Oliver's merciful fate, however, proved to be the exception rather than the rule; when Moore Haven's floodwaters finally began to drop, they revealed far more casualties than survivors. Although the Great Miami Hurricane's official death count at Moore Haven stands at 150, this represents only the number of bodies, badly decomposed and half-eaten by vultures, which rescue workers actually managed to pull from the muck of the Everglades. The real death toll was almost certainly far higher. The force of the water, which scattered bodies deep into the sawgrass of the Everglades, combined with the speed of organic decomposition in the Florida subtropics, ensured that many corpses were never recovered and melted forever into the swamps south of Moore Haven. Furthermore, the southern rim of the Okeechobee was the home of many transient black workers and swampland squatters, but since historians have little idea as to how many such people lived in Moore Haven at the time of the hurricane, there is no way of knowing how many died. As a result, a total death toll of 300 at Moore Haven seems quite reasonable, and contemporary estimates rose as high as 600 casualties. One fact is certain: a fresh set of skeletons had now joined the ancient Kreamer and Ritta island skull fields on the bottom of Lake Okeechobee.

In the meantime, about a hundred miles to the southeast, metropolitan Miami was beginning to count its own corpses, and the tally was appalling. According to the official Red Cross figures, 115 people were killed in Miami alone, in addition to 17 on Miami Beach, 26 in Hialeah, and 39 in the flattened suburb of Hollywood. As was the case in Moore Haven, however, these statistics record only recovered bodies, and they do not include the hundreds of people known to be missing and presumed to be dead. What is more, these statistics do not include the unknown missing, such as tourists and transients, who left little record of themselves in Miami before disappearing entirely during the ravages of the storm. As a result, the total actual death toll for south Florida as a whole may have approached 1500, though it is impossible to know for sure.

Why were casualty figures so high? In part, this grim body count can be attributed to the sheer fury of the Great Miami Hurricane, which contemporaries believed was "probably the most destructive storm in the history of the United States." During the hurricane, weather instruments measured sustained winds as high as 138 mph, and single gusts of wind might have topped 175 mph, which suggests that the 1926 storm almost reached the terrifying status of a class-five tropical cyclone. This incredible wind velocity was the highest ever recorded in the United States up to that time. During the passage of the storm's eye, Richard Grey recorded a barometric pressure reading of 27.61 inches, which also set a new U.S. record. What is more, the hurricane produced a storm surge that topped eleven feet along much of the Biscayne Bay shore. During the height of the storm, in fact, Miami Beach temporarily became ocean bottom, and downtown Miami was flooded several blocks inland by the wind-driven sea. Perhaps most incredibly of all, the hurricane pushed a massive fifteen-foot-tall wall of water up the Miami River, flooding all of downtown Miami alongside the river to a depth of four feet. These awesome storm tides managed to sink every single boat in the harbor and the river, with one bizarre exception: the *Prince Valdemar,* which had earlier jeopardized the boom by sinking at the mouth of Miami harbor, somehow managed to safely ride out the Great Miami Hurricane.

The ferocity of the hurricane alone, however, cannot explain the massive scale of the casualties produced during the 1926 storm. Hurricane Andrew, after all, packed even stronger winds when it made landfall near Miami in 1992, but only fifteen people were killed directly by Andrew's passage. What made the Great Miami Hurricane so deadly, in the end, was the near-total lack of hurricane preparedness in the young city of Miami. With the exception of the sturdily built homes of Coral Gables, which acquitted themselves quite well during the storm, most houses in Miami were of flimsy construction, having been clapped together quickly for rapid resale during the boom. Small wonder, then, that the air was filled with timbers, awnings, and broken pieces of houses during the worst of the storm. Worse yet, the thousands of Northern transplants who inhabited Miami had virtually no experience with hurricanes, and as a result, the return of the storm following the "lull" proved to be a fatal surprise. Many Miami residents were touring the storm damage, attempting to find loved ones, or even heading off to work when the "second storm" hit on the morning of the 18th. Other Miamians were caught while crossing the two causeways between Miami and Miami Beach when the storm returned; witnesses estimated that as many as forty motorists and pedestrians were washed off of the causeways by the "recurving disturbance." Others were luckier, and made a narrow escape from the causeways just ahead of the wind-driven tide.

Although Miami's hurricane naïveté helps to explain the high death toll, it does not excuse it. There were plenty of old-timers in the Miami area, including outspoken old Commodore Monroe of Coconut Grove, who could have been tapped for information concerning the realities of living in the hurricane-prone American subtropics. Indeed, Munroe had been complaining publicly for years that south Florida's developers were toying with disaster. What is more, Miami was blessed with a number of prime examples of responsible building techniques. Miami's older houses survived the hurricane quite well—even though many were mere driftwood shacks—since they had been designed with hurricane winds in mind. Sensible structures of this sort, however, were antithetical to the boom-time spirit of glitz and glamour that captivated Miami minds during the 1920s. Instead, developers specialized in showy, multi-story structures, with an eye to speed and profit rather than quality of construction.

In the aftermath of the hurricane, in fact, some critics laid the blame for the massive loss of life squarely upon the shoulders of the Florida real estate industry. According to Stella Crossley, who wrote a damning article for *The Nation* magazine several weeks after storm, realtors in Florida had made fortunes by gambling callously with human lives. "Florida is on the edge of the tropics," she reminded readers, "and hurricanes are to be reckoned with in the tropics. The best man can do there is to admit calmly to himself and others that such things are always likely to happen and to take such precautions as are possible. But in Florida," Crossley charged, "the realtor's cupidity . . . forbade this. So in a land where human habitations should be constructed for strength they are generally constructed flimsily for huge profits; and where the public should have a full understanding of the possibilities of such hurricanes and severe storms," she concluded, "it is considered sacrilege to speak of them." Florida developers, therefore, had put real estate profits before human lives, and the inevitable result was written unmistakably in "Death's black letters over Florida."

〰 〰 〰

Although the exact author of "Death's black letters" is open to debate, the impact of the Great Miami Hurricane on Miami's fortunes is not. In all, the 1926 storm inflicted as much as $75 million in property damage to the Miami area, a figure equal to sixty-four percent of the value of Miami real estate at the boom's height. Since few homes and businesses were insured, little was rebuilt after the storm, and as a result, the city of Miami entered into over a decade of profound depression. Land prices plummeted—plots that had sold for $60,000 in 1925 were now on the market for $600. Bankrupt developers abandoned their half-finished subdivisions, and jungle reclaimed the land. Not until two decades later, during the next era of expansion in Miami, would builders rediscover the streets and sidewalks of these lost housing developments beneath the dense subtropical foliage alongside Biscayne Bay.

In desperation, Miami boosters tried to put a brave face on the disaster, declaring the storm to be "Miami's wonderful hurricane," which had cleared the way for urban renewal in the Magic City. The *Miami Herald,* which was a virtual organ of the real estate industry, joined in the chorus of optimism as well, reporting that Miami would "continue her course of building to be a greater city than ever before." This new burst of hot air, however, could not reinflate the shattered bubble of the Miami boom.

Desperate to save their troubled city, Miami boosters turned to taunts and threats; the *Miami Herald,* for instance, reprinted the sermon of pastor R. N. Merrill, who advised that "persons who are so pessimistic as to believe that Miami will not rebuild a more beautiful, a cleaner, and a more righteous city than existed before the hurricane . . . [are] advised to take the first train north." To the dismay of the Miami boosters, however, a large number of Miami residents called Reverend Merrill's bluff and did exactly that. In the days after the storm, hundreds of homeless Miami citizens took advantage of an offer of free transportation by the FEC and boarded trains for points north, fleeing the physical destruction and economic desolation which the hurricane had wrought in Miami. As a result, Flagler's East Coast line, once the pulsing artery of progress for Biscayne Bay, was now the primary vehicle for escape by those who had lost faith in the Miami dream.

If there was ever any doubt before, there could be no doubt now: the Miami boom was over. Worse yet, it seemed that time was actually running backwards, draining Miami of its population and reducing the town to an earlier and more primitive state of economic development. Perhaps "recurring disturbance" was an apt name for the storm after all—except that it was the city of Miami, and not the hurricane itself, that suddenly reversed direction in that storm-wracked September of 1926

10

Poverty in Paradise

On a spring day in 1924, the New York novelist John Dos Passos was resting his weary feet in a small station of the Florida East Coast Railway. For the past few weeks, he had been bumming his way down the Florida peninsula, hitching rides when motorists were friendly and walking when they were not. On this particular day, though, Dos Passos was hot, thirsty, and tired—and he was ready for a change. When a train entered the station bound for Key West, therefore, Dos Passos decided on a whim to climb aboard.

In his later years, Dos Passos was very glad he opted for the train on that steamy spring day. Key West, he found, was like nowhere else in America, and Dos Passos loved everything about it.

The people, for instance, were a marvelous and varied bunch. Railroad men and old Florida settlers coexisted with Conch fishermen from the Bahamas and transplanted New Englanders, who helped give an oddly northern feel to America's southernmost town. Dos Passos' favorite Key West residents, however, were the Cuban and Spanish cigar rollers, whom he described admiringly as "well informed and often surprisingly well read," in large part because of the entertaining orations by the *lectores* in the cigar factories. Indeed, Dos Passos found that Key West Cubans "listened with avidity not only to the Socialist newspapers, but to the nineteenth-century Spanish novelists and to translations of Dostoevski and Tolstoy." And what is more, these literature-loving Cubans could cook: Dos Passos had fond memories of Key West's splendid little Spanish restaurants, all "well furnished with Rioja wine."

Dos Passos loved the look of Key West, too. He appreciated the simple beauty of the island's unpainted frame houses, nestled in the cool shade of "palms and pepper trees." Unlike the New York megalopolis he left behind, Key West sported few large structures outside of the old cigar factories and "a couple of drowsy hotels where train passengers on their way to Cuba or the Caribbean occasionally stopped over." Dos Passos even found beauty at the old abandoned navy yard, which boasted a pool of "deep azure water" perfect for swimming. "You had to watch for barracuda," Dos Passos remembered in his memoirs. "Otherwise it was delicious."

And the smells! Key West boasted quite a few, and all were exotic. Cayo Hueso's subtropical air, Dos Passos remembered, was often heady with the salty tang of the Gulf Stream. The Key West docks contributed other odors to the mix, including the pungent smell of fish and the odd aroma of green turtles awaiting shipment or slaughter in the Key West turtle kraals. The most sublime scent of all, however, was the "unbelievable sweetness" of the blossoming key lime trees that were scattered through the mangroves outside of town. The same mangroves were also home to predatory clouds of mosquitoes, however, so it was not advisable to linger long while enjoying the citrus fragrance of the limes.

For Dos Passos, then, Key West was paradise. The food was cheap, the lodgings were quaint, and the liquor ran freely—despite the passage of the Eighteenth Amendment five years earlier, Dos Passos found that no one in Key West "ever seemed to have heard of . . . prohibition." After a while, pressing obligations forced Dos Passos to tear himself away from Key West's pleasures, but in the years following, he constantly talked up the virtues of Key West to his circle of friends, inviting them to return with him to the "Garden of Eden" he had discovered at the end of the Florida Keys. One of Dos Passos' most appreciative listeners, as we shall see, was Earnest Hemingway, whom Dos Passos called "Hem," and who was fast becoming the most celebrated American writer of the age.

Still, though Dos Passos may have been only barely aware of it himself, there was trouble in paradise, and his glowing depiction of this island Eden ultimately conceals as much as it reveals. The cigar workers Dos Passos so loved, for example, were in reality a dying breed, the last remnants of an industry that was being throttled by competition from both large Tampa manufacturers and from the growing popularity of cigarette smoking, a nasty habit that American doughboys had brought back with them from the battle-fields of France. The turtles in the Key West kraals were a dying breed as well, quite literally, since unrelenting harvests had already reduced turtle populations to critically low levels. The abandoned naval yard may have provided Dos Passos with a nice place to take a dip, but its closing also deprived Key West's permanent residents of a vital source of income. And as for the unpainted Key West houses that Dos Passos so admired, these were left unpainted for economic rather than aesthetic reasons: simply put, few of Key West's strapped residents could afford paint.

Indeed, other observers of the period painted a far gloomier picture of Key West. Only a few years after 1924, one resident complained that "in the afternoons all the streets [of Key West] are empty and most everyone dozed behind closed shutters, as if daylight would expose our conditions." When night came, our observer continued, Duval Street became a "carpet of shadow," since the municipal government was too poor to pay to light the streets. Not that lights would have been of much use—"Everyone knew where everything was," our observer continued, "and there wasn't much of anything anyways." One Florida editorialist went so far as to claim, in 1934, that "Key West has been dead for fifteen years; the funeral procession had just been held up for someone to pay the undertaker." Scratch below the bright surface of Dos Passos' Key West, then, and you would find a city on its knees.

k k k

For many, Key West's decline into despair came as an unexpected shock. The 1910s, after all, had started on a positive note, with the completion of Flagler's Overseas line to the distant Florida main. Many Key West stalwarts assumed the rail line would bring prosperity, and in the short run, there were reasons to believe that it would. In 1912, the year of the railway's completion, Key West boasted a new electrified streetcar system, two movie theatres, and a population of twenty thousand, which was an all-time high. What is more, the town vas visited by a growing number of wealthy fishing addicts, drawn to the region by the fashionable fishing camp that Flagler had built on nearby Long Key. Key West also catered to a different type of addiction, gambling, which thrived behind closed doors throughout the town. Add in a generous serving of bootleg booze, which was still widely available despite official persecution, and you had all the makings of a tourist wonderland. Those in the know confidently expected that Key West, the "Queen of the Southern Seas," would boast a population of fifty thousand before the close of the decade.

Key West's hopes for rapid expansion were buoyed still higher by the coming of World War I. During this conflict, "America's Gibraltar" became the nation's foremost military base on the Caribbean, and federal authorities poured funds into the island city, building a barracks, a seaplane base, and even a blimp hanger. Between 1917 and 1918, a thousand military men swelled Key West's shops, theatres, and bars, and they gambled away their wages at cockfights, a Latin tradition brought to Key West by expatriate Cubans. For years after, both the citizens of Key West and the directors of the FEC remembered the war years as a golden age.

When the war ended, Key West erupted with joy. Soldiers and sailors ran wild through the town, stopped the streetcars, and jumped up on the stages of the movie theaters. In the meantime, daredevil pilots from the seaplane base buzzed the town; an observer present at the celebratory scene later remembered how the planes flew "down low over the street going straight for houses" before "suddenly zooming over barely missing them." One imagines that quite a few Key West residents were sick to death of the military on that day and wished good riddance to these rambunctious servicemen. If so, they soon got their wish. Almost immediately after the war ended, the government began to downsize its military operations in Key West, and within a year or so both the soldiers, and the money they had lavished on Key West, were fading memories.

The departure of the military from the island deprived many Key West residents of an income, but most people in Key West were not worried: after all, they still had Flagler's Overseas Railway. As they soon discovered, however, the railroad was a bust. Despite all the hopes of its builders, the railway brought little trade or tourism to Key West, and never turned a profit for the FEC—indeed, the Overseas never even earned enough money to cover the costs of its own maintenance. To the dismay of Key West, Flagler's attempt at immortality proved to be an economic disaster.

Why did the Overseas turn out to be such a dud? Part of the answer lies in the economic realities of long-distance trade. One of the axioms of the shipping business is that it is cheaper to transport goods by sea than by rail, since ships require less expenditure of energy than trains. Trains are faster, true, but international shippers generally make their money by keeping their volumes high and their costs low, not through speed. What is more, shippers who made use of the Overseas Railway would have had to pay to transfer their cargoes from train to ship, or vice versa, and that would have made the trip still more expensive. Even after the completion of the Overseas Railway, then, Key West had little to offer the shipping business.

The only cargoes that the Overseas could carry profitably, in fact, were perishable articles, where speed of transport *was* a significant consideration. One such commodity was Cuban pineapples, which had to be transported quickly to northern markets before they spoiled and lost their value. During the height of the Overseas, thirty-five hundred carloads of fruit passed though Key West every year, usually during a single eight-week period after the Cuban harvest. Another perishable product was pigs, which were in great demand in pork-loving Cuba. Still another was ice, shipped from northern icehouses to the overheated residents of the Florida Keys. Outside of these few articles, however, it made little economic sense to use the Overseas for international trade, even for trade with Cuba. You were better off just using a boat.

But what about tourists? Vacationers, after all, are a perishable article of a sort—tourists, like pineapples and pigs, are highly sensitive to the speed of their transport. And who was better equipped to cater to the needs of vacationers than the FEC, which had already built its livelihood on the Florida tourist trade? Even if other cargoes brought little profit, FEC officials hoped, Flagler's "Eighth Wonder" would pay its way through tourist traffic alone.

In the end, however, such hopes proved fruitless, as several factors conspired to prevent the Overseas Railway from carrying the vast throngs of tourists that Flagler had anticipated. Part of the problem was that the Overseas was not, in the end, a particularly fast railroad. The FEC advertised that "there is no change of cars between Key West and the Pennsylvania Station in the very heart of New York City," and this was true, as far as it went. But FEC advertising failed to mention the fact that the "Havana Special" actually made innumerable stops at miniscule local stations, each serving only a few settler families, as it crept down the line of the Keys.

What is more, FEC engineers were under orders to cross the Overseas' many bridges at the languid pace of fifteen mph, and during windy conditions, they were unable to cross the bridges at all—indeed, FEC policy prohibited trains from crossing the bridges entirely whenever wind speed topped fifty mph, not an uncommon occurrence in thunderstorm-prone Florida. As a result, what should have been a four-and-a-half-hour jaunt down the Keys often became a seven-hour ordeal, and some trains from New York arrived in Key West a full day after they were expected. Small wonder, then, that the Overseas Railway never became the darling of American tourists.

Even if the Overseas Railway had operated like clockwork, it is likely that the new-found popularity of the automobile and airplane would have prevented it from being a great success with travelers. As the glum and war-torn 1910s gave way to the roaring 1920s, Americans fell in love with their cars, and the nation's interstate roads, such as Fisher's Dixie Highway, were clogged with ever more vacationing motorists. Other tourists turned, not to wheels, but to wings. At the same time that the automobile was gaining dominion over the ground, commercial airlines began to conquer the sky, and south Florida was an American epicenter of this breakthrough; indeed, Key West was the original home of Pan Am Airlines, the nation's first international passenger air carrier.

As a result of this stiff competition from both roadway and skyway, passenger traffic on railroads began to decline sharply, and the Overseas Railway suffered accordingly. It is one of the ironies of history that the Overseas Railway, which arguably represents the pinnacle of American railway achievement, was completed just as American railroads in general were beginning to become obsolete. Although the line still operated regularly until its dramatic death in the mid-1930s, it became increasingly clear to Key West's residents that the Overseas offered no solution to Key West's problems.

As 1918 gave way to 1919, then, everything seemed to be conspiring against Key West's prosperity. The Overseas

Railway, which backers had envisioned as a bustling highway of trade, had proven to be a dead end. Key West's military installations, which once echoed with the footsteps of a thousand servicemen, now stood still and empty under the subtropical sun. And then, at that moment of greatest vulnerability, the hurricane decided to make yet another unwelcome appearance on the Florida Shore.

One of the first to notice that something was amiss was F. Addison, the supercargo officer of the large passenger steamship the *Corydon.* As his vessel passed through the Florida Straits on Sunday, September 7th, Addison noticed "a tiny black speck [that] appeared against the sun and then gradually grew larger." Once the speck finally chased down the vessel, Addison realized that it was a vulture, a bird with a sinister reputation. As Addison watched in dismay, the vulture spun in menacing circles around the *Corydon,* and then landed briefly on the spar of the vessel before ascending and circling again. "I knew something was going to happen to that ship when I saw that bird," Addison later claimed, "and when it kept following us mile after mile, I told the captain and the crew but nobody would listen to me."

Was Addison just falling prey to a sailor's superstition? Or is there any real science behind Addison's premonition of disaster? Historians of hurricanes have long recognized that animals often behave unusually in the prelude to cyclonic weather. Coastal birds seek the shelter of inland forests, ants reinforce their hills, alligators seek the relative safety of deeper water, and land mammals set out for higher ground. Indeed, the Seminoles were reportedly quite adept at predicting bad storms by watching animal behavior—when all the animals of the ecosystem begin to flee at the same time and in the same direction, the Seminoles knew that a hurricane was approaching and took the necessary precautions. It may be, then, that Addison's vulture was not so much an omen of destruction as a terrified fellow refugee, driven to the safety of the *Corydon* by fear of the approaching storm.

As it turned out, however, the *Corydon* provided no safety. Soon after the vulture made its ominous appearance, the weather began to worsen, and by the 8th of September the crewmen of the *Corydon* found themselves fighting for their lives against towering seas and wailing winds. Finally, at around noon of September 9th, "mountain-like billows" began to roll over the vessel, and the crew lost control. According to an account of the tragedy published in the *Miami Herald*, the vessel was first knocked to one side by the force of the waves, then swamped by another, which washed deep into the hold of the ship. When the flood of cool seawater reached the hot metal of the engine room, "the boilers exploded, finishing the work of destruction."

A few sailors survived, mainly through the efforts of Addison himself, who managed to cut a lifeboat free at the last moment and leapt aboard it with nine other men just as the *Corydon* was going down. Even after escaping the sinking liner, however, their own fate was by no means assured. "Three times the lifeboat was capsized and they were thrown headlong into the cauldron of smashing seas," the *Herald* article proclaimed, "but each time they desperately fought their way back into the boat and succeeded in righting it." Only one man was lost on the lifeboat, apparently due to insanity—he made no effort to protect himself from the waves, so was washed overboard and never seen again. The ordeal of the remaining nine survivors did not end until several days later when the keeper of the Fowey Rock lighthouse, located a few dozen miles southeast of the city of Miami, spotted their battered craft as it drifted by. Addison and his fellows are lucky the lighthouse keeper had a sharp eye; past the Fowey Rock light lay only open water and almost certain death by exposure and dehydration.

In the meantime, while Addison and his fellows were bobbing eastward in the Gulf Stream, the westward-tracking hurricane continued its deadly work. All told, the storm sank ten vessels as it passed through the Florida Straits, including the Havana-bound Spanish steamship *Valbanera*, which went down with as many as 488 people aboard. Twenty-seven more died on the *Corydon*, including the poor fellow who succumbed to madness. The hurricane then recurved northward and struck Corpus Christi, Texas, which was first inundated with the storm surge waters, and then sucked dry by the outflowing seas. As a result, many Corpus Christi landmarks were lost, dragged off of their foundations by the receding tide and deposited unceremoniously in the open waters of the Gulf of Mexico. It seems almost miraculous that only 284 Texans lost their lives to this powerful class-four storm, which is still regarded today as the fourth most powerful hurricane ever to strike the United States.

As for Key West, the Corpus Christi storm did not strike the city directly—the eye apparently passed about thirty of forty miles to the south—but as is often true of a storm of this magnitude, even that glancing blow packed an enormous punch. The winds of this slow-moving storm began to pick up in Key West on the early morning of the 9th, and they did not finally die down until late evening on the 10th, which means the beleaguered citizens of Key West suffered though an unbelievable thirty-eight hours of gale or hurricane force winds. At their height, these winds probably topped 110 mph, though it is difficult to be sure, since the same gusts also toppled the instrument tower at the local Weather Bureau station. To top it off, the Corpus Christi storm inundated the island with over thirteen inches of rain, and three drowning deaths were later attributed to the rainwater alone. As a result of this combination of wind, rain, and storm-surge flooding, virtually every structure on Key West was damaged, if not utterly obliterated.

Contemporary newspaper accounts provide vivid descriptions of the scale of the destruction at Key West. According to a headline in the *Tampa Morning Tribune,* "Terrific Wind Topples Houses as Though Stack of Cards," and the same newspaper declared that the Key West waterfront now resembled "a mass of shipping jammed together, with much damage to craft which remain afloat. There is a mass of interlocked fishing vessels, yachts, and other small craft." As for downtown Key West, "all the show windows in the stores on

Duval Street . . . were blown in and goods displays destroyed." Key West's already-fading cigar industry suffered the worst damage of all: "cigar factories sustained a total loss of over a million dollars, and cannot resume operations under two to four weeks." Even the boom-boosting *Miami Herald,* which normally had only good things to say about happenings in Florida, wrote candidly about the disaster which had overcome their near neighbors. "The waters receded today [from Key West] leaving the streets strewn with fallen leaves and debris," the *Herald* declared, and they guessed that the property loss would amount to "not less than 2 million dollars."

Indeed, the 1919 hurricane all but ruined Key West. In the morning after, Key West's citizens discovered that their beautiful red brick courthouse had been seriously damaged, that most of the still-active cigar factories were damaged or ruined entirely, and that the electricity would be off indefinitely, since the power plant had been demolished during the blow. Still, most Conchs expected the setback to be only temporary. Key West had suffered hurricanes before, after all, and had rebounded every time. Why should this time be any different?

As it turned out, however, this time *was* different. In the aftermath of earlier storms, such as the 1910 blow and the Great Hurricane of 1846, Key West had always enjoyed a solid economic foundation on which to rebuild. But in the years after 1919, the days of prosperity were over, and the citizens of Key West were forced to try to rebuild their lives upon a proverbial foundation of sand.

The statistics tell the story. In the decade following the Corpus Christi hurricane, the number of manufacturing plants in the city declined by over half, from a high of sixty-nine in 1919 to a mere thirty by 1928. During the same time period, manufacturing salaries dropped even more dramatically, from $2 million in 1919 to only a little over $.6 million a decade later. Most astoundingly of all, this decline occurred *before* the great stock market collapse of 1929, which propelled the entire nation into a decade-long financial tailspin. Even before the Great Depression further clouded Key

West's tropical skies, then, old Cayo Hueso was on the teetering on the edge of economic collapse.

Not surprisingly, many residents opted to emigrate from Key West during this troubled time, and sought their fortune else-where—some, no doubt, in the "Magic City" of Miami, where the boom was coming into full swing just as Key West's luck was turning sour. In all, at least five thousand Conchs and Cubans took a ship or a train to the mainland during the 1920s, never to return. It is one of the ironies of south Florida history that the Overseas Railway, which was supposed to restore Key West's prosperity, actually contributed to its decline, since it served as an escape valve for Key West's poorest and most desperate inhabitants. The temptation to step on the train in poverty-stricken Key West and then off again in the modern metropolis of New York must have been almost irresistible.

Those citizens who decided to remain in Key West did what they had to in order to survive. Prostitution thrived, as did lottery rings and other forms of gambling. If you had access to a boat, you might try your hand at smuggling in immigrants from Cuba, a dangerous yet potentially lucrative enterprise. Other Key West residents ventured to Cuba, not for immigrants, but for alcohol, which the Eighteenth Amendment had transformed into an illegal yet highly valuable commodity. During this period, in fact, Key West gained a reputation as a town where speakeasies abounded and where Prohibition agents ventured at their own risk. Even the Overseas Railway participated in the bootlegging business. Rod Bethel, a long-time employee of the FEC, remembered how quite a few tourists to Havana "died" while visiting Cuba and were shipped back by rail to Northern relations in sealed coffins that clinked and gurgled suspiciously when moved. Bethel even admitted that, while working the "Havana Special," he himself had succumbed to the temptation to smuggle a bottle or two of hooch. The dry-minded Flagler, had he lived to see the 1920s, would no doubt have been absolutely appalled.

Although booze, whores, and lottery tickets attracted a few

One of the Overseas Highway's wooden bridges under construction. (Florida State Archives)

thrill-seeking tourists to Key West, these illicit pleasures were hardly the basis of a respectable and sustainable economy. What was required, Key West's city fathers decided, was an automobile link to the mainland, which would attract some desperately needed vacationing motorists to the island city. To this end, Monroe County borrowed $2.6 million to fund an ambitious scheme: the construction of a combination roadway-car ferry link between Key West and Miami. Once the roadway was completed, tourists would able to drive their way to Lower Matecumbe Key, take a ferry across forty miles of water to No Name Key, and then putter along the last thirty miles to the city of Key West. It would be like no other highway in the world—and its very uniqueness, the city fathers hoped, would capture the imagination of tourists.

When the project was finally completed in January of 1928, the city fathers held a lavish ceremony to greet the first few cars from the mainland, in hopes of attracting the attention of the national press. Civic boosters proclaimed it a "red-letter day" in the city's history, and predicted grandiloquently that the road's completion would usher in a period of "unprecedented activity and growth," transforming Key West into "one of the leading industrial and resort cities of the state." One wonders if any of those present at the festivities recalled that many of the same unfulfilled promises had been made at the opening of Flagler's Overseas Railway, almost exactly sixteen years earlier. It was a new wineskin, but the same old wine.

Indeed, history would prove that this "Overseas Highway" was even more of a bust than Flagler's Overseas Railway. Some motorists were attracted by the road's novelty, but many soon regretted their decision, as the slow-moving ferry between Lower Matecumbe and No Name Key wasted at least five hours of precious vacation time—both going out and coming back. One imagines that quite a few ferry passengers on the way to Key West looked across the water with envy as FEC trains clattered over the Seven-Mile Bridge at the relatively brisk pace of fifteen mph. Next time, I'll take the train, they probably thought. Or better yet, next time I won't go to Key West at all.

In the end, the Overseas Highway probably did more harm than good to Key West's fortunes. With its industries failing and its tax base fleeing to the mainland, Key West proved unable to repay the loan it had taken out for highway construction, and the municipal government began to fall behind in its obligations to employees and creditors. On the day before the Overseas Highway's opening, in fact, the city council was forced to cut city worker salaries by ten percent, and six public servants, including four police officers, lost their jobs entirely. The city council hoped to restore these jobs as soon as the Overseas Highway began to earn dividends, but that time never came, and the start of the Great Depression less than two years later shattered the city's hopes of economic recovery. The Overseas Highway, then, proved to be a millstone rather than a miracle for the sinking island town.

The Overseas Highway did attract one tourist of some importance, however, whose mere presence on the island changed Key West forever. That visitor was the man Dos Passos called "Hem," but the rest of America knew as Ernest Hemingway.

◕ ◕ ◕

Hemingway first visited Key West in early 1928, on Dos Passos' recommendation, with the intention of scouting the place out and determining whether he and his wife Pauline could stomach the island town as a long-term residence. The Hemingways, after all, had spent much of the last few years wandering restlessly through Europe, so the idea of settling down permanently on American soil was an attractive yet somewhat intimidating proposition. Hemingway, you see, was not overly fond of America—he abhorred the glitz, the bustle, and the pretence of his native land. As it turned out, however, he needn't have worried. As Dos Passos noted, "The place suited Ernest to a T," and after a few weeks at Key West, Hemingway decided to make the place his home.

Ernest Hemingway spent much of his time in Key West drinking, fishing, and boating with his "mob" of friends; despite the island's distractions, Hemingway's years in Key West were some of the most productive of his career. (Florida State Archives)

Why was Hemingway so fond of Key West? Certainly not because of its wealth—indeed, Hemingway was far more aware than Dos Passos of the town's economic distress. In a letter to his editor, Max Perkins, Hemingway noted that "there was a penciled inscription derogatory to our fair town in the toilet at the [train] station and somebody had written under it, 'If you don't like this town get out and stay out.' Somebody else had written under that 'Everybody has.'" Hemingway, in fact, would later exploit the town's misery for artistic purposes: his 1937 novel *To Have and Have Not* chronicles the life of a Key West fisherman named Harry Morgan who is forced by hard times into running bootleg liquor and smuggling Chinese from Cuba. Over the course of Hemingway's dark tale, the ill-fated Morgan loses his boat to the law and his right arm to a gunfight, before being fatally wounded by Cuban Marxists while serving as an unwilling accomplice to a bank robbery. Morgan's dying words, uttered while in a fever-induced delirium, may represent Hemingway's attempt to give voice to Key West's post-1919 despair: "A man ain't got no hasn't got any can't really isn't any way out."

Hemingway may have sympathized with the town's troubles, but they didn't prevent him from having a grand old time in Key West. Before long, Hemingway became the ringleader of a tight-knit "mob" of close friends, including Charles Thompson, an affable young man who belonged to Key West's wealthiest family, and "Captain Bra," a Conch fishing guide from the Bahamas who might have been the model for the ill-fated Captain Morgan. Hemingway and his cronies amused themselves by drinking heavily at the local bars, fishing for tarpon along the Florida shore, and swimming at the old submarine basin at the naval base, where Hemingway perfected a combination swan dive/belly flop that his friends dubbed the "Hemingswan." Hemingway spent so much time enjoying himself, in fact, that some Key West residents decided that he did no real work at all: "Nobody believes me when I say I'm a writer," he confided to his editor. "They think I represent Big Northern

Bootleggers or Dope Peddlers." Small wonder that Hemingway, in his later years, would remember his Key West days as some of the best in his life.

A few locals may have resented Hemingway's freewheeling ways, but nearly all Key West residents were deeply thankful for his royalty money. In 1930, Hemingway was still not yet a full-time resident of Key West, but that did not stop him from spending up to $1,200 a month in Key West—a sum equal to that earned by the average American family for an entire year's work. Following Hemingway's purchase of a stately old house on the corner of Whitehead and Division in the spring of 1931, even more Hemingway family money found its way into the needy hands of Key West's indigent citizens. And then there was the income earned from feeding, housing, and entertaining Hemingway's many friends and admirers, who arrived from the mainland in a steady stream. By the mid-1930s, therefore, catering to the needs of Ernest and his hangers-on had become a significant part of Key West's economy.

In the meantime, at the other end of the Overseas Highway, the city of Miami gained a sugar daddy of its own at almost exactly the same time: "Scarface" Al Capone, the legendary boss of the Chicago crime syndicate. Capone bought a house on Miami Beach in 1928 and soon transformed it into a veritable fortress, protected by high walls and staffed by twenty well-armed bodyguards. In the process, Capone injected much-needed money into the stagnant Miami economy, but unlike Hemingway, Capone received little praise for his financial contribution. Indeed, soon after he arrived, the city fathers of Miami launched a legal crusade to expel him from Miami's sunny shores. One of the most vocal of Capone's opponents was none other than Carl Fisher, who had been ruined by the collapse of the Miami boom, but who nonetheless still carried a lot of moral weight in post-boom Miami. Not surprisingly, given Fisher's history as a real estate developer, one of Fisher's chief complaints about "Citizen Al" was that his mere presence on

Al Capone (right) and his ill-gotten wealth stirred up a great deal of controversy in his new hometown of Miami Beach. (Florida State Archives)

the Beach dragged down property values.

The campaign against Capone eventually collapsed, however, largely because Capone's money ended up speaking with a louder voice than Capone's opponents. As one Florida historian has noted, "restaurants, ice houses, haberdashers and florists all seemed to flourish when Capone and his entourage were around. His arrival was accompanied by civic outrage and by the jingle of cash registers." When the case against Capone finally came to court, it rapidly became clear that nearly all of his detractors had actually done business with Capone at some time or another, or else had attended one of the lavish parties at Capone's Miami Beach estate. As the judge trying the case acidly observed, "if a community is embarrassed by the mere presence of an individual, it certainly does not have to deal with him either socially or in business. . . . However, to some," the judge concluded, "the smell of money is good, regardless from whence it cometh." In the hard times following the Great Miami Hurricane, the lure of Chicago Al and his ill-gotten millions proved almost irresistible.

In the meantime, while the court case against Capone lurched towards its absurd conclusion, the city of Miami itself sank to new depths. Hotels stood empty, and good jobs became nearly impossible to find—the only positions available were in sales, and all of those were on commission. The University of Miami, which had been founded with such high hopes during the Great Miami boom, was forced to abolish four departments and reduce its staff to a bare minimum just to keep afloat. During these days of deprivation and want, in fact, quite a few Miami residents relied on fruit trees, many of which had been originally planted for ornamental purposes, to fill their bellies on a day-to-day basis. Although few were aware of it, some Depression-era Miamians probably owed their lives to the soursops, Barbados cherries, and key limes that early Bahamian settlers had brought with them to Biscayne Bay a century earlier.

As the Depression deepened, Miami's residents hoped desperately for the return of better days, and local newspapers such as the *Miami Tribune* featured optimistic headlines such as "Rush of Florida Tourists Heralds Record Season." But wishing wouldn't make it so, and cruel reality kept spoiling the best efforts of the Miami boosters. Only four days after predicting a tourist bonanza, for instance, the same newspaper was obliged to print a headline declaring, "Tent City for Idle Vetoed by County." The county commissioners of Miami, the paper proclaimed, were unwilling to publicize the fact that "there are so many unemployed here that they have to be housed in tents." Willful inaction in the face of human misery, however, was hardly likely to bring better days to the city on Biscayne Bay.

If things were bad in Miami, they were even worse in Key West. As the troubled 1920s gave way to the nightmarish 1930s, unemployment in Key West reached epidemic levels: by the mid-1930s, in fact, as many as 6,000 people were without a job, and no less than eighty percent of the city's 11,600 inhabitants relied on government relief. While Miami's citizens scrounged for fruit to survive, Key West residents subsisted on coconuts and fish, and according to one observer, some residents were reduced to shooting the island's songbirds in their quest for food. As in Miami, the newspapers clung desperately to any scrap of good news: the January 31, 1935, issue of the *Key West Citizen,* for instance, printed headlines praising even the smallest civic accomplishments, such as "Missouri Folk Enjoy Sojourn" and "Visitors Enjoy Fishing Outings." If you read past the front pages, however, you could catch revealing glimpses of Key West's plight. In the very same issue, the *Citizen* printed an article entitled "Lack of Food Brings Tramp Back to Jail."

As time went on, in fact, "tramps" became an increasingly frequent feature of life in Key West. Some were drifters and hoboes who hopped the trains to Key West every winter to escape the bitter winds of the frigid North. A larger number, however, were veterans of the First World War—the so-called bonus marchers—who had been exiled to Florida by President Roosevelt and had been put to work building the roadway that would eventually become U.S. 1. Back in 1924, these veterans had been promised a substantial "bonus," payable in twenty years, in return for their admirable service in the Great War. By 1932, however, many of these veterans found themselves in desperate need of cash, so they pleaded for early payment of their promised bonus. When fiscally conservative President Hoover refused to comply, veterans from all over the country descended on Washington to protest his decision, and by June of 1932, as many as twenty thousand veterans and their families were living in Washington-area "bonus camps." Spooked by the threat of insurrection, Hoover overreacted and ordered Army Chief of Staff Douglas MacArthur to disperse the camps with armed force. The result was a political fiasco. Newspaper readers opened their papers on July 30th to stories of unarmed men and women fleeing from tanks and tear gas. By the time the smoke cleared, Hoover was politically dead, and Roosevelt easily ascended to the presidency in the 1932 elections.

Hoover had cleared the camps, but the bonus issue remained, and Roosevelt wanted to make sure that the bonus marchers did not destroy his presidency as they had that of his predecessor. To that end, Roosevelt promised the bonus marchers regular jobs and good pay in various government-run work camps—camps which, coincidentally enough, were all hundreds of miles away from the politically sensitive environs of Washington D.C. As a result, by the mid-1930s, several thousand veterans of the Great War ended up living and working on the upper Florida Keys.

By all accounts, these unfortunate ex-servicemen led miserable lives—not unlike those of the FEC workers who had built the Overseas Railway four decades before. The camps they inhabited were hot, crowded, unlit, and uncomfortable. Fresh water was available for drinking, but not for bathing, and sanitation was virtually nonexistent. And as always on the Florida Keys, mosquitoes were a constant torment. Small wonder, then, that these veterans relished the opportunity to abandon the camps each weekend in favor of the bars and brothels of Miami and Key West.

The citizens of Key West appreciated the bonus marchers' money, but not their behavior; indeed, the veterans soon gained a reputation for being totally out of control. Their drunken brawls in Sloppy Joe's bar were the stuff of legends. According to Hemingway scholar Michael S. Reynolds, "on any Key West Saturday night," those veterans who were "not yet annoying enough to be arrested or crazy enough to be exported [would] curse, carouse, and brawl, leaving the floor slippery with spilled beer and blood." Nor did the veterans confine their mayhem to the bars: on one occasion, a liquored-up bonus marcher climbed upon a Duval Street front porch, took off his clothes, and loudly denounced the living conditions up on Matecumbe Key. One of the few Key West residents with any sympathy for these rough customers was Ernest Hemingway, but even he recognized that some of these veterans had been permanently damaged by the awful experience of war. A few were "hard working and simply out of luck," Hemingway claimed, but others were "punch drunk" or even "close to the border of pathological cases." In the end, you can hardly blame Roosevelt for wanting to get these unstable men out of Washington—though in retrospect, it might have been better to send them somewhere else than the hurricane-prone Florida Keys. For far too many of these bar-brawling drunks, the exile that Roosevelt had imposed upon them was about to become a sentence of death.

🌀 🌀 🌀

By the spring of 1934, the writing was on the wall for all to see: Key West was on the verge of total collapse. The municipal government was in default of $1 million in bonded debt and another $300,000 in interest, and there was no end in sight, since Key West's citizens had no income with which to pay the $1 million they owed collectively in back taxes. Key West's public servants had not been paid in months, and though a few police officers and firemen had stayed on the job, garbage collectors had quit, so piles of rotting trash now lay haphazardly throughout the city. Unemployment had become so bad that the Federal Emergency Relief Administration, one of the showcase programs of Roosevelt's "New Deal," was handing out rations of food to Key West's hungry and dispirited citizens. Finally, in July of 1934, the city councilmen gave up, pronounced that their community was hopelessly bankrupt, and turned the town over to the state government in Tallahassee—which in turn handed it right over to the FERA. For all intents and purposes, Key West was now a helpless dependent of the federal government.

So what was to be done? One possibility, which the FERA seriously considered, was to depopulate the town entirely and send its citizens to Tampa, but this plan foundered after Tampa's leaders made it clear that they wanted nothing to do with Key West's impoverished inhabitants. Instead, the FERA resolved to "rehabilitate" the town, and transform it into a tourist mecca. This was, of course, far from a new idea—civic boosters had tried to attract vacationers, with relatively little success, ever since Flagler first built his railway to the island. But the local FERA administrator, a man

Some of Julius Stone's FERA workers, making repairs on Catherine Street. (Florida State Archives)

named Julius Stone, had a plan. The trick, he decided, was to recognize the features that made Key West unique. And what did Key West have that other towns did not? The answer was clear—Key West had Ernest Hemingway.

Indeed, Hemingway had left an indelible mark on the island ever since his first arrival in the spring of 1928. Because of Papa's presence, Key West had become something of a pilgrimage site for America's artistic set: writers, painters, and poets from throughout the country had come to visit the island town, and some of them chose to stay. Key West, Stone realized, was already halfway to being another artist's colony like Montparnasse or Provincetown—and if Stone could advertise this fact to the nation at large, then Key West might finally become the fashionable tourist destination it had long aspired to be.

But first things first: before any tourists could be persuaded to make the long trek to Key West, the town would have to be spiffied up. Recognizing that the FERA did not have nearly enough resources to tackle the job itself, Stone convinced the residents of the town to donate their own labor to the town's revitalization, and after more than a million man-hours of collective effort, the town boasted a new swimming pool, a new sewer system, and (perhaps most importantly) a new sense of purpose. Fixing up Key West's unpainted and dilapidated wood-frame houses proved harder, since Stone was forbidden from using public money to improve private property, but he did invent a clever system whereby Key West's citizens could trade man-hours of labor for paint, lumber, and electrical fixtures. To top it off, Stone worked hard to give the town a more artsy feel, hiring painters to decorate Key West walls with murals, actors to perform open-air theatre, and musicians to greet tourists at the train station. If Key West was going to become an artists' colony, Stone figured, then it had better look the part.

Stone's efforts did not please everyone—indeed, many of the "artists" themselves were appalled. Katy Dos Passos, John Dos Passos' wife, complained in a letter that "Key West is now a Greenwich Village Nightmare . . . they're painting murals on the café walls, and weaving baskets, and cutting down plants and trees, and renting all the homes (with Washington money) and arranging sight-seeing tours, and building apartments for tourists so that they can observe the poor Hemingways." Ernest himself was so irritated by all the gawkers—his family home was listed as a tourist attraction on brochures—that he hired a handyman to build a brick wall around his home. Another novelist and long-standing Key West resident, Elmer Davis, complained that since so many tourists were invading this "artists' colony," the real artists were being forced "to move out, and hunt for some place as yet undiscovered by the public where they can get some work done." In the end, however, Davis conceded that Key West's transformation was probably for the best: "You cannot ask people to starve," he admitted, "for the sake of being quaint."

Despite the bitter opposition of the artistic community, Stone's plan to revitalize the town worked. During the 1934–35 tourist season, eight thousand guests booked rooms in Key West's hotels—so many tourists came, in fact, that locals were able to rent out their recently-refurbished houses to the overflow visitors. Although none in Key West could have known it at the time, Stone and the FERA had successfully laid down two of the foundations of Key West's modern economy: Key West's present-day identity as a Bohemian art town and a Hemingway shrine dates back to Stone's intervention in the summer of 1934. The only element still absent was gay culture, which would not become a significant factor of Key West's identity until after the Second World War and the coming of the gay playwright Tennessee Williams.

This is not to say that all of Key West's problems had been solved overnight with a wave of the FERA's wand. Times were still tough for Key West's residents, and it would take years of hard work before Key West finally regained the population and prosperity it had enjoyed before the First World War. And what would happen if another storm hit? Everyone knew about the terrible hurricanes of 1919 and 1926, which had shattered the prosperity of the Florida shore. Even a minimal hurricane, Conchs knew, would ruin Key West's fragile recovery, and return the island town to the days of economic ruin. So Key West watched the southern skies for gray clouds, and prayed that the next hurricane would pass Key West by.

As we shall see, they had cause for concern. Barely a year after Julius Stone began his experiment in Cayo Hueso, a new hurricane began to curve northwards towards the Florida Keys. And this was no minimal hurricane; indeed, the Labor Day Hurricane of September 1935 would prove to be the most awesome and terrifying storm ever to inscribe itself into the annals of American meteorological history. The time to pay the undertaker had come.

11

No Return

If you do not mind stepping once more into another man's shoes, I would like to transform you into yet another south Florida voyager and send you on a third and final imaginary journey along the Florida shore. This time, the date is August 31, 1935, and you are a Depression-era vacationer who has been attracted to the swaying palms and cheap off-season room rates of Depression-era Florida. Perhaps you were also drawn south by memories of the great Florida boom—let us suppose that you are one of the quarter-million Americans who thronged into boom-time Miami exactly one decade before, and you have now returned to explore familiar haunts in the "Magic City."

To your great disappointment, however, you discover that Miami of the mid-1930s is just a dim reflection of what it used to be. The heady optimism of the boom has entirely abandoned the city on Biscayne Bay, and many thousands of unemployed Miami citizens are now so desperately poor that they have become dependent on local tropical fruits like grapefruits, mangos, avocados, and sea grapes for their basic sustenance. "A mango," you overhear the hungry inhabitants of Miami assuring each other, "is five times more nourishing than a whole steak." You cannot help but chuckle; boosterism is still alive and well in Miami, you realize, and local inhabitants are still trying to spin perception into reality by means of the spoken word.

So, like many a disappointed tourist before you, you decide to move on. But where should you spend your Labor Day holiday? Well, why not Key West? For the past year, Florida New Deal officials have been advertising Key West heavily in national newspapers, and you remember seeing a newspaper photograph of Dizzy Dean, the star pitcher for the St. Louis Cardinals, enjoying himself on the Key West waterfront. Perhaps you might even rub shoulders with that famous writer Ernest Hemingway, Key West's resident author and most well-known inhabitant. If the fancy strikes you, and your funds hold out, you could even take a side trip to the old Cuban city of Havana, which is just a half-day's sail across the Florida Channel from Key West. Your decision made, you book yourself on the FEC's Havana Special and set your alarm clock so that you will not miss the train's 6:45 departure the following morning.

As it turns out, however, you should have slept in. The September 1st Havana Special doesn't actually arrive from West Palm Beach until about two in the afternoon, which you later learn is a common occurrence on the FEC rail lines. In fact, you ought to count yourself lucky—FEC trains often arrive at their stations more than a full day after they were expected, though the FEC tries hard not to advertise this fact. The Depression had already driven Flagler's once-proud railroad into bankruptcy proceedings, and the line is on the brink of total economic collapse; small wonder, then, that the desperate railway is less than honest with the general public about its chronic lateness.

Since you know little and care even less about the FEC's financial difficulties, however, you board the train in a huff, annoyed that the late arrival of the Havana Special has cost you half a day of vacation. Seeing your displeasure, a train porter tries to cheer you up: why, due to the tardiness of the train, you might even be able to see the glory of a Florida Keys sunset from atop the Bahia Honda Bridge!

But surely, you ask him, we will arrive in Key West before sunset? According to the railroad timetables, after all, the Miami–Key West leg is at most a five-hour trip!

The amused porter snorts with suppressed laughter. "That would be a first," you hear him mumble to himself as he clomps off.

Well that's just great. More annoyed than ever and realizing that you might be in for a long ride, you try make yourself comfortable in a seat on the left side of the rail car, guessing that the side of the train facing the Florida Straits will enjoy the lion's share of beautiful scenery. In this, at least, you are not disappointed. True, the first leg of the journey is relatively monotonous, as the railway cuts arrow-strait through grassy swamps and tangled mangrove-land entirely devoid of human habitation. Once you reach Key Largo, however, the scenery improves dramatically. Thick tropical foliage alternates with scattered groves of fruit and small homestead settlements, and at intervals, you are able to catch tantalizing glimpses of the turquoise blue of the Atlantic Ocean through the trees. Not since the garden of Eden, you imagine, has man lived in such beauty and simplicity.

As the train moves onwards into the mid-afternoon, you spy several sunburned residents of Eden's garden, and you briefly envy their relative shelter from the economic storms of the Depression-wracked North, where former millionaires have been reduced to hawking apples on street corners. Although few crops now grow in the Keys' thin soil, which has been depleted by years of pineapple and lime harvests, local Conchs can still eke out a living collecting sponges and catching fish. What does poverty matter, you muse, if you live in paradise?

As you entertain yourself with fantasies of abandoning your office job in the North for an untroubled life as a fisherman on the Florida shore, the miles clack by, and Key Largo gives way to Plantation Key. The change of island, however, brings no change of scenery, and you soon find the voyage becoming monotonous once again. As if in response to your boredom, the Havana Special suddenly emerges into open space, and as it clatters across the Snake Creek Bridge, you have your first clear view of the mighty Atlantic Ocean on the left side of the train. In your appreciative eyes, the sparkling waters of the Florida Straits undulate like a sea of sapphires beneath the still-powerful sun of a lengthening Florida afternoon. John Dos Passos, you recall, had described the railroad journey across of the Keys as a "dreamlike crossing." Now you can see why.

Moments later, however, the dream gives way to reality of the basest sort: your view of the sea is abruptly blocked by a small city of shacks, storage sheds, trucks, and outhouses, strewn haphazardly across the narrow shelf of land between the railway and the Atlantic Ocean. Is this a town? If so, where are the women? There is barely a female to be seen; instead, this village of tents and wooden shacks seems to be inhabited almost entirely by shabbily dressed middle-aged men. After a moment of confusion, you realize that you must be looking at one of those work camps that Roosevelt has been erecting for the benefit of unemployed veterans in the Florida Keys. You remember reading about these encampments in the newspapers; critics of the New Deal, you recall, have heaped scorn on these costly concentration camps, where lazy bonus marchers are sent to "play, putter and carouse at Government expense." Pleased by your brush with history in the making, you wave to the tired, grim-faced veterans and then watch as their rickety work camp recedes in the distance behind the clattering train.

Following the unexpected appearance of the veterans' camp, your voyage becomes more interesting. The train passes next through the two Matecumbe Keys, the upper of which contains the small town of Islamorada, and the lower two more ramshackle camps filled with miscellaneous veterans and bonus marchers. Soon after, the Havana Special clatters onto the world-famous Long Key viaduct. While crossing this marvel of modern railroad engineering, you are able to look straight down from your Pullman car into the azure waters of the Atlantic Ocean, and you swear that you can discern the sinister outline of a ten-foot shark keeping pace with the train in the waters below. About an hour later, after chugging through a scattering of small keys and the bustling little town of Marathon, the Special reaches the Seven-Mile Bridge, which takes your breath away. From your point of view on the train, this endless bridge seems to disappear into an eternity of unbroken blue water. You are almost disappointed when, a mile or so into the bridge, you spy a low smudge of land emerging from the approaching horizon.

The highlight of your journey, however, is undoubtedly the crossing of the Bahia Honda Channel. From atop this stately bridge, which soars more than thirty feet above the rippling ocean, you bear witness to a subtropical sunset of unimaginable beauty. The sky is bedecked in shimmering, opalescent colors, filling the horizon with an unearthly pearly hue. As the sun disappears below the horizon, it launches flares of multi-colored light into the darkening sky. Awestruck, you can only sit and wonder at the majesty of the spectacle.

Later, while disembarking the train into a humid Key West evening, you happen upon the same uniformed porter you had spoken with before. Lord almighty, you tell him, you were sure right about that sunset! Are all Florida Keys sunsets like that?

To your surprise, the formerly-sarcastic porter seems bewildered, almost frightened. "No," he tells you, "they aren't. I've been working the Overseas for years, and I've never seen anything like it."

Troubled by the porter's obvious anxiety, you carry your bags through the nearly deserted Trumbo Island Terminal at Key West and hire a taxi. As the cabbie drives you to your Duval Street hotel, you ask him, "what's going on? Anything I should know about?"

"Well," he says, "I hate to be the one to ruin your vacation."

"Just tell me!"

"What I heard is that there's some nasty weather brewing out on the Great Bahama Bank. They put up the storm warning flags at the naval station sometime last night. From the looks of it, we might be in for a bad blow."

As you sink back into the seat of the taxi, you notice disturbing signs of hurricane preparation all around you. Nightfall has come to Key West, but despite this, the populace is busily at work, taking down signs, stowing furniture, closing shutters, and sealing up windows with wooden planks. Your vacation, you realize, has taken you to a city at war, preparing desperately for a siege by the elements. Perhaps coming to Key West was not such a good idea after all.

"Look on the bright side, the cabbie tells you as he pulls up to your hotel. The storm warnings are for the entire coast of south Florida between Ft. Pierce and Ft. Myers. That's a lot of real estate, and it tells me that they don't have a clue where this thing is going. Why, it might not even get within a hundred miles of us!"

The taxi-driver's words are meant to be calming, but for some reason, they call to mind those veterans' camps you saw earlier in the day out on the middle Keys. You remember the narrow shelf of land between the railroad and the sea, the flimsy wood-frame shacks, and the utter lack of any shelter on those low-lying islands. Despite the clammy heat of the subtropical night, a chill runs down your spine.

If the hurricane hits those veterans, you pray, may God have mercy on their souls.

Like all hurricanes, the Labor Day storm of 1935 started small. It first came to the attention of the Weather Bureau at midday on Saturday, August 31, as a tiny but intense tropical disturbance on the other edge of the Bahamas. By 9:30 that night, when it passed over Cape Santa Maria on the north end of Long Island in the Bahamas, the depression had been upgraded to the status of a tropical storm by virtue of its gale-force winds. At that point, the developing cyclonic storm disappeared into the little-traveled triangle of water between Exuma Sound, Man-of-War Channel, and a deep-water gut with the colorful name of Tongue of the Ocean. When it reemerged off the southern end of Andros Island on the morning of the September 1, it had strengthened further, and the weather service guessed that it had "probably" developed winds of hurricane force in a small area near its spinning heart. So far, there were no indications that this marginal hurricane, which seemed on course to pass well to the south of the United States, posed much of a threat to anyone other than Cuban fishermen, though the weather service did issue a cautionary warning to vessels passing through the Florida Straits. No one could have foreseen that this modest hurricane would soon explode into a category-five monster so powerful that one recent author has dubbed it the "storm of the century."

At the time of your departure from Miami for Key West in the early afternoon of September 1, during your imaginary vacation, the still-minor storm had begun to drift south and west in the direction of Cuba, and it seemed to be passing even farther away from the North American continent. Over the course of the next five hours, not much changed; the storm crept gradually to the west, loitering about thirty miles to the south of an underwater shoal in the Bahama Bank known, appropriately enough, as the Hurricane Flats. By the time you reached Key West, and began your disconcerting conversation with the cab driver, the slow-moving storm had wandered only a few dozen miles westward. All the signs seemed to indicate that this weak hurricane would meander its way slowly across the north coast of Cuba and then twirl off into the empty expanse of the Gulf of Mexico.

On Labor Day morning, however, the hurricane's course began to change dramatically. As the storm inched towards the coast of Cuba, it grew rapidly in strength, most likely due to the energizing effect of the tepid water that the hurricane discovered south of Hurricane Flats. Tropical hurricanes feed on warm water, and meteorologists now speculate that the Labor Day Storm of 1935 must have come across a rare migrating pocket of heated water off the Great Bahama Bank. This sun-simmered water triggered an extremely rapid period of intensification—some scientists have dubbed this process "bombing out"—which transformed it into a fearsome category-three hurricane within mere hours.

To make matters worse, as the hurricane began to gain momentum, it started to recurve to the north, away from Cuba, directly towards the small town of Islamorada on Upper Matecumbe Key. The storm's new path brought it into the Florida Straits, where it drank deeply of the warm waters of the Gulf Stream, and "bombed out" once again, gaining still more wind speed and strength. By the time this small but ferocious storm roared into the middle Florida Keys, it had become a category-five meteorological nightmare, unquestionably the most powerful hurricane ever to strike the coast in the history of the United States.

In a way, the United States was lucky. By chance, the Labor Day Hurricane happened to run aground on a relatively unpopulated portion of the vast American coastline. If the storm had veered another few degrees to the west, it would have caused catastrophic damage to Key West; indeed, the Labor Day Hurricane might have all but scraped the island clean of human habitation. Luckily for you, while the rain and wind of the storm's edge would put a damper on your Key West vacation, you would live to tell the tale of your brush with the Labor Day disaster. Had the storm angled a few more degrees to the east, it would likely have leveled the city of Miami, killing thousands in the process. Indeed, if the Labor Day storm had struck already-struggling Miami, it is quite possible that the sodden ruins of the "Magic City" might have been abandoned *en masse* by the storm-weary survivors, and Miami might very well have joined the bypassed town of Juno as a forgotten chapter of Florida history.

The nation was lucky in another sense as well. Since September 2 was Labor Day, those veterans working on the Overseas Highway who could afford it had abandoned the mosquito-tormented Keys for the relative comfort of Key West and Miami. As a result, out of a total contingent of 684 men, only about 400 veterans remained on the Keys at the time of the storm's arrival. If the storm had touched down on a normal workday, when the camps housed a full contingent of laborers, the casualty figures would almost certainly have been far worse.

The nation's good fortune, however, was little consolation to the veterans and native residents who found themselves trapped on the Keys on Labor Day, 1935. The storm was approaching, and their luck was about to run out.

As always, when it comes to understanding hurricanes, there is no substitute for the personal testimony of eyewitness observers. Classifications, numbers, and statistics each have a story to tell, but such sterile facts often tell us little about the lived experiences of people caught in the storm's path. Unfortunately for historians, however, the Labor Day Hurricane produced relatively few comprehensive eyewitness accounts. Unlike the Great Miami Hurricane, which left behind thousands of articulate survivors, the Labor Day storm killed more than it spared as it howled over the middle Keys, and the small handful who survived were shell-shocked veterans, many of whom were depressed, alcoholic, or downright insane. As a result, the first-hand accounts of the storm that have survived for the use of modern-day historians have a distinctly fragmented character; they provide glimpses rather than a full panorama of the events of that fateful day. The goal of the remainder of this chapter, then, will be to collect the storm's debris, and piece together the scattered recollections of the survivors into a coherent narrative of the Labor Day Hurricane of 1935.

⑥ ⑥ ⑥

By all accounts, the veterans and native Keys dwellers awoke on September 2 to an especially dark and forbidding

Monday morning. One observer later said that the clouds were so "muddy and close" that "it looked like you could reach out and get hold of them." Elsewhere in the Keys, the storm-frothed seawater had developed a sinister milky appearance, and exceptionally large waves were spilling over offshore reefs and crashing heavily onto south Florida beaches. Those who owned barometers had further warning of the coming trouble: on Labor Day morning, barometers all over the Keys were registering a gradual but continuous drop in air pressure, a telltale sign of the approach of a tropical storm.

At this point, the Weather Bureau had not yet predicted that the storm would wash up on the Keys, or anywhere else in the United States for that matter. At 9:30 A.M. on Labor Day, in fact, the Bureau was still guessing that the storm was "probably" a hurricane, and they anticipated that it would continue to amble slowly to the west. For the Overseas Highway workers on the Keys, however, these pronouncements from a distant federal agency were far less convincing than the steady fall of water and mercury in their own barometers, and some began to worry. This feeling of anxiety increased on Labor Day morning as the storm began to treat the middle Keys with a preview of its arrival, sending gusting winds and drenching rains into Islamorada and the veterans' camps. Finally, at about 11:00 A.M. on Labor Day morning, Ray Sheldon, the ranking official of the Overseas Highway project, made a belated decision: the time had come to order a rescue train to evacuate the veterans and camp officials from the storm-threatened islands.

What happened next would have been a comedy of errors, if the result hadn't been so tragic. Because of a phone call the night before to FEC officials, Sheldon was working under the influence of a false impression: that a rescue train could reach the Keys from Miami in about four hours. In actuality, the FEC officials had informed him that a train could be Islamorada in four hours *if ordered immediately*, since a train happened to be ready at the Miami station at that moment, but Sheldon apparently misunderstood the caveat. As a result, Sheldon did not bother to call Fred Ghent, his boss in

Jacksonville, until about noon, by which time Ghent had disappeared for a two-hour lunch break. Ghent finally returned the call to Sheldon at around 2:00, and shortly after, Ghent phoned the FEC dispatcher with orders to prepare a rescue train. At this point, however, another obstacle presented itself—since it was a holiday, the FEC was running with a skeleton crew, and it took time to assemble the personnel and equipment needed for the train. Consequently, the rescue train didn't start out for the veteran's camps until about 4:30 in the afternoon.

All told, then, five and a half hours elapsed between Sheldon's decision to order the train and the actual departure of that train from Miami station. Perhaps, if the storm was still meandering westward as the Weather Bureau had predicted, these five hours would not have been critical. Unfortunately, however, the "bombing-out" storm had begun a remarkable change in speed and direction. Between 1:30 and 4:30 P.M., the Labor Day Hurricane began what would eventually prove to be a sixty-degree turn to the north, and it increased in speed from a walk to a trot, accelerating from a languid six mph to the brisker pace of twenty-five mph in a matter of hours. As a result, the recurving hurricane would smash into the Keys almost a half day earlier than expected, and the "rescue" train would arrive just in time to become part of the unfolding catastrophe.

Even after the train was actually under way, delays and poor decisions continued to dog its progress. The eleven-car train had hardly built up a head of steam, for instance, before it was stopped cold by an open drawbridge on the Miami River. Strange as it may seem, the rescue train, on which so many lives depended, was not given priority over the pleasure boats of holiday merrymakers which were streaming into and out of Biscayne Bay on that Labor Day evening. The train was delayed once again at the Homestead switching yards, since the engineer in charge of the evacuation expedition, J. J. Haycraft, thought it wise to put the engine on the back of the train so that the train could make a speedier exit from the Keys once it had collected the imperiled veterans. Although a good idea in theory, this cost the rescue expedition fifteen more minutes that they could ill-afford to lose. The switch-over in Homestead was costly in another sense as well; during this stop, a number of people, including a newspaper reporter, a telephone repair crew, and several veterans, decided to board the southbound train. As a result, what was supposed to be an "evacuation" train ended up carrying yet more victims to a deadly rendezvous with the most terrifying storm in American history.

In the meantime, the situation had become very bad on the middle Keys, and it was getting worse by the minute. By 5:00 P.M., the eye of the storm was about seventy or eighty miles from the veteran's camps, and edge of the hurricane was already bringing blinding rains and battering winds to Upper Matecumbe, Lower Matecumbe, and Windley Keys. Still, the prevailing mood on the camps was one of optimism. The rescue train, after all, was expected at any moment—Sheldon had ordered it at 11:00 A.M., hadn't he? And hadn't the camp administrators tacked bulletins to the notice boards promising that a special train was at constant readiness in Miami to evacuate the veterans from the Keys? Some misinformed veterans were so complacent about the coming bad weather that they actually welcomed the hurricane; one later admitted to an interviewer that "we all hoped it would blow the mosquitoes away and cool things off." Confident that they had already left the worst days of their lives behind them on the shell-torn fields of France, many veterans vastly underestimated the danger posed by a tropical storm; even if the storm did sweep the Keys, they assumed, it would be at most a mild irritant. As these veterans would soon discover, however, there are even more dangerous places in the world than the trenches of the Great War, and no one in their right mind was fool enough to welcome the arrival of a Florida hurricane.

Still other veterans were simply too drunk to care. The veterans had been paid on Friday, so many of these hard-drinking men were now on day three of a post-payday alcoholic stupor and planned to stay drunk until their funds ran out. According to one eyewitness, "Those men who didn't leave the camp for the holidays were drinking more heavily than I had seen them over a period of about a year since the camp began." It is a testimony to the woeful incompetence of the veterans' camp administrators that the canteens of the camps continued to sell booze through much of Labor Day, despite the threatened approach of deadly weather. One low-level administrator did issue orders to stop the sale of alcohol on the morning of the 2nd, but his decision was countermanded by Sheldon, who pronounced it "silly." When the storm did arrive on the evening of the 2nd, therefore, many of the veterans had to contend with their own drunkenness along with the wind and water in their struggle to stay alive.

As for the local residents of the Keys, they were better prepared for the coming of the hurricane, though of course there is only so much that can be done to make ready for a category-five monster. Loose items were strapped down and stowed, windows were boarded shut, and boats were tied up tight. In addition, most Keys families abandoned their regular homes, which were generally built along the vulnerable Atlantic coast side of the Keys, and bunkered down in their hurricane shelters, reinforced wooden structures built on higher ground. If this had been an ordinary hurricane, perhaps such measures would have sufficed.

The Labor Day storm was no ordinary hurricane, however, and as evening approached, this fact became appallingly clear. As early as 2:00 P.M., hours before the rescue train had even left the station, the wind was already so strong that it was all but impossible to walk upright, and the flimsier structures in the camps, such as the tents, were beginning to blow to pieces. Between 5:00 and 6:00, as the veterans waited impatiently for the coming of the evacuation train, the wind started to howl, and survivors later reported that debris began to batter their wood-frame shacks. By 7:00, the mounting winds had begun to tear apart even the larger, better constructed buildings on the Keys. The Matecumbe Hotel in Islamorada, for example, began to shake violently by 6:00 P.M., forcing its evacuation, and it was smashed flat by the storm winds soon afterwards. At Camp Three on the south end of Lower Matecumbe Key, survivors reported that, at about 7:00, the "roof of the mess hall went flying off into space," which compelled the veterans inside to scatter desperately in search of cover. But there was little cover to be had; the wooden-frame structures in all three camps were already beginning to disintegrate in the face of the remorseless power of the hurricane gales.

If the evacuation train had arrived in the camps at this point, it might have saved a few lives. At the very least, the sturdily built train cars might have provided some shelter to the poor unfortunates on the Keys, if not a means for escape. Unfortunately, the doomed train continued to be plagued by unexpected delays. By the time the train reached Cross Key, which was little more than a raised embankment between Blackwater and Barnes sound, four-foot waves were crashing over the tracks, forcing J. J. Haycraft to slow the train's advance. Once the train reached the Keys proper, the going was easier, but Haycraft was still obliged to keep the throttle at about 20 mph in order to keep the swaying train on the tracks. At 7:00 P.M., Haycraft finally crossed over to Windley Key, and was just short of Camp One, when he happened to spot a group of storm-battered refugees standing near the track, desperate to hitch a ride on the passing train. Although Haycraft was eager to reach the veterans' camps before the storm worsened further, he didn't have the heart to leave these men behind, so he stopped the train briefly to take them aboard.

Big mistake. When Haycraft put his hand back on the throttle, the train started forward, then lurched to a sudden halt. What had happened?

One of Haycraft's subordinates soon discovered the problem. While the train was idling to pick up the unexpected passengers, the crane belonging to a nearby rock quarry had been buckled by the storm, and the drooping boom cable of the crane had somehow become entangled between the engine and the tender car. Haycraft tried backing the train up to dislodge the cable, but to no avail; the steel cable, it seems, had become all but fused to the engine by the force of the impact. In the end, it took nearly an hour for the train crew to cut the cable and free the leashed train.

By that time, the eye of the hurricane was approaching landfall, bringing high seas and 200 mph winds in its deadly wake. All hell was about to break loose on the middle Keys.

On one issue, nearly all the eyewitness accounts of the Labor Day Hurricane agree: the late evening hour of 8:00 marked the real start of the hurricane. According to one survivor, "suddenly things seemed to break loose—the cabins-timber-trees-shells and rocks. They might have been bullets, the way they cut through the air." Another shocked survivor reported that "I saw bodies with tree stumps smashed through their chests—heads blown off—twisted arms and legs, torn off by flying timber that cut like big knives." By this point, the shrieking wind had snatched up so much sand from the beach that observers claimed the gusts could peel the skin right off your body, and one survivor later told interviewers that "you could not look toward that storm at all; it would gouge your eyes out." At Camp Three, the gusting wind ripped the tracks right off the railroad embankment and hurled them into the air, along with a large number of men who had been holding on desperately to the railroad ties. They landed in a "tangle of whirlpools and debris," and most were never seen alive again.

Elsewhere in Keys, the storm's ferocious winds were performing feats of strength that left observers astounded. According to one witness, the hurricane winds picked up a six-by-eight-inch, eighteen-foot long wooden beam, which must have weighed about a ton and a half, and hurled it over three hundred yards into his house, smashing the home to pieces upon impact. In the meantime, the blasting winds broke the protective glass surrounding the lamp at the Alligator Reef Lighthouse and snatched away the lamp's heavy glass lenses. According to one hurricane historian, one of the lenses was later found, miraculously unbroken, on a beach almost eight miles away.

At the same time that the winds were reaching their terrifying crescendo, the water began to rise alarmingly throughout the middle Keys. Survivors later recalled that seawater had been slowly advancing on the camps ever since the early evening, but after 8:00 P.M., the water level rose rapidly; one veteran later claimed that "I saw the sea creep up the railroad elevation like it was climbing a stairway." Before long, the surging seawater had risen to roughly the same height as the railroad embankment throughout the middle Keys; as a result, the water level on the south side of the Keys was now several feet above that of the north side.

There is reason to think, in fact, that the railroad embankment greatly worsened the coming disaster. Because of the solid immensity of the raised railway, millions of square meters of seawater became trapped south of the Keys, thus magnifying the power of the developing storm surge. If not for Flagler's Overseas Railway, the storm tide would likely have spilled over and through the Keys and into Florida Bay, releasing and dispersing its force in the process. As it was, however, the railway embankment caused the water to pile higher and higher along the line of the middle Keys, much as the dike guarding Moore Haven served only to stack up the storm-swept waters of Lake Okeechobee during the Great Miami Hurricane of 1926. It was just a matter of time before all that bottled-up seawater would reach critical mass and explode.

Before that could happen, however, the storm abruptly fizzled to nothing and was replaced by a sudden and unexpected calm. According to one veteran, "the wind stopped, the stars came out, and it seemed that the most wonderful thing in the world was happening." A kitchen worker at the camps described the same phenomenon. "It quieted down just like that," he told an interviewer, "just stopped, and the stars came up and the wind seemed to get warm, and it was [so] still, a piece of paper wouldn't flutter in the air." Thankful to still be alive, the kitchen worker and several other like-minded men huddled together and congratulated each other, celebrating their survival of the storm. They had no clue that the worst was still to come, and that they were enjoying nothing more than a temporary respite in the eye of the tempest.

Meanwhile, back at the approach to Camp One, J. J. Haycraft and his crew finally disentangled themselves from the quarry boom shortly before 8:00 in the evening, and the rescue train lumbered forward once again—or really backwards, since (after all) Haycraft had placed the locomotive at the engine's rear. Within moments, the train reached Camp One, but to the amazement and dismay of the veterans assembled there, the train clattered past without stopping.

Why did Haycraft leave these veterans behind? Perhaps Haycraft missed the camp in the inky darkness; by this point, the evening's normal gloom had been compounded by dense, low clouds and rain-choked winds, reducing visibility to nearly zero. Or perhaps Haycraft bypassed the camp because conditions had deteriorated to a point where rescue was nearly impossible. William Johns, the news reporter who had boarded the train at Homestead, later remembered that "the wind was too high for a man to walk" by the time the train reached Camp One that evening, which would have made the evacuation of the camp an exercise in futility. Furthermore, what was the point of picking up these men, only to carry them into deeper danger father down along the Keys? Far better, then, to leave the veterans in their camp for the time being, and then retrieve them upon the return, just before the train made a mad dash for safety and salvation. But it was not to be. As William Johns later pointed out, "There was no return," and few of the veterans at Camp One ever saw the rescue train again.

Whatever Haycraft's plan might have been, one point is incontestable: as it rumbled its way south past veteran's Camp One, the rescue train finally began to lose ground in its desperate struggle with the elements. By the time the train began its approach to

Islamorada station, waves had started to wash over train tracks that normally rose seven feet above sea level. As one historian of the Overseas Railway has written, "Haycraft was now piloting a rocking train—at one to two miles an hour—across the surface of the ocean itself." For all intents and purposes, Haycraft had been transformed from the engineer of a train into the captain of a ship.

Despite the train's incremental pace, it managed to arrive at Islamorada station at around 8:20 in the evening. At first, however, Haycraft was not aware that the train had reached its destination; as a result of the midnight black that surrounded him, he didn't notice the station's approach until he began to see the desperate faces of Keys residents passing by in the gloom. By the time Haycraft managed to stop the train, he had overshot the station by several hundred feet, forcing the desperate crowd of veterans and Keys natives that had cowered near the station to venture out into the tempest to reach the promised shelter of the train.

Even as they approached, however, the storm surge began to rise in earnest. One of the Islamorada refugees was none other than Ray Sheldon, now a victim of the storm that he had so badly underestimated. Sheldon had sought shelter from the storm in a freight car near Islamorada's storm-battered railway station, but after he saw the lights of the train blinking in the darkness, he started out against a punishing headwind to reach the train. As he approached, the frothing ocean water began to slosh across the Matecumbe Keys. "When I first left the box car," Sheldon later remembered, "the ground was dry," but by the time Sheldon approached the train, "the water [had risen] to my waist." The surging floodwaters had now reached a height of about ten feet over normal sea level, and they continued to mount by the minute.

As the waters boiled up around him, Sheldon pulled himself into the cab of the locomotive, nearly ecstatic over the arrival of the rescue train. Thus did Ray Sheldon, the negligent administrator who had jeopardized hundreds of lives, meet J. J. Haycraft, who was risking his own safety by piloting his locomotive into the teeth of the worsening storm. "You're the man we've been looking for," Sheldon reportedly told Haycraft, his voice no doubt choked with gratitude and relief. Sheldon had been waiting all day for the arrival of the rescue train, and now that it had arrived, he probably assumed that his long ordeal was nearly at an end. As both Sheldon and Haycraft were about to learn, however, the worst was still to come.

About eight miles away from the rescue train, at Camp Three on the south end of Lower Matecumbe Key, a group of perhaps seventy veterans had sought shelter from the rising tides atop a railway tanker car. One of the veterans perched on the car, B.E. Davis, later reported hearing a bizarre noise sometime after 9:00 in the evening, during the climax of the storm. At first, the Davis remembered, the sound was oddly pleasant, like a "rustle of leaves" somewhere out in the Atlantic Ocean. Within minutes, however, the approaching sound rose dramatically in volume, and soon developed into a "deepening roar." As Davis watched in mixed horror and amazement, a towering wall of water emerged from the surrounding gloom, and bore down on the helpless veterans. "It was at least twenty-five feet high," the supervisor later claimed, and when it reached the tanker car, "it completely submerged us with approximately five feet of water." Although by this point their hands were almost numb from the strain, the veterans on the tanker car held on for dear life, unwilling to put themselves at the mercy of the swirling floodwaters. And for good reason—although a small number of veterans survived the night clinging to the mangroves on the northern end of Lower Matecumbe Key, the majority of those who succumbed to the storm surge at Camp Three were washed to sea and killed by the raging storm tide.

In the aftermath of the storm, survivors all up and down the Keys bore witness to the incredible destructive power of the Labor Day Hurricane's murderous "tidal wave," which ranks was one of the strongest storm surges ever to strike the United States. Back at

Camp One, a veteran who had sought shelter in a storage hut remembered how the merciless flood had picked up the building in which he was hiding and tumbled it end over end "three or four times," forcing the hapless veteran to dodge a huge spool of heavy steel cable which bounced around freely in the storm-tossed shack. Other veterans at Camp One remember how the storm surge washed them over the railroad embankment and towards certain death in Florida Bay; they survived only by grabbing on to something—anything!—which could prevent them from being swept to sea. Luckily for the veterans of Camp One, the north side of Windley Key was thick with mangroves, and these storm-resistant trees provided handholds, and salvation, for a number of desperate veterans.

Camp Five, on the other hand, lacked this safety net of mangroves, and as a result, the death toll there was catastrophic: out of a normal contingent of 185 men, only twelve were later found alive, and several of those survived the storm by fleeing to marginally safer camps before the worst of the hurricane struck. Those who remained first sought shelter in the flimsy buildings of the camp, but by the height of the storm, these crude structures lost their roofs and began to disintegrate, spraying the area with deadly debris. As a result, the Camp Five veterans tried to save their lives by clinging to the north side of the railroad embankment, which offered at least some meager protection against the punishing winds. Their perch on the leeward side of the embankment, however, put them at the mercy of the storm surge, which "came bubbling over" the embankment at sometime around 9:00 and "swept the men right over the island into the gulf." A few lucky survivors saved their lives by clinging to trees, but there were few trees at this camp, and most veterans disappeared below the storm-troubled waters of Florida Bay.

One Camp Five veteran managed to survive only after a harrowing ordeal that almost made him envy the dead. When the "heavy sea came along," this veteran clung desperately to the railroad tracks, even after they were lifted up by the surging water. Moments later, the railroad track sank back down, but to the veteran's horror, the heavy rails and cross ties settled upon his left foot, pinning him beneath the tracks. The ill-starred veteran later told interviewers that, "after lying there for what seemed countless ages, suffering horrible agony, I decided to try to cut my foot off." He couldn't reach his knife, however, and was soon knocked unconscious by the pain. When he came to, he found that the railroad track had released him, but he had only fallen from the proverbial frying pan into the fire: the storm tides were now washing him away towards certain death in the open waters of Florida Bay. Luckily for the veteran, his flailing body happened to strike a mangrove, and he managed to survive by holding on to it for dear life all the rest of that terrible night.

At about the same time, back at the railway station in Islamorada, J. J. Haycraft decided that it was time to move on, and he pressed down on the throttle to start the train in motion. Authorities on the Labor Day Hurricane disagree as to where Haycraft intended to go next: Les Standiford suggests that Haycraft had decided to escape from the Keys before it was too late, but Willie Drye claims that Haycraft intended only to return to the water tower at Islamorada station to refill the steam train's boilers, after which the train would continue to Camps Three and Five. Either way, the point is moot. Despite Haycraft's best efforts, the train refused to budge, and stood immobile on the flooded tracks.

What was going on? Haycraft's crew jumped out of the train into chest-deep water to look for the problem, and they discovered that the wind had blown one of the train's boxcars off of the rails, thus activating the train's automatic braking system. Unless the boxcar was removed, the rescue train was dead in its tracks, and until the water receded, there was no way that Haycraft's crew could cut loose the wayward boxcar. Rendered powerless by the storm, the crew waited anxiously for the floodwaters to drop.

Instead of receding, however, the floods mounted still higher, until the waters were flush with the floors of the passenger cars and waves began to batter the sides of the train. Then the waters rose higher still and extinguished the flames in the locomotive engine's firebox. At this point, Haycraft must have realized, the knocked-askew boxcar was the least of his concerns. The Labor Day Hurricane had already transformed Haycraft from a train engineer to a boat captain; now he began his final transformation, into just another victim caught in the path of the most powerful tropical hurricane ever to strike the United States.

And then it happened. As Haycraft and Sheldon watched in horror, a towering swell heaved itself out of the ocean and smashed itself into the helpless train. Sheldon later claimed to interviewers that "the waves were of such height that they beat over the heads of the engine crew who were in the cab of the locomotive." For a few desperate moments, Sheldon, Haycraft and the rest of the crew struggled for their lives against the surging water that swept through the cab. Luckily for them, the 106-ton steel locomotive stayed firmly planted on the tracks, and the handholds it provided saved the men inside it from being swept away by the flood.

The passengers in the rest of the train were not so lucky, however; unlike the heavy locomotive, the wood-frame Pullmans and boxcars proved no match for the awesome power of the storm surge. William Johns, the reporter who had joined the train at Homestead, later published a vivid account of the affect the "tidal wave" had on the would-be rescue train. "A wall of water from about 15 to 20 feet high picked up our coaches and twirled them about like straws," he wrote, and the passengers in his own car were "tossed . . . across seats, against windows, and in crazy heaps on the sidewalls that suddenly became floors." To Johns' dismay, water began to pour into the shipwrecked rail car from both the shattered right-side windows below him, which had now become yawning holes in the floor, and the smashed windows of the trains' left side, which the storm had transformed into skylights in the ceiling. It must have seemed to Johns that the entire world was being turned upside-down.

Desperate to avoid being drowned like a rat in a trap, Johns

Aerial view of rescue train, showing the distance the storm surge carried the train cars from the railroad tracks. (Florida State Archives)

removed bits of broken glass from the train window above him in case the water rose dangerously high and he needed to swim for safety from the flooding car. In the meantime, Johns remembered, "the waves and rain nearly beat the breath out of me. . . . I couldn't see an inch away, so thick was the spray blowing through the car." As it turned out, Johns did not drown—the water receded as quickly as it had risen—but Johns still spent a desperate, shivering night in the capsized ruins of the train, terrified that another monster wave would smash the remains of the train into splinters, and sweep the survivors into oblivion.

ⓑ ⓑ ⓑ

Even the most catastrophic disaster generally produces some moments of black humor, and the Labor Day storm of '35 is no exception. In her delightful book of Key West legends, Jeane Porter records the story of an elderly, eccentric old Conch who lived alone on the Keys. According to Porter, this venerable gentleman

. . . had ordered a barometer from Abercrombie and Fitch in New York. When it arrived on what became one of the last trains from the mainland, its needle was pointing to 'Hurricane' and he thought the instrument had been broken in transit! Being a recluse, he hadn't heard any of the messages of storm warning. When the hurricane struck, he climbed up and lashed himself to his tallest coconut palm and rode out the storm. They found him two days later, semi-conscious and still up the tree. He had been stripped naked by the wind, dazed but quite alive, and he was still clutching the barometer.

Not all of Jeane Porter's memories of the Labor Day Hurricane were so whimsical, however. In her later years, Porter still remembered stories that she had heard in '35, while still only nine years of age, about the gruesome piles of swelling corpses that the storm had piled up on the Matecumbe Keys. When these rotting cadavers were doused in kerosene and set aflame, Porter was told, some of the bodies reacted against the heat, and "were seen to crawl out of the fire." For months after the '35 storm, whenever she saw a black cloud drifting towards Key West from the north, Porter thought of the burning, desperately crawling dead, and was sure that she could smell the lingering stench of mass cremations on the middle Keys.

Porter's story of writhing corpses is likely apocryphal—it is not supported by any other source I am aware of—but it is characteristic of the horrors that rescuers discovered when they arrived on the storm-wracked Windley and Matecumbe Keys. One of the first to the scene was Key West's resident writer and tourist attraction, Ernest Hemingway, who sailed to the middle Keys along with Charlie Thompson and Captain Bra on the second day after the disaster. He found the islands almost entirely devoid of foliage and vegetable matter, and covered with heaped-up piles of sand, looking like "the abandoned bed of a river where the sea had swept it."

Hemingway described one key as "absolutely swept clean, not a blade of grass, and over the high center of it were scattered live conchs that came in from the sea, craw fish, and dead morays. The whole bottom of the sea blew over it."

And everywhere, Hemingway wrote, there were bodies. Corpses were bobbing in the water at the ferry slip on Lower Matecumbe Key where Hemingway landed his sailboat. The leeward sides of the Keys especially were littered with the dead, "face down and face up," tangled in the brown, "autumn" branches of the wind-stripped mangrove trees. Farther along "you found them high in the trees [where] the water had swept them." On one key, Hemingway came across the bodies of two women, "naked, tossed up into trees by the water, swollen and stinking, their breasts as big as balloons, flies between their legs." After reflection, Hemingway realized that these bloated corpses belonged to the "very nice girls who ran a sandwich place and filling station three miles from the ferry." As for the road-side sandwich shop they once worked at, not a trace remained.

No matter where the storm had deposited them, the bodies of the dead were beginning to decompose, badly, in the subtropical sun. When Hemingway got to the Keys, the standing order from President Roosevelt was that the veterans should be packed in coffins for burial at Arlington National Cemetery, but this task became increasingly difficult as time progressed. Hemingway, who helped in the recovery of the dead, remembered that the bodies had become so swollen with corruption that they "burst when you lift-ed them, rotten, running, putrid, decomposed, absolutely impossi-ble to embalm . . . the whole thing stinking to make you vomit." Not long after Hemingway wrote this, the governor of Florida real-ized that the task of collecting veterans' corpses for Arlington had become hopeless, and in defiance of FDR's decree, he ordered the cremation of the remaining bodies where they lay.

Hemingway was far from the only contemporary observer to be shocked at the death and devastation the storm had wrought on the middle Keys. Possibly the most vivid account by an eye-witness to the storm was penned by Henry Cavendish, a staff writer for the *Miami Herald*, who toured Windley, Upper Matecumbe, and Lower Matecumbe Keys on the morning of the 4th, two days after the storm. After crossing Snake Creek, where "the water was still swirling like a millrace through the railway culvert," Cavendish came across a drowned body, stretched out on the landing, which was "turning green in the early morning sunlight." This grisly corpse was a preview of things to come, and it would prove to be just the first of thirty-two cadavers that Cavendish would see with his own eyes on the middle Keys.

As Coast Guard planes buzzed overhead, searching for the living and the dead, Cavendish continued onwards to Windley Key, where he encountered scenes of "utter desolation." He located the site of veteran's Camp One and discovered that "four houses alone of the twenty or more which were formerly there remained either intact or partially intact." Outside of those few lucky structures, Cavendish discovered, Camp One had been reduced to a tangled heap of debris, in which "boards of the buildings and their furnishings all mixed up in an unholy mélange of materials and bodies."

Farther along on Windley Key, Cavendish crossed paths with three exhausted railway workers, including none other than J. J. Haycraft, who had abandoned the useless wreckage of the rescue train he had once commanded and was now making the return trip to the mainland on foot. Haycraft and the others told Cavendish that the cars of their train had been knocked as far as four hundred feet from the tracks by the power of the tidal wave, which they claimed had washed over the tall driving wheels of the locomotive. If true, this suggests that waves on the crest of the storm surge might have reached over thirty-five feet in height. As for Islamorada, Haycraft claimed, "not a house was left standing on the island." After a short interview, Cavendish allowed these tired railway workers to continue their weary march back to Miami, and he continued onwards, anxious to see Islamorada for himself.

As Cavendish picked his way across the ruined roadway on

Windley Key, he was struck by the incongruity of the scene around him. To his left, late summer sunlight sparked upon the tranquil waters of the Atlantic, which was as "calm as a lake in the light morning breeze." Windley Key itself, however, looked as if had been subjected to an artillery barrage. In some places, Cavendish wrote, "the jungle was sheared off close to the ground as though some grim reaper with a gigantic scythe had passed that way, swinging his malevolent instrument." Automobiles were "mashed up and scattered about," Cavendish reported, and bodies lay everywhere, all bearing visible testimony to the fury of the storm. One of the corpses Cavendish passed was "doubled up and twisted," with "one arm almost torn off." Another body was found impaled by a wooden board, and still another lay totally naked in a thicket of swamp grass. Nearly all the corpses he saw had been "battered, bruised, and twisted" by the wind, and "gangrening spots marked where the flesh had been bruised by flying timbers." After a while, Cavendish became almost inured to the scale of the carnage; as he later wrote in the *Miami Herald,* "death in such large numbers" left him with "a benumbing feeling."

Cavendish's numb heart was broken, however, by his interview with the remnant survivors of the Russell family, who had gathered together at the southern end of Windley Key. Before the storm, the seventy-four-member Russell family of Islamorada had been one of the largest clans on the Florida Keys. The storm, however, had taken a horrific toll—only five family members had been rescued so far from the blasted wreckage of Islamorada, and two of them were so critically injured that they had been transferred from Upper Matecumbe Key to Windley Key "on cots placed sideways on the gunwales of the boats." Cavendish listened attentively as John Russell, eldest surviving member of the family, poured out his anguished story. "We've lived in Islamorada all our lives," John Russell told him. "The barometer started falling Monday about noon. We stated making preparations about the same time." But the preparations were not enough. "About 8 to 8:30 P.M.," Russell continued, "the water got so high it broke the house down and we were all washed out. The wind was raging, and it was so dark we couldn't see anything. We were all left," he concluded, "to the mercy of the Lord."

Cavendish eventually left John Russell to his sorrow, and took a rescue worker's ferry across to Upper Matecumbe Key, where he found "more than a hundred refugees," some bearing terrible injuries, all waiting to leave the island for the mainland. He did not stop to talk to the crowd, but continued onwards, past palm trees that had been snapped in half like matchsticks, and eventually located the capsized rescue train and the ruined remnants of Islamorada. "What had formerly been the Islamorada railway station and warehouse across the street," Cavendish wrote, "was now merely rough board planks piled up in an indescribable tangle about the overturned coaches." Further underscoring the power of the storm was the looming presence of the *Leise Maersk,* a three-thousand-ton Danish freighter caught up in the hurricane, which had run aground almost within shouting distance of the wreckage of the train at Islamorada. Such was the power of the Labor Day storm; the same forces that had transformed a train into a boat had also hurled a seagoing vessel onto dry land.

Awestruck by the scene, Cavendish paused and surveyed his surroundings. Not far from the wreckage of the station he discovered two small houses that had been reduced to a "shambles" by the storm, one of which still contained "an elderly man . . . sitting peacefully in death." Cavendish then crawled through the shattered remains of one of the overturned rescue train coaches, perhaps to see what the storm might have looked like from the perspective of the passengers on the doomed train. While in the coach, Cavendish came across a small sign, still "spick and span" despite the catastrophe, which reminded passengers on the Overseas Railway that "Spitting is Unlawful." All Cavendish could do is marvel at the absurdity of it. Amidst such death and devastation, it must have seemed inconceivable to him that some distant authority could care

Such was the power of the 1953 hurricane that it washed away entire communities, such as the Caribbee Colony Resort. (Florida State Archives)

so deeply about the problem of spitting.

After crawling out of the ruin of the train, Cavendish made his way still farther down Upper Matecumbe Key, and he continued to be dumbfounded at the sheer scale of the destruction. The roof of the Matecumbe Hotel had been blown away, he noted, and the second story had collapsed down upon the first. A sandwich shop also stood nearby, ruined but recognizable. Other than that, "the country looked as though a mowing machine had passed over it . . . nothing was left but debris." Still farther on, Cavendish came to the former site of the "Caribee Colony" tourist camp, a roadside attraction, famous for its coconut pies, which George Merrick had built on the Keys after the post-boom collapse of Coral Gables. But the pies were now gone, along with the rest of the camp—not even boards or debris remained. Cavendish looked around for Mr. and Mrs. Dumas, the Caribee's proprietors, but found only their automobile, which had been reduced to "a scarred wreck in a ditch." The only human being he found at the site was George Henderson, a "Negro" cook at the Colony, whose lifeless body was "flattened against a telegraph pole" that had somehow remained standing through the storm. Other than that, there was simply nothing left.

In the days after the storm, the names of Mr. Dumas, Mrs. Dumas, and George Henderson were all added to a growing list of killed and missing—George Henderson with the notation "colored" next to his name, in keeping with the pervasive institutional racism of the time. The hurricane, however, proved to be colorblind and killed black and white quite indiscriminately as it rampaged through the middle Keys. All told, the storm slew at least 423 people in southern Florida: 259 veterans, 164 civilians. Several hundred bodies were discovered on the Keys in the aftermath of the storm and were either shipped to the mainland for burial, burned on the site in funeral pyres, or (as the decomposition worsened) simply doused with kerosene and incinerated where they lay. Others were swept to sea and washed ashore on distant mangrove keys. Mary Russell of the Russell clan, for instance, was found dead nine miles north of Islamorada on a small island that is still called

The slain veterans, here already enclosed in coffins, at first received a full military burial, but such niceties had to be abandoned due to the rapidity of decomposition in Florida's subtropical climate. (Florida State Archives)

"Russell Key" today. A few even were found on the distant Florida mainland, including the bodies of two unidentified veterans that washed up on Cape Sable, about twenty miles as the crow flies to the northwest of Lower Matecumbe Key.

As always with a tragedy of this nature, the official numbers are just a best estimate, and reflect only the known dead. No one really knows exactly how many veterans were in the camps when the hurricane struck. No one knows the precise number of civilians, homesteaders, passers-through, and temporary visitors who might have been on hand in the middle Keys that Labor Day weekend. What is more, it is impossible to say how many civilian and veteran corpses were never recovered, either because they were washed into deep swamp grass or mangrove thickets, or because they sank to the bottom of Florida Bay. As a result, the actual death toll of the storm was likely far higher. Hemingway, who knew the Florida Keys well, was convinced that the total number of fatalities was "between 700 and 1000." Historians of the storm claim variously that the real loss of life was as high as five, six, or even eight hundred people. The truth will never be known.

What is certain, however, is that the hurricane killed at least as many as it spared as it passed over the middle Keys. The Russell family alone suffered an eighty-five percent casualty rate as a result of the storm—only eleven out of seventy-four total family members eventually emerged alive from the wreckage. At Camp Five, located along a vulnerable spit of land between the Florida Channel and Florida Bay, the casualty rate probably exceeded ninety percent. More sheltered locales on the middle Keys, such as Camp One, recorded fewer casualties, and the presence of the huge tanker car at Camp Three, which provided hand-holds for about seventy veterans against the storm surge, reduced the mortality rate to only about forty percent at that camp. Still, an overall casualty rate of about fifty percent in the middle Keys seems like a reasonable estimate. By way of a contrast, the Great Miami Hurricane produced just 243 known dead in a metropolitan area with a total population of over

100,000, yielding a casualty rate of only about one-quarter of one percent. In terms of mortality rate, then, the '26 Miami hurricane was the meteorological equivalent of the common cold, while the Labor Day storm matched the wholesale carnage of the Bubonic Plague.

What made the Labor Day Hurricane so deadly? Geography no doubt played a significant role. Rising barely above sea level and open to the sea on both the north and south, the Florida Keys are particularly vulnerable to the high winds and high tides which a hurricane brings in its wake. Still, given the sheer power of the Labor Day Hurricane, it is likely that the storm would have caused catastrophic damage and appalling fatalities no matter where it struck. The Labor Day Hurricane packed sustained winds of at least 160 mph, making it the most powerful of the three category-five hurricanes that have struck the coast of America. Based on the available evidence, scientists believe that the gusts circling the storm's eye probably reached 200 mph. If true, this suggests that the Labor Day Hurricane boasted wind speeds that exceeded those of all but the strongest tornados.

The unearthly intensity of the Labor Day Hurricane was further demonstrated by the astounding barometric pressure readings that accompanied the storm's passage. Air pressure measurements as low as 26.35 inches were recorded in the '35 storm, and these readings still hold the record for the lowest barometric pressure ever recorded on American soil. Indeed, the Labor Day's barometric pressure reading enjoyed the dubious distinction of being the lowest ever recorded anywhere within the entire Western Hemisphere until the arrival of Hurricane Gilbert in 1988. Some observers reported seeing washed-ashore fish burst open during the passage of the Labor Day storm's eye, most likely because the hurricane's record-breaking lack of air pressure caused the swim bladders of the fish to explode. Small wonder, then, that so many storm victims reported having difficulty breathing. The storm's low pressure was sucking the air right out of their lungs.

If the gray, glowering clouds of the Labor Day Hurricane had any silver lining at all, it was that they passed relatively quickly from the Florida shore. By 3:00 A.M. of the morning of September 3, the storm was already brushing past Cape Sable on the southernmost tip of the Florida peninsula, and conditions began to improve markedly in the Keys, though few veterans or civilians dared to venture far from their places of refuge until dawn came at about 6:00. By mid-morning of the day after Labor Day, the storm was already well on its way to Tampa Bay, which it would sweep past in the late evening of the 3rd; as it roared by, the storm first blew most of the seawater out of the bay, then flooded the bay with an impressive storm surge that submerged Tampa's Bayshore Boulevard under six feet of water. The hurricane then crossed the Florida Panhandle and passed into Georgia, where it lost its hurricane strength, but not its power to kill: the tornadoes and heavy downpours that accompanied the storm claimed several more lives.

As if seeking to return to the ocean where it was spawned, the storm then angled back towards the Atlantic coast, passed over the Carolinas and Virginia, and finally spun back out over the ocean near the state of Maryland. But its saga was not yet over. Once it reached the open waters of the Atlantic, this seemingly unstoppable storm intensified once more, regaining hurricane status by virtue of 90 mph winds. Thankfully, the rejuvenated storm never made landfall again, and once the prevailing winds carried it to the cold waters near the Arctic Circle, the great Labor Day Hurricane weakened, sputtered, and finally dwindled away. No one mourned its passing.

6 6 6

Despite all the sound and fury, then, the Labor Day storm had a total lifespan of just over a single week. A mere ten days elapsed between its unwelcome appearance at the eastern edge of the Bahamas and its anticlimactic demise southwest of the icebound island of Greenland. The hurricane's effect on southern Florida, however, would prove far more long lasting. The middle Keys, for instance, were stripped almost to the bedrock by the storm, destroying much of what was left of the declining citrus and pineapple industries. What is more, the tourist camps on the middle Keys, including both the Caribee Colony and the world-famous Long Key Fishing Camp, were all but obliterated. The Red Cross did what it could, but it could not replace the topsoil, resurrect the dead, nor change the minds of would-be vacationers who now associated the Florida Keys with corpses and cremations. It would be years before the middle Keys recovered from the storm.

As for Key West, it was not struck directly by the Labor Day storm, but it was nonetheless hard-hit by the hurricane's aftermath. For all of Key West's financial problems in the 1930s, the town could still rely upon Flagler's Overseas Railway, and the Conchs had grown accustomed to receiving news, goods, food, and water by rail. When this umbilical cord to the mainland was suddenly severed by the Labor Day Hurricane, however, Key West reacted with a sort of mass hysteria. According to the novelist James Leo Herlihy, in the days after the Labor Day storm, "many people [took] to eating grass and weeds, boiling the stuff with nothing to flavor it but a bird shot out of the tree with a BB gun. . . . One old man took off all his clothes, ran into the swamps and died there a week later, stark-naked and alone; a middle-aged teacher surprised her students and colleagues one Monday morning by walking into the grade school dead-drunk, her hair freshly dyed in the color of ripe tomatoes and twirling a loaded pistol around her forefinger; and so on. Nothing made sense anymore." The city of Key West, it seemed, was now on the verge of psychological as well as financial collapse.

The most notable casualty of the '35 hurricane, however, was Flagler's Overseas Railway, which was put out of commission forever by the Labor Day storm. When railway repair workers visited the Keys after the hurricane, they discovered that forty-two miles of railroad embankments had been washed out, and much of the track that remained had been twisted ninety degrees by the force of storm surge, creating what one historian has called "a devil's jest of a picket fence." Still, the wound that had been inflicted upon the railway was not necessarily mortal. The railway bridges, which Flagler had built to withstand the test of both time and the elements, managed to survive the storm almost unscathed. Since these bridges were by far the most expensive part of the project, it probably would have been possible to restore service on the Overseas in a matter of months if the FEC had been willing to do so.

But the FEC, as it turned out, was inclined to let the Overseas Railway become one more casualty of the storm. The Key West Extension, after all, had never even paid for its own maintenance costs, much less produced a profit. With the railway already teetering on the edge of total financial insolvency, the directors of the FEC made a fateful decision: they sold the remnants of the Overseas Railway to the state of Florida in exchange for $640,000 in cash and $160,000 in payment of back taxes. Really, who could blame them? The Overseas Railway was Flagler's most cherished dream, but that dream meant little to Depression-era FEC executives fighting a desperate battle to keep their company alive—and when a body is dying, it is sometimes necessary to lop off the gangrenous limb.

Thus, with a single stroke of the pen, Flagler's enduring monument was transformed from a working railway into a picturesque antique, a quaint leftover relic of Gilded-Age America. Although few recognized it at the time, the same pen stroke also sounded the death knell for a fascinating era of Florida history. Only a few years before, south Florida had been awash with seemingly unlimited human ambition. The "Magic City" of Miami, for instance, had dreamed of rivaling New York City in size and influence, and Key West had aspired to become the Queen of the Southern Seas. George Merrick had tried to create a "master suburb" of one hundred thousand souls in the pine ridge west of Biscayne Bay, and "Crazy Carl" Fisher had built an American vacationland upon the mangroves and mudflats of Miami Beach. But by the time of the Depression, all these dreams were dying or already dead, swept away by the new economic realities of the twentieth century, or by the raging fury of the hurricane. Only Flagler's Overseas Railway had survived the 1920s, and even that dream perished forever on that fateful Labor Day of 1935. The abandoned arches and trestles of Flagler's railway survive to still impress and bewilder tourists on their way to Key West. But time has passed them by, and the south Florida shore will never be the same again.

Epilogue

September, Remember

As a general rule, historians prefer to conclude their tales with laurels of victory, with days of wine and roses, or with glorious accomplishments that blaze like lampposts above the triumphant path of human affairs. Our own one-hundred-year journey through the history of southern Florida, however, has followed a much gloomier path to a far bleaker destination.

The fateful year of 1935, in fact, marks the nadir of a century of human history on the south Florida shore. The old Florida industries of sponges, cigars, turtling, wrecking, and Indian trading, which had once been the region's lifeblood, had already been swept from the stage of history by the inexorable economic forces of the modern world. But there was reason for hope: in the first decades of the twentieth century, a new and greater Florida appeared to be rising from the ashes of the old. Flagler's marvelous Overseas Railway seemed to offer Key West a gleaming steel escape route from its turn-of-the-century economic doldrums. Meanwhile, about 150 miles away, ambitious Miami developers like George Merrick and Carl Fisher were building castles in the air alongside the warm, subtropical waters of Biscayne Bay. In the end, however, the promises of the Overseas Railway and the Great Miami Boom proved hollow, thanks in part to the repeated ravages of September hurricanes along the south Florida shore. By the winter of 1935, both cities were in a state of despair, and the future seemed grim.

But, the reader may ask, why end the story in 1935? Isn't this a bit misleading? Both Miami and Key West, after all, have since fully recovered from the turbulent events of the late '20s and early '30s. Key West, once just a "dusty old town," is now a fashionable tourist destination, attracting legions of visitors from both throughout the nation and throughout the world. Miami's recovery since the 1930s has been even more spectacular: the Miami metropolitan area now claims over two million residents, more than any other urban center in Florida, and Miami has become the virtual business, financial, and commercial capital of the entire Caribbean basin. Indeed, at the time of writing, Miami was enjoying an impressive real estate boom which, if not quite up to the standards of the '25–'26 phenomenon, was nonetheless bringing great prosperity to this former Seminole Indian trading post on the banks of the Miami River.

What is more, Miami and Key West are not alone in their good fortune—the entire state of Florida is currently enjoying quite an impressive upswing. Florida, which could claim only a little more than half a million residents in 1900, boasts over seventeen million today, a rate of population growth well over five times the national average. During the same period, Florida rose from being only the thirtieth most populous state in the country to the fourth most populous, after only California, New York, and Texas. What is more, the population of Florida is still swelling at an astounding rate: over the last decade alone, Florida gained three million residents, which represents nearly a twenty-five percent increase in only ten years. If the present rate of growth continues apace, the population of Florida will top that of New York within fifteen more years, and eighty-five years after that, even California might take second place to Florida in overall population.

Florida's boom has impacted the realm of politics as well; as a result of its rapid demographic expansion, Florida is fast becoming the single most crucial battleground for American presidential elections. True, three other states currently have more votes than Florida in the electoral college, but elections in New York, California, and Texas are generally foreordained: the Democratic candidate nearly always prevails in California and New York, while Republicans habitually carry Texas. In Florida, however, the margin of electoral power between Democrats and Republicans is quite narrow, and as a result, the swing of a few thousand or even a few hundred votes in Florida might determine which candidate receives Florida's twenty-five electoral votes, and with them, the presidency of the United States. True, Bush was elected by a more comfortable margin in 2004, but Clinton won the state by nearly the same margin in 1996. The pivotal role that Florida played in the bizarre 2000 presidential election, therefore, might just be a prelude of things to come.

In any case, whether or not Florida is destined to be the kingmaker of the twenty-first century, one fact is clear: the "Sunshine State," as Florida prefers to call itself, is currently enjoying a population boom which rivals even the Great Miami Boom of the 1920s. It is important to realize, however, that the geographic constraints that undid Florida's earlier boom, and which helped to mire Florida into two decades of depression, have not disappeared. Stella Crossley's warning, first issued in 1926, still has a lot of currency today. "Florida is on the edge of the tropics," Crossley reminds us, "and hurricanes are to be reckoned with in the tropics. The best man can do there is to admit calmly to himself and others that such things are always likely to happen and to take such precautions as are possible."

Indeed, Crossley's warning is more relevant now than ever before. When Crossley originally wrote her diatribe against the Florida boom, the state as a whole boasted only a million and a half inhabitants. Today, over ten times that many people are crammed into the Sunshine State, which means that the task of evacuation is ten times as difficult, the potential for property damage is at least ten times as high, and the list of possible storm victims is ten times as long. What is more, due to a recent spike in North Atlantic Ocean temperatures, meteorologists expect above-average hurricane seasons in America for as many as three decades to come. Hurricane seasons like that of 2004, when Florida was punished by a record-topping four major hurricanes, are likely to become an ongoing trend. All the preconditions are in place for a catastrophe.

My goal in presenting these facts is not to terrify Florida residents, nor is it to dissuade would-be tourists from vacationing in the Sunshine State. There is far more to Florida, after all, than the potential threat of cyclonic weather. Indeed, Florida's current boom is based on a very real foundation: Florida's climate is a delight, its beaches are unmatched, and its wilderness areas are national treasures. Still, Florida's residents and visitors should keep in mind that Florida's booms have collapsed before, and will likely collapse again, as boom-time ambition inevitably gives way once more to the shattering reality of the Atlantic hurricane. So if you find yourself in Florida during the hurricane season, make sure you keep one eye on the Weather Channel; failing that, stay close to a good old-fashioned barometer. And always remember: Florida sunsets are at their most spectacular right before the coming of the storm.

Index

Mallory, Stephen R., 4, 6, 28
Man-of-War Channel, 305
Manatee River, 50
manchineel tree, 128, 178
Manning, Warren H., 206
Manufacturer's Record, 182
Marathon, 303
Margarita (Caribbean isle of), 22
Martí, José, 99, 113–114, **114**
Maryland, 331
Massachusetts Savings Bank
    League, 227
Matecumbe Hotel, 311, 327
Matecumbe Key(s), 294, 302,
    306, 322
Maxwell House coffee, 253
Meade, Lt. George Gordon, 109
Mediterranean ear sponges *(see*
    sponges)
Merrick, George Edgar, 203–6,
    216–17, 222, 227, 232, 233,
    234, 333, 336 *(see also* Coral
    Gables)
    Coral Gable office of, **204**
Merrick, Solomon, 203
Merrill, Reverend R. N., 273
Miami, 157
Miami, 3,41,63,72, 73, 120, 153,
    154, 158, 170, 174, 183,
    185, 186, 193, 195, 199,
    206, 209, 210, 213–15,
    220–21, 222–28, 269, 270,
    271, 285, 290, 294,
    299–300, 305, 308, 309,
    324, 333, 334 *(see also* Great
    Miami Hurricane of 1926)
    2000 presidential elections in,
    44
    advertising for, 206–8, 211–12,
    220–21, 273
    beginnings of, 86, 123–34
    boom *(see* Great Miami Boom)
    bust, 228–237
    Flagler's "park" conflict,
    144–46
    Government Cut, 146–47, 230
    growth of, 74, 90, 205–6
    hurricanes in *(see* hurricane)
    Little River section of, **247**
    naming of, 131
    passenger trains in, **131**
    population of, 130, 142, 148
    shipping in, 229–31
    soldiers in, 140–42
    violence in, 137-39
Miami Beach, 66, 201–3, 205,
    206, 214, 215, 219,
    223, 226, 229, 231, 269,
    270, 290, 333
Miami City Council, 143, 196
Miami Herald, 182, 208, 214,
    216, 239, 273, 282, 284,
    324, 325
Miami Metropolis, 130, 140
Miami Minute Men, 139–40
Miami River, 22, 39, **45**, 57, 58,
    59, 60, 63, 65, 72, 86, 87,
    123, 124, 126, 127, 128,
    130, 131, 132, 134, 136,
    137, **146**, 148, 154, 239,
    270, 309, 336
    plantations on, 41–43
Miami Tribune, 240, 245, 292
Miami Weather Bureau, 245, 249
Mississippi River, 162
Missouri Key, 176
Mitchell, Gus, 262
Mobile, 166
Model T, 220
Monroe County, 286

If you enjoyed reading this book, here are some other Pineapple Press titles you might enjoy as well. To request our complete catalog or to place an order, write to Pineapple Press, P.O. Box 3889, Sarasota, Florida 34230, or call 1-800-PINEAPL (746-3275). Or visit our website at www.pineapplepress.com.

The Florida Chronicles by Stuart B. McIver. A series offering true-life sagas of the notable and notorious characters throughout history who have given Florida its distinctive flavor. **Volume 1** *Dreamers, Schemers and Scalawags* (pb); **Volume 2** *Murder in the Tropics* (hb); **Volume 3** *Touched by the Sun* (hb)

The Florida Keys by John Viele. Three volumes include fascinating accounts of two centuries' of island and maritime history in southernmost Florida, organized by topic. *Volume 1: A History of the Pioneers* (hb); *Volume 2: True Stories of the Perilous Straits* (hb); *Volume 3: The Wreckers* (hb)

Florida's Great Ocean Railway: Building the Key West Extension by Dan Gallagher. The completed F.E.C. Key West Extension stands as a monument to those who planned it. Much of this book deals with the planners and their plan, a masterpiece of both engineering and administrative design that made the Key West Extension one of the major construction projects of the early twentieth century.

Key Biscayne: A History of Miami's Tropical Island and the Cape Florida Lighthouse by Joan Gill Blank. This engaging history of the southernmost barrier island in the U.S. tells the stories of its owners and would-be owners. (hb and pb)

Lighthouses of the Florida Keys by Love Dean. Intriguing, well-researched accounts of the shipwrecks, construction mishaps, natural disasters, and Indian attacks that plagued the Florida Keys' lighthouses and their keepers. (hb and pb)

Miami, A Backward Glance by Muriel V. Murrell. From the lavish parties and the innovative architecture to the mosquito bites and the hurricanes, Muriel Murrell captures in a series of charming vignettes Miami's earlier days—from the Roaring Twenties, the Depression and Deco Days, on through the war and into the Fifties.

Iosco - Arenac District Library
East Tawas, Michigan

AG 12-15-05
PL 2-16-06
BT 4-20-06
WH 6-22-06
OM 8-24-06
TC 10-26-06
SF 1-11-07
OS 3-15-07

DISCARD

OS 3-15-07 KP